The Cloak of
Competence

D0206877

The Cloak of Competence

Revised and Updated

Robert B. Edgerton

UNIVERSITY OF CALIFORNIA PRESS

Berkeley / Los Angeles / London

University of California Press
Berkeley and Los Angeles, California

University of California Press
London, England

Copyright © 1993 by The Regents of the University of California

Library of Congress Cataloging-in-Publication Data

Edgerton, Robert B., 1931–
    The cloak of competence / Robert B. Edgerton, — Rev. and updated.
      p. cm.
    Includes bibliographical references and index.
    ISBN 0-520-08225-7. — ISBN 0-520-08226-5 (pbk.)
    1. Mentally handicapped. I. Title.
HV3004.E3   1993
362.3—dc20   93-5292
                                             CIP

Printed in the United States of America

1 2 3 4 5 6 7 8 9

The paper used in this publication meets the minimum require-
ments of American National Standard for Information Sciences—
Permanence of Paper for Printed Library Materials, ANSI
Z39.48–1984 ⬚

Contents

Acknowledgments
for the Revised Edition

In addition to those associates of mine mentioned in the acknowledgments to the original book, I owe a great debt to the following people for their skill, dedication, and compassion in conducting field research: Sylvia Bercovici, Marsha Bollinger, Thomas Browner, Alex Cohen, the late Gordon Creed, Marcia Gaston, Patti Hartmann, Barbara Herr-Harthorn, Karen Joseph, Hilarie Kelly, Paul Koegel, Frank Marlow, Lynne Pettler, Donald Sutherland, Thomas Ward, and Robert Whittemore.

I also wish to thank once again the late Harvey Dingman and the late George Tarjan for endorsing this research in the first place, and Richard Eyman, Georges Sabagh, and the research staff at Pacific State Hospital for their help and encouragement. I am also indebted to the staff and faculty of the Mental Retardation Research Center at the University of California, Los Angeles, especially its director, Nathaniel Buchwald and my colleagues in its Socio-Behavioral Research Group. I most gratefully acknowledge research funding from the National Institutes of Child Health and Human Development, Grants Number HD 04612, HD 05540–02, and HD 11944–02. Ellen Lodge, Dana Stulberg, and Tina Tran helped with the preparation of the revised material in various ways.

Most of all, I thank the people whom this book is about. Their humor, good sense, and courage are a continuing inspiration to me.

Introduction to the Revised Edition

For several years, various of my academic colleagues, students, and professionals in the field of developmental disabilities have suggested that I revise *The Cloak of Competence* to include the several follow-up studies of the people described in this book which have taken place since the publication of the first edition. They have also suggested that I address some of the criticisms the book has evoked and comment on the significant issues that I have encountered during more than thirty years of research with these and other persons with mental retardation. I was flattered by these suggestions and often tempted to begin such a revision but some other research project always seemed to take priority. But now that over twenty-five years have elapsed since *The Cloak of Competence* was first published, and over thirty years have passed since I began my research with the people described in the book, it seems to me that now is the time to say more about the lives of these people and to comment on the issues that their lives illustrate. The story of their lives deserves to be told for many reasons, not the least of which is that what they have accomplished since the original version of *The Cloak of Competence* was written dramatically changes the way in which a reader would think of them as people with mental retardation. In growing older most of them have grown wiser and stronger and happier. All of these people have had much to overcome; some have not done so, but most have, and in doing so they have helped to change the way in which we think about people with disabilities.

The field research on which the original book was based was conducted throughout 1960 and the first half of 1961. In July of 1961, I left the United States to fulfill a previous commitment to conduct anthropological research in East Africa (Edgerton, 1971). It was not until the spring of 1965 that I was able to begin analyzing the "Cloak of Competence" data, as this material eventually came to be known. These materials had been stored in the form of extensive narrative field notes as well as audio tape recordings. Although my memories of the sample members were not as vivid in 1965 as they were in 1961, a review of all the notes and tapes did much to refresh them. I felt then as I do now, that by delaying the analysis of all this material, I had achieved a more objective perspective on these people and their lives than I had earlier. In 1961 I was perhaps too involved with these people, too concerned about them, or in some cases, too confused by the emotional impact their life circumstances had made upon me to be very objective. I am not sure that I could have written the book in 1961; by 1965 I could. Perhaps I should note parenthetically that what I wrote was not intended to be a book. It was a final report to my supervisor at Pacific State Hospital, the late Dr. Harvey F. Dingman. I lacked any conceit that this report was a "book." However, in addition to sending a copy to Harvey Dingman, I showed one to my former mentor in the Department of Anthropology at the University of California, Los Angeles, Dr. Walter R. Goldschmidt, who liked it enough to recommend it to the University of California Press and to write a foreword to it.

Despite my unexpected good fortune in having this manuscript published, I was acutely aware that there was much about the people I had studied that I could not know, just as there was much about the condition known as mental retardation that I did not understand. Before beginning my research at Pacific State Hospital in 1959, I had never knowingly met a person with mental retardation, and all I knew about people who had been given this dismal-sounding diagnosis came from my hurried reading of the recently published book, *Mental Subnormality*, by Masland, Sarason, and Gladwin in 1958. The third author, Thomas Gladwin, was an accomplished anthropologist, but still, the book contained little about the social or cultural considerations that influenced the etiology or diagnosis of the various conditions that were lumped under the category of mental retardation, and still less about how such factors might affect the life course of people who received this diagnosis. No viable test of adaptive behavior existed then and there was little discussion of the concept. It was known that the measurement of IQ could be affected by social and cultural factors, but at the level of clinical practice, the IQ score was still treated as largely immutable and highly prognostic. The idea of the "six-hour retarded child"—retarded in school, but normal in other social settings—had not yet arrived; Jane Mercer had not yet published her work on the relationships between ethnicity, IQ scores, and adaptive behavior (Mercer, 1973). The term "deinstitutionalization" was not in common currency and the concept of normalization was not put forward until a decade later (Nirje, 1969). Although the idea that a stigmatizing label could serve as a self-fulfilling prophecy had been around for some years, serious work on what came to be known as "labeling theory" had not yet begun either.

At that time, it was still common to find scholarly references to "mental retardates" and even "morons." The preferred terminology today is "persons with mental retardation," a cumbersome but less pejorative designation. For the same reason, "disability" replaced "handicap," and terms such as "client" or "resident" have replaced the earlier term, "patient." Advocacy groups for persons with mental retardation were a thing of the future as were the Special Olympics and the federally funded centers for research on mental retardation that were initiated during the Kennedy presidency. Very little about mental retardation was taught in our medical schools or departments of psychology or education and there was virtually no interest at all in the subject by social scientists.

With so little guidance from social science, I chose to do the only thing that seemed to be self-evidently necessary, that is, look closely at the patient population of a hospital (people in such institutions were then referred to as "patients"). I quickly learned that these patients were not at all alike. Among them were children and adults who spent their entire lives lying in cribs, unable to speak or to control their bodily functions. Some understood a little speech but others did not. All had to rely on hospital staff to care for all their needs. Other patients were physically active but had no measurable IQ and few communicative skills. Many others were less severely handicapped and some, at least on superficial acquaintance, appeared to suffer from no physical or mental disability. Although I studied and wrote about patients of all these kinds, I was most intrigued by the apparently normal people. I quickly learned that they had developed a hospital-based culture of some complexity; they had their own values, customs, and systems of social control. They were mortified to find themselves in a hospital that seemed to them to be intended for severely handicapped people, but they had developed means of repairing their lost self-esteem and of finding ways of living relatively normal lives despite their confinement. It also seemed to me that people like these could and should be able to live outside the hospital, or on the "outs" as they put it. It seemed to me that they had been incarcerated less because of their low measured IQs than because someone—parents, neighbors, teachers, police—found their behavior difficult to manage. I wanted to know how people like these would succeed if they were released from the hospital.

I did not have to wait for them to be released before I could address this question, because as I indicated in the original edition of the book, I found that Pacific State Hospital had been releasing patients like these to vocational placements in the community for some years and that 110 of these people had done well enough on this leave program to earn a discharge from the hospital, or the "state," as the former patients put it. Like the people I had known in the hospital, these former patients had IQs in the mildly retarded range, came from depriving home environments, and a few had physical or emotional handicaps. In the climate of that time, when state agencies willingly provided the addresses of former patients, it was not difficult to locate most of these people, and it was obvious that they were willing, and sometimes eager, to discuss their experiences both in the hospital and after leaving it.

Unfortunately, although many studies of former patients similar to these had been published by that time, they were of remarkably little help in guiding the research I hoped to do. For one thing, they provided virtually no details about the actual day-to-day activities of the people being studied, and they offered even less insight into the personal thoughts and feelings of former patients. What they did offer was the frustrating but still hopeful finding that substantial numbers of former patients were able to maintain themselves in the communities to which they were released. For example, during World War I, Walter E. Fernald conducted the first significant follow-up study of former patients when he examined the post-hospital adjustment of 1,537 persons discharged from the state school at Waverly, Massachusetts, over a twenty-five-year period. Despite the fact that many of these people had not been recommended for release by the institution and were thought likely to fail, Fernald found that only 34.4 percent of the men and 40.8 percent of the women had been rehospitalized or imprisoned. Reflecting the conventional wisdom of his day, Fernald had predicted that fully 85 percent of these people would have to be reinstitutionalized, and he was so shocked by the their surprisingly good adjustment that he delayed publication of his findings for two full years (Edgerton, 1983). He also found that success in community adjustment was related to finding someone in the community who would take an interest in their welfare. I was not aware of this study before I began my own research, but the critical role of helpful community members, whom I came to call benefactors, was so obvious that my ignorance of Fernald's work was not a handicap.

Subsequent follow-up studies of former patients continued to find such high rates of successful community adaptation that Henry V. Cobb (1972:145) was moved to write that "the most consistent and outstanding finding of all follow-up studies is the high proportion of the adult retarded who achieve satisfactory adjustments, by whatever criteria are employed." Other major reviews of the post-hospital adjustment of former patients reached a similar conclusion, but none was able to identify variables that would allow one to predict successful community adaptation. Moreover, this early literature lacked anything approaching a consensus about how to define successful community adaptation (a problem that persists to this day). By default, then, the operative criteria when I began my research were typically whether or not the formerly institutionalized persons with mental retardation can avoid reinstitutionalization either in a therapeutic, custodial, or correctional institution. By these criteria, it was clear that many former patients could succeed in community living, but how they did so and why some had to be reinstitutionalized was unknown.

I was most limited in the research I was about to undertake by the absence of information concerning the extent to which success or failure in community adaptation was due to social, cultural, and economic factors rather than attributes of the individuals themselves. The assumption at that time was that successful adaptation was primarily a function of a person's intelligence or personality rather than the social and economic environment in which they found themselves. I was not aware in 1960 how dramatically rates of reinstitutionalization varied from one time period to the next, from one state to another, from poor economic conditions to better ones, and among various criminal jurisdictions. Of course, it was apparent even then that race, class, gender, religion, and other sociocultural factors could influence success or failure, but evidence of just how powerful a role these factors played would not become compelling for some years to come (Edgerton, 1983). As a result, although I thought of the people whom I was about to study as victims of inequitable social and cultural circumstances, I may not have been as sensitive to the power of those factors in their lives as I should have been.

It is difficult to be certain about what one's preconceptions were at a time more than thirty years in the past, but one important preconception of mine is quite clear. That has to do with whether I thought of the people in my sample as mentally retarded, as people with significant cognitive limitations, or rather as products of a process of social labeling whose disabilities, if any, could be overcome by the experiences of more or less social living. I believed then, as I do now, that these people had significant cognitive limitations that were a product of an interaction between environmental and biological factors. I believed, too, that although experience would greatly increase their social competence, their cognitive limitations would persist. As you evaluate the materials presented here, you may judge how accurate these preconceptions were and whether they biased my collection, presentation, or interpretation of the data, as some critics of the original edition of this book have alleged (Bogdan and Taylor, 1982; Gerber, 1990).

Another question of some importance in assessing my approach to this research was my use of hospital records. I read the hospital records of each person in the sample searching for relevant information such as the presence of epileptic seizures, psychological evaluations indicating serious psychiatric disorders, and psychometric tests indicating how their IQs had been determined and whether they were notably strong or weak in some particular subscale. I also recorded the names and addresses of relatives whom I might be able to contact, and I took down the names of anyone else who might have useful information. When it came to the rest of the record—parents' comments, social workers' opinions, court decisions, or narratives about their conduct while in Pacific State Hospital—I maintained a healthy skepticism. I routinely took the position that records of this kind are notoriously inaccurate, reflecting institutional needs and perspectives to the neglect of the patients' point of view, or, for that matter, the truth. When the records indicated that a patient underwent a tubal ligation, I was inclined to regard this as a fact. But when the records said that someone had been sexually promiscuous as an adolescent, unless there was corroborative evidence, I took this to be one possible interpretation among many and suspended judgment.

With regard to the actual conduct of the data collection, it is important to recall that in terms of formal practices of human subjects' protection procedures, 1960 was the dark ages. There was no such thing as requiring written informed consent. Nevertheless, I always told the people in the sample that they did not have to talk to me or my assistants. I frankly doubt that they believed me. I was seen as being "from the state" and they almost certainly felt at least some pressure to cooperate with me. I also told them that if they agreed to have some conversations tape-recorded they could listen to whatever was on the tape and have it erased if they chose to. Few chose to listen and no one asked to have anything erased. Most striking from today's more humane perspective was the willingness of agencies of all sorts to release their records to us in an attempt to locate former patients whose addresses were not current. In retrospect, it is more than a little chilling to realize how freely telephone companies, public utilities, collection agencies, various state agencies, and law enforcement officials cooperated in providing information. It is chastening to me to admit that at the time I did not then see my use of this information as an invasion of the former patients' privacy.

One of the most important steps taken with regard to the data collection procedures was my decision to make certain that each individual in the sample would be visited by at least two field-workers, including at least one man and one woman. I would also visit each sample member in an attempt to provide another perspective. These precautions proved to be important because although there was much about each person in the sample that we all agreed about, there could also be differences of interpretation, particularly between male and female field-workers. When these differing views arose, I would visit the sample member in an attempt to form my own opinion. Later, I would try to resolve the issue by discussing it with the field-workers. Despite these measures, some issues remained vexed until the end, and when this happened, I tried either to indicate in the text of the book that a certain interpretation was questionable or I omitted it altogether.

Another significant issue involved my attempts to reduce the effects that the presence of field-workers would have on the lives of sample members. My assumption was that by meeting with these people and telephoning them between meetings, we could have an influence on the course of their lives. Because our purpose was not to intervene in their lives but simply to record them in a nonreactive way, as if from behind a potted palm as it were, this was worrisome. As a result, I instructed field-workers to avoid being judgmental about the sample members' conduct or beliefs, to be certain they were not intruding into their lives at a time that could prove to be inconvenient, and under no account to take any action that could reasonably be expected to lead to a change in a sample member's life circumstances. Therefore, although we regularly drove sample members to visit a friend or relative, we refrained from expressing any judgments about those people. We did not offer advice about changing jobs, finding new housing, dealing with agencies, or changing eating habits. If asked for an opinion about something of potential consequence in the lives of sample members, the field-workers were supposed to indicate that they had no opinion, indeed, that all they were interested in was the opinion of the sample member. Needless to say, it was not always possible to follow these rules to the letter. When a slip occurred and I found out about it, I made it a point to look carefully for any changes in behavior or attitude that might have resulted. In fact, I found none.

I later came to understand that it was a form of hubris to think that either I or one of my field-workers was so salient a person in the lives of these former patients that anything short of reporting that person to some official agency would have any measurable effect on his or her life. Indeed, when I undertook later follow-up studies of these people, I instructed field-workers to be more forthcoming in expressing their own opinions, in answering questions, and in providing assistance with emergent problems such as a request for help in finding medical or dental care, in answering a letter from a welfare agency, or in dealing with a minor financial matter. By the early 1970s this practice of offering a *quid pro quo* to research subjects in return for their cooperation had become an ethical requisite in anthropology so I applied it to my work with these sample members. We still did not intervene in their lives on our own initiative, but we became friends more than we had earlier, we sometimes provided help when it was requested, and we sometimes offered advice when it was clearly called for. We have continued to follow these guidelines to the present day and all the evidence available to me indicates that although our help and friendship are appreciated and even sought, with one exception we have brought about no major changes in the lives of these people that would not have taken place regardless. (That exception consisted of helping a woman qualify for Social Security Insurance [SSI] on the basis of mental retardation; she might not have done this on her own.)

After twelve months of intensive and costly data collection, the initial field research successfully documented a number of main points about the community adaptation of the former patients. But I had no illusions that the research had uncovered everything of significance about these people, and as subsequent research was to demonstrate again and again, a year of research, no matter how intensive, is never adequate to reveal all the major patterns of thought, emotion, or behavior in a person's life. What is more, as I shall indicate in chapter 7, many sample members changed their behavior in dramatic and unpredictable ways in response to changes in their life circumstances. That they did so should hardly be surprising. They are complex people whose lives have truly been in flux, and like many other people, will continue to be. In what follows, it will be possible to glimpse various aspects of their lives but never the whole story. And, of course, for surviving members of the sample, the whole story has not yet been lived. In addition to this introduction, this revised edition contains updated information about the lives of the individuals whose lives were highlighted in chapter 2, as well as two new chapters. Chapter 7 reviews the findings of the subsequent follow-up studies and chapter 8 addresses a number of issues about people with mental retardation that the original book helped to raise.

Foreword

If it may be said that it is the professional duty of an anthropologist to travel to strange lands, then we may say that Dr. Edgerton has returned from a most exotic journey and brought back a report of both great practical and great theoretical value. His cultural description of the land of the mentally retarded, based upon detailed interviews of post-hospitalized patients, enables us to escape from the stereotypes by which this world is known. Only through a realistic understanding of the actualities in the lives of these unfortunate people can meaningful programs for them be developed. For that reason this book will become a necessary item in the armamentarium of all who work with the mentally retarded, either within the hospital setting or outside it.

The cultural study of a population which, unlike that of a small homogeneous community, is of diverse origins and experiences encounters many special problems. It is necessary to discover what, in the mass of that experience, is the central and consistent element in the life activities of the population under consideration. Dr. Edgerton has found this commonality in the efforts of these people to envelop themselves in a "cloak of competence," in their need to deny to themselves the reality of their condition, and in the closely related requisite that they hide—or convince themselves that they have hidden—the fact that they have been adjudged deficient. This is their inner commonality; it reflects the dual commonality of their external experience: inadequate mental competence and the fact of their past hospitalization. The matter is of great theoretical importance, and since a practical program requires adequate theoretical understanding as well as accurate factual appraisal, it will be necessary to give attention to these theoretical matters.

We are beginning to appreciate the fact that all cultures provide a set of values for their adherents. These values, which are the shared conceptions of the proprieties of life, give meaning to individual acts and a unity to cultural experience. In normal communities, particularly in tribal societies, values are related to the economic activities necessary for survival, and are thus functional in a sociological sense. Inasmuch as they are shared, they have a public aspect, and are expressed symbolically by means of titles, possessions, public roles, or other externally visible designata. But these values have an inner meaning as well; they form the basis for self-evaluation, reinforcing for each individual his sense of personal worth. I believe that most students of individual psychology and social behavior recognize, implicitly at least, that a positive self-evaluation is a requisite for the mental health of the individual in any culture. It is not quite as frequently recognized (though it has long been expressed) that such a positive self-evaluation can come only through social interaction, through the responses of others to one's own action and behavior. It is this, which I have elsewhere called "the need for positive affect," which I believe is a central and essential dynamic in the human motivation system. It is this hunger that binds each of us to his fellow man and thereby serves as cement in the formulation of society. But what is important to us here is that this matter has both a public and a private aspect; that is, there is the matter of our privately held self-image and its adequacy in relation to the generally held standards of our society, and there is also the public presentation of the self, our management of interpersonal relationships so as to obtain a satisfactory appraisal from the outside world. These two aspects are intimately related: the private image is created and reinforced through the responses received from this public response; and this self-image is built out of the public reactions to behavior.

None of us is perfectly adequate in terms of our culturally established expectations, and all of us manage our affairs so as to hide from others those imperfections we know to exist. Furthermore, as Anna Freud made clear, we all develop psychological mechanisms to hide imperfection from ourselves—by suppression or repression or by diverting our attention to new strengths. We all, it may be said, in varying degrees manage fictional lives through a fictional world. In a measure, we are all passing, and we are all denying.

But among the mentally retarded this problem is doubly exacerbated. First and foremost, their problem lies in the fact that their stigma—of all possible stigmata—is closest to what we may call the soul. Of all the attributes of man, mind is the quintessence; to be found wanting in mental capacity—in general intellectual competence—is the most devastating of all possible stigmata. (At least this is manifestly true for American culture; perhaps there are other cultures in which the self is less closely tied to intellective potential, and sheer physical strength, sexual prowess, or good looks take a preeminent part. It may be of interest to examine the mentally retarded in other cultural settings to discover whether their cultural concerns take on the same character as those described here.) Because of the totality of the impact, to have been certified by the society of which they are a part as being mentally deficient is entirely too destructive to the ego. The condition cannot be accepted for what it is.

For this reason, as the pages of this book make clear, these patients must deny the implication of their public defamation. The mechanisms are diverse: they were placed in the hospital by persons of evil intent or through misdiagnosis; their "problem" really lay elsewhere; the hospital experience itself is the cause of their post-hospitalization inadequacy, and so forth. They engage in a kind of psychological metonymy, letting a particular attribute—nervousness, illness—stand in substitution for the whole, because to recognize the totality of their incapacity would deny the self-image completely.

These difficulties are compounded by the fact that their incompetence itself hampers their ability to manage their public life so as not only to hide from others the reality of their stigma but—even more important, in my belief—to receive confirmation of their own competence. It is this inadequacy and the valiant subterfuges by which they endeavor to overcome it that give pathos to the story of their behavior.

These efforts by the retardates in face of their inadequacy have significance for a theory of human behavior, as well. The very defenselessness, the naïveté of these subjects, makes this matter of self-evaluation so clear, that one cannot fail to see the importance it has in the management of human lives. These mental retardates have, one might say, less cultural clothing to hide the naked drives which motivate their actions; they are less capable of dissembling the actual in their desires, thus giving clearer expression to the generic orientation in man, the need for positive affect. Elsewhere I have suggested that it is necessary to return to a recognition of the existence of a common substratum of human motivations underlying the diverse cultural manifestations of human behavior. I believe Dr. Edgerton's study of mental retardates, because of their intellectual transparency, is an especially valuable contribution to such an enterprise. It is for this reason that I consider *The Cloak of Competence* a contribution to theory as well as to the more mundane—but perhaps more important—practical concern with programs for the mentally deficient.

It is to these practical considerations that I want now to direct a few words. Dr. Edgerton is an anthropologist, and he has wisely eschewed the programmatic. Nor will I endeavor to suggest a program of action. But a knowledge of the culture of these people suggests some of the ingredients that must go into any program for alleviating the unnecessary distresses of the population here being examined.

First, a program of rehabilitation should help them to weave their garment of concealment, so that they may escape the psychological inroads that their past makes upon them. In this, training in those areas of life that are requisite for minimal competence—but which escape the attention of the competent as being too trivial—would be the first step. One wonders how many of these people could have been taught, had the effort been made, to tell time or to make change, and how much such knowledge might have helped them dissemble their past, to meet the challenges of everyday life, and to have thus avoided further erosion of their egos. Those of us who are competent are generally unaware of the cues to which we respond automatically, for they are not in our consciousness. We do not even have to train our normal children in the ordinary demands of behavior, except when they are very young or as they enter into new situations, for they rapidly learn the cues to appropriate behavior. But the mentally inadequate must not only be told, they must repeatedly be told; indeed they must be drilled in proper social responses to normal social situations. In this context, too, one should supply these people with an acceptable rationale—a cover story, if you will—for their hospitalization; one which takes the defamation off the total person and places it in some more limited context, allowing the ego to be retained relatively intact. This should not, of course, be a delusory "you are like everybody else." Rather, it should be in the form: "You are as good as anybody else, you just can't. . . . " It is an impressive fact that, repeatedly, the truly meaningful result of sterilization lies not in the deprivation of parenthood but in the fact that this surgery has engraved permanently upon them the fact that they have been judged incompetent, and they live in constant dread that this mark of their incompetence will be discovered. It would not be hard to devise means by which they could disclose the fact of sterility without indicating the reason. It is a remarkable fact that these people, with their limited capacity, have found such stories for themselves, and have clothed them with the semblance of reality sometimes by the acquisition of the lares and penates of a normal life. They should be helped in the performance of those small deceptions which all of us engage in to preserve our public image so as to protect our private one. It seems to me that these illusions should be fostered and reinforced so long as they do not create unrealistic levels of aspiration.

A second and equally compelling requisite to rehabilitation is the establishment of a social universe in which the mental retardates can fulfill their needs for human contact and response. Here one cannot help but wonder whether those energies and interests of normal persons, which these mentally deficient persons have captured on a hit-or-miss basis, could not be more effectively harnessed. Leaving aside the occasional minor economic exploitation, one is impressed by the fact that the benefactors so frequently are meeting that same need for positive affect that the retardates are endeavoring to satisfy; perhaps but the one-eyed in the kingdom of the blind. That their own needs are being met makes their benefaction that much more valuable. If chance can bring about so much satisfaction in these relationships, it would seem that planning might multiply the opportunities for finding benefactors, to the mutual advantage of each. At the same time, machinery to prevent exploitation—by "friends" as much as by benefactors—should be maintained.

Finally, though social agencies have long made efforts to provide social life for these and other handicapped people, it is clear that, however much they are needed, they are not used. This can only mean that such efforts to date are wanting in some significant way. Part of the difficulty in establishing social programs lies in the fact that participation in them by retardates is a reaffirmation of the stigma of incompetence which these ex-patients almost universally avoid; but it must also be because these social groups do not adequately meet the needs of the retardates themselves. What these needs are—despite the variegated life-patterns of these ex-patients—forms a major part of the content of this book; the problems in meeting them do not seem to be insoluble.

Such then are some of the essential and more compelling ingredients for the development of programs to help the post-hospitalized mental patient. They derive directly from the understanding of the cultural and social attributes of the mental retardates, and from an understanding of the central dynamic to their lives. One cannot make of these people what they are not, but one can make their lives more comfortable, more nearly satisfying, and more useful.

The major impact of this ethnography, as it is with all ethnographies that reach deep into human motivation, is: how like us they are after all. They are like us in their diversity as well as their similarities; above all, however, they are like us in their desires to be human, and to be seen as human; in this their humanity appears in all its nakedness.

Walter Goldschmidt

Preface

Anthropologists are known for their propensity to visit strange places where they study curious people and their still more curious customs. But even within anthropology, whose practitioners have long felt free to study everything and anything about man and his culture, the subject matter of this study is novel. Despite the undeniable fact that mild mental retardation is a social and cultural phenomenon, the social and cultural sciences have paid it scant heed. Sociologists have devoted little time to mental retardation, and cultural anthropologists, virtually none at all. That this should be so seems to me an unfortunate accident of academic history whereby certain subjects have become known as the preferred province of certain disciplines and not others. And so the study of mental retardation has remained as a problem for medical men, psychologists, or educators; more often, it remains a *tertium quid*.

Since I cannot view mild mental retardation outside of the social and cultural webs within which it takes on its meaning and becomes a problem, I must conclude that it is a proper subject for anthropological inquiry—quite as proper, in fact, as some of the traditional anthropological concerns. Of course, there is no denying that mental retardation is a serious practical problem for many people, in many cultures.

My purpose is not to harangue my colleagues concerning what they ought to be studying, for obviously, only they should make that choice. What I wish to argue is that the study of the cultural and social phenomena relating to mental retardation is a legitimate anthropological enterprise, one that serves an important and unmet need.

The presentation of this study is organized so that it proceeds from a general description of the lives of mentally retarded persons in the community to a specific discussion of the problems they face, and the techniques they employ, in dealing with their stigma and their incompetence. Chapter 1 presents the plan of the study as briefly and nontechnically as possible. Chapter 2 is a detailed introduction to the lives of a few selected persons who represent typical modes of living, and chapter 3 is a broad overview of some critical aspects of the lives of all the retarded persons in this study. Chapters 4, 5, and 6 concentrate upon the problems these retarded persons face in coping with the demands of life in a city and in attempting to maintain their self-esteem in the face of great stigma.

Of the many at Pacific State Hospital to whom my gratitude is due, I am most indebted to Dr. George Tarjan, Dr. Sebastian Casalaina, Dr. Georges Sabagh, Dr. Jane Mercer, Mr. Jack Brown, Mr. Lee Rader, and especially to Dr. Harvey Dingman. For their skill and tact in fieldwork I thank Mr. Allan Simmons, Mr. Dan Gilmore, Mr. William Poole, Miss Wanda Baker, Miss Jan Clarke, and Miss Cecile Mairesse. For assistance in analyzing the data I am grateful to Miss Michelle Wilson and Miss Mary Wynn. For typing portions of the manuscript I thank Mrs. Mary Schaeffer, Miss Kay Kataoka, Miss Sherry Rose, Mrs. Shirley Grossman, and Miss Juanita Baiz. Grateful acknowledgement for support is due NIMH Grant Number 3M-9130.

To the former patients who gave me such free access to their lives and their problems, I reserve the final thanks. These people were told that the information they gave me might some day help others who would face similar problems. I hope that it will.

R. B. E.

CHAPTER ONE

The Study
and Its Background

An Introduction to Mental Retardation

Although the human tragedy surrounding mental retardation is understood only too well by those persons whose lives have been touched by it, few persons who have not been directly involved are fully aware of the magnitude or the character of the problem that is mental retardation.

The most generally accepted estimate of the numbers of mentally retarded persons in this country—the one employed by the President's Panel on Mental Retardation in 1961—is 3 percent of the total population. On this basis it is estimated that there are well over 5 million mentally retarded persons in the United States today, and by 1970 this figure will increase to over 6 million. By this same 3 percent estimate, there were 540,000 mental retardates in the State of California in 1965. Another perspective can be gained by considering that each year in this country, over 130,000 mentally retarded children are born. Further, during the Second World War, over 700,000 American men were rejected for military service because of "mental deficiency."

Even though this estimated incidence of mental retardation is not yet confirmed by epidemiological research—some studies have suggested a lower rate, others have suggested a higher one—it is certain that mental retardation is an enormous problem. In fact, only mental illness, arthritis, heart disease, and cancer afflict a greater number of Americans. The cost of mental retardation can be estimated in dollars—it runs to well over a billion dollars per year in public funds alone—but the human cost can never be calculated.

"Mental retardation" is the currently approved term for the designation of persons who have also been referred to as mental deficients, mental defectives, mental subnormals, exceptional children, aments, and, perhaps most generally in the past, feebleminded. What mental retardation is called, however, is far less variable than what mental retardation *is*. One thing is obvious. Mental retardation is not a unitary disorder in the sense that all persons who are so designated share a common condition that is produced by a specifiable etiology. There are over one hundred known "causes" of mental retardation, and the condition so named embraces several constellations of varied syndromes. For example, the term mental retardation applies to persons who are so profoundly physically disabled and intellectually enfeebled that they must spend their entire lives lying inert in cribs where they are literally able to do nothing more than vegetate. A profoundly retarded condition of this sort can be the product of any number of causes, such as degenerative neurological disease, genetic anomaly, or anoxia. Mental retardation also applies to those persons who suffer a specific, but less profoundly disabling, genetic disorder such as mongolism (more properly, Down's syndrome), which is now known to be caused by chromosomal imbalance, namely, trisomy for chromosome 21. But the term mental retardation is likewise applied to persons who have no noticeable physical defect, and whose intellectual abilities, although inadequate for some tasks, are perfectly adequate for many others. For such persons it is only rarely possible to specify the cause of their relatively lesser intellectual abilities. Both etiologically and descriptively, then, mental retardation is heterogeneous.

Nonetheless, there is a "semi-official" definition of mental retardation, the one adopted in 1959 by the American Association on Mental Deficiency. The definition reads as follows: "Mental retardation refers to subaverage intellectual functioning which originates during the development period and is associated with impairment in adaptive behavior."[1]

Not only does this definition take into account "adaptive behav-

1. Heber (1958), p. 3.

ior," but it also adds, in a later section, that an individual may be mentally retarded at one time and normal at another as a result of changes in his own performance or in "social standards or conditions." Thus, it is explicitly recognized that mental retardation is a relative concept, the limits of which have meaning only in terms of *social* conditions.

Diagnosis of so variable and socially relative a phenomenon as mental retardation is understandably difficult. Concerning the more severe cases of retardation, medical tests and common sense usually agree, and the validity of this agreement is beyond question. However, most cases diagnosed as mental retardation are *not* severe, and neither medical test nor common sense can provide a consensually acceptable diagnosis. What is required for the diagnosis of these, the less severe, cases is an operational test of "adaptive behavior," "intellectual functioning," or both. There are tests of adaptive behavior—principally the Vineland Social Maturity Scale—but few workers in the field would contend that such tests alone are sufficient as diagnostic devices. For one thing, tests of adaptive behavior are markedly unstable, for they are subject to varying shifts in subcultural norms, and are sensitive to all manner of changes in social and cultural conditions. Furthermore, they are too global, for a deficit in adaptive behavior may be the result of any number of psychological and organic conditions which may be entirely unrelated to mental retardation. For example, deafness and psychosis are but two conditions that could cause an inadequacy of "adaptive behavior" in a person of normal intelligence.

What is required is an operational test that is more directly a measure of intellectual functioning. The answer to this need has long been taken to be the IQ test, in one or another of its versions. Nevertheless, even its most zealous advocates admit that IQ testing is both relative and fallible. It is no secret that errors in IQ assessment do occur, and sometimes spectacularly. For example, there are well-documented cases of persons who were institutionalized on the basis of an IQ test performance below 70, only to be found some years later to be partially deaf, or emotionally disturbed, and to have, upon retesting, an IQ in the genius range. Consequently, while there are many psychometricians who have confidence in IQ testing and who feel that its use is misunderstood by those who malign it most, few practitioners would defend IQ tests as perfect devices for determining who is or is not mentally retarded. However, this is not the place for an extended discussion of the concept of tile Intelligence Quotient, nor of its suitability as a measure of subnormal intellect. The problem is complex and an enormous literature on the subject is available.[2] The essential point here is that despite the recognized imperfections of IQ tests, virtually all diagnoses of mental retardation rely upon these tests. Indeed, legal statutes often require such testing. IQ is *the* operational tool, and both medical and legal terminologies and classifications of mental retardation are based upon discriminations in IQ.

There are many variants of the IQ classification of mental retardation. Older classifications spoke of "idiots" (IQ less than 25), "imbeciles" (IQ 25–49), "morons" (IQ 50–69) and "dull normals" (IQ 70–89). Subsequent versions have altered both the descriptive terms and the IQ ranges. One of the most widely employed current classifications is that of the American Association on Mental Deficiency: (Table 1).

In considering these levels of mental retardation, it should be borne in mind that the range of "normal" IQ in the United States is generally considered to be 90–110, with the national average being approximately 100. From an inspection of Table 1 it should be obvious that only relatively slight changes in IQ would be necessary to move an individual from one level to another, for example, from "borderline" to the "mildly retarded" level. A shift of ten IQ points could make a great difference.

No one seriously questions the proposition that experience, especially early experience, affects one's IQ. It is, for example, generally accepted that the longer individuals, especially children, live in conditions of intellectual deprivation or isolation, the lower, on the whole, their IQs will tend to be. Undeniably, then, the influence of social and cultural factors upon IQ is great. This point is crucial for an understanding of mental retardation. Most persons who are defined as mental retardates are not profoundly, severely, or even moderately retarded. Quite the contrary, fully 85 percent of all mental retardates are only mildly retarded. Indeed, Tarjan and Dingman (1960), basing their estimates upon a population in the United States of 175 million, concluded that there were 5,276,755 persons in the United States with IQs between 50 and 70.

Even if we conclude that most, or even all, persons who have IQs

2. For example, see Robinson and Robinson (1965).

Table 1 *Levels of Mental Retardation*[a]

Levels	Description	IQ range
I	Borderline	70–84
II	Mildly retarded	55–69
III	Moderately retarded	40–54
IV	Severely retarded	25–39
V	Profoundly retarded	0–24

[a]After Heber (1961).

in the mildly retarded range suffer some degree of organic impairment of the brain or central nervous system—and this has never been demonstrated—it is nevertheless the case that their disorder is first and foremost an inadequacy in social conduct. Such persons do not become diagnosed as mental retardates because some specific organic cause has been located. Causal diagnoses of this kind are rare exceptions. Rather, diagnoses are typically made by recourse to IQ testing *after* some degree of social incompetence has been demonstrated. This is not to suggest that one or another program of social engineering can greatly elevate the intelligence of all, or even many, of our more than 5 million mildly retarded. It is the case, however, that the relative competence of these persons is judged by social and cultural criteria. It is therefore the case that changes in social and cultural criteria, and thus in IQ test performance, would shift numbers of persons either out of, or into, the range of mild mental retardation. Furthermore, it is the case that changes in social and cultural conditions, especially as they affect early experience, might alter the adult IQs of large numbers of persons.

In short, most mental retardation is mild mental retardation, and mild mental retardation is a social phenomenon through and through.

Background to the Study

It has been said that there is no sin except stupidity—a view which, though it may appeal to some, is not likely to receive universal approval. If there be sin relating to stupidity, it more properly resides in the fact that the social sciences have failed to make a concerted effort to develop a sociology, or social psychology, of stupidity. The concern of this research is with the perception and management of incompetence—stupidity, if you will—among the mildly retarded. This study of incompetence is not simply an effort to increase our understanding of mental retardation, it is also an attempt to contribute knowledge toward a sociology of incompetence. The study of mental retardation is essential for obvious practical reasons, but it also offers basic theoretical insights for the social sciences, insights which are as yet largely unexploited. As long as the social sciences allow mental retardation to remain in some dark arcanum, our knowledge of mental retardation will lack sociological perspective. It cannot honestly be argued that this sociological perspective will serve as the long-sought philosopher's stone, transmuting mental retardates into persons of superior intellect, but it is undeniably the case that mild mental retardation has its roots in social and cultural phenomena, and thus far these phenomena have received only the most rudimentary study.[3]

An outstanding void in existing sociological knowledge of the mentally retarded is a detailed description of the everyday lives of such persons outside of custodial or treatment institutions.[4] Neither the details of their everyday conduct nor their own thoughts and emotions concerning their life circumstances have been documented. The present study is an effort to provide information about the life circumstances of a number of mildly retarded persons living in a large city.

This study has proceeded upon the belief that in order to understand the behavioral features of the everyday lives of these retarded persons, as well as their own feelings about themselves and their lives, it would be necessary to establish prolonged and direct personal contact with them. Insofar as possible, it would be necessary to see these people through their own eyes and to hear them in their own words. This approach has been the quintessence of the anthropological tradition since the days of Boas—perhaps its first exponent—and Malinowski, who gave it his most eloquent and forceful endorsement. This study, then, was an effort to urge certain mentally retarded persons to discuss their behavior, their thoughts, and their

3. See Edgerton (1963), and MacAndrew and Edgerton (1964).
4. The same void exists within institutions, although here, at least, there has been a beginning, e.g., Abel and Kinder (1942). Edgerton (1963), and MacAndrew and Edgerton (1964).

feelings as they themselves comprehend and experience them. Additionally, the goal is to provide a reasonably detailed account of the life circumstances of these persons and the ways in which they perceive and manage their relative incompetence. Finally, the study concentrates upon the crucial relevance of stigma and passing for an understanding of the lives of these persons.

Despite an impressively bulky literature dealing with the lives of the mentally retarded in the community, no existing report deals at all adequately with the details of their everyday lives or with their own reactions to themselves and their lives. The literature fails to provide us with an appreciation of what the lives of retarded persons are like in communities across the United States, and it fails totally to give us any understanding of the social-psychological dimensions of their lives and their problems. We search the literature in vain for some indication of what it might be like to live in a city or town as a mentally retarded person.

What we find when we examine the existing research is an immense accumulation of studies concerned with the relative adjustment of such persons in the community. Scores of studies since the 1920s offer information on the community lives of retardates released from sundry schools, colonies, and hospitals throughout the country.[5] These studies relate a host of details about marriage statistics, occupation, law violation, and, almost inevitably, some measure of "success" or "failure" in community living. Few, however, go beyond a statistical, demographic survey of the most gross and impersonal sort. Only a very few (e.g., Raymond, 1923; Camp and Waite, 1932; Hiatt, 1951; Charles, 1953) offer even brief case studies of the retarded persons who are being studied; most do not even interview the retardates themselves, but instead concentrate upon their parents, guardians, teachers, or employers.

The best available account of the texture and emotion of life among the mildly retarded is Abel and Kinder's *The Subnormal Adolescent Girl* (1942). The authors devoted considerable time to the study of the life experiences of some eighty-four adolescent girls who were being given industrial training in New York City. They suc-

5. Some of the more notable of these studies include: Town and Hill (1929), Foley (1929), Doll (1930), Powdermaker (1930), Olin (1930), Fairbank (1933), Hay and Kappenburg (1931), York, (1939), Kinder *et al.* (1941), Abel and Kinder (1942), Whitney (1948), Hilliard (1954), O'Connor and Tizard (1956), Saenger (1957), O'Connor (1957), Shafter (1957), Tarjan *et al.* (1960).

ceeded in portraying something of the substance of the lives of these girls and something of their personalities, but very little case material is offered and the girls' own perceptions of their efforts to cope with their relative incompetence are dealt with only very sketchily. We still see too little of the mentally retarded persons' efforts to adapt their deficient intellects to the demands of city life. Much, much more is needed, even for a beginning. The following study is offered as a step toward that beginning.

The Study

Since the purpose of this study was to examine some of the ways in which mentally retarded persons manage their lives and perceive themselves when left to their own devices in a large city, the choice of a population for study was decidedly limited. Most such persons are either formally institutionalized or have their lives managed for them by their own relatives, by foster families, or by other parental surrogates.

However, the facilities of Pacific State Hospital offered an opportunity to reach a suitable population. Pacific State Hospital is a large California state institution for the mentally retarded. Opened in 1927, it gradually increased in size to an inpatient capacity of over 3,000 patients served by a staff of over 1,500 employees at the time of this research. As the institution grew, it changed its orientation from custodial care to intensive therapy, both medical and psychological.

By reviewing the records of this hospital it was possible to select patients who met the required conditions for inclusion in the study. There were several conditions. First, a substantial number of retarded persons was required. In addition, in order to select persons who had a reasonable chance of success in independent city living, persons would have to be selected who were near the upper limits of the mildly retarded range, both in terms of their measured IQs and their estimated social competence. These persons also needed to have been discharged from the hospital and to have remained free from any formal supervision either by Pacific State Hospital or any other social agency or institution. Finally, at the time of their release, these persons must have been free of the supervision or guardianship of parents, relatives, or friends; they must have been released with the explicit understanding that they were expected to live on their own resources.

Such a population of incompetent persons was available. One of Pacific State Hospital's training and rehabilitation programs involved vocational training and experience both within the hospital and in supervised work placements in the community. Patients selected for this program represented the upper stratum of the hospital's mildly retarded patients in regard to their IQs, their demonstrated social competence, and their demonstrated emotional stability. Each patient in this program progressed from simple, undemanding jobs within the institution to a supervised job placement in the community. Most patients in this program returned from "work leave" in the community to the hospital several times before they succeeded in demonstrating that they were competent to manage their own lives without the aid or control of the institution.

During the period 1949 to 1958, 110 patients successfully graduated from this vocational training program and were discharged from the hospital without any reservations on their freedom. No guardians were appointed, and no restrictions were specified. These 110 persons were free to conduct their lives with the same freedoms enjoyed by any other citizen. As far as was known at that time, their lives were free from the influence of parents, relatives, or institutions.

This population of 110 former patients of an institution for the mentally retarded was the research cohort selected for study. Of this cohort, 55 were men and 55 were women. Their ages ranged from seventy-five to twenty, but the mean was thirty-five. Eighty-one were Caucasian, twenty-two were Mexican-American, 5 were Negro, 1 was American Indian, and 1 was Nisei. The mean IQ of the cohort was 64. The characteristics of the cohort are shown in Table 2.

Thus, members of the research cohort are near the upper limit of the mildly retarded range in intelligence, they have a demonstrated ability for self-support, and they are old enough to have achieved some emotional stability. In short, the members of the cohort are the most competent socially and most able intellectually of the patients to have been hospitalized at Pacific State Hospital over the ten-year period prior to the research. If there were any group of persons once institutionalized as being mentally retarded who could be expected

Table 2 *Characteristics of the Cohort*

Sex		Race				Mean age	Mean IQ	Mean days in hospital before discharge	Mean date of discharge
		White	Negro	Mexican-American	Other				
Male	55	44	2	8	1	33.7	66.5	6,935	1954.4
Female	55	37	3	14	1	35.6	62.9	8,086	1954.2
Total or mean	110	81	5	22	2	34.6	64.7	7,510	1954.3

to have an opportunity for successful independent living outside an institution, it would be this group. In fact, thirteen of these persons had IQs over 70, but since they were formally institutionalized for mental retardation, and were defined as such, they were retained in the cohort. The relationship between IQ and social competence will be discussed in chapter 5.

RESEARCH PROCEDURES

In June, 1960, the search for the 110 members of the cohort was begun. All available sources were utilized in the effort to locate the former patients: Pacific's records, living relatives, former employers, hospital-affiliated social workers, Los Angeles welfare agencies, training schools, police files, coroners' records, state and private hospital admissions, private physicians and dentists, telephone directories, credit agencies, credit departments of large retail stores, and finally, the advice of a retired private investigator.

Most of the former patients were relatively easy to locate. Within six months, 85 percent had been located. But when the search was terminated after twelve months (May, 1961), 12 of the original 110 had still not been located. No ingenuity or diligence of detective work was sufficient to provide leads on these remaining 12 persons.

Nothing is known about the post-hospital careers of these twelve persons, but as a group, their known pre-hospital and hospital experiences and their general characteristics do not differ notably from those of the entire cohort. For example, five have IQs above the cohort IQ mean of 64; seven are below the mean. Four are over the cohort mean age of thirty-five; eight are below it. Six were discharged before the cohort mean date of 1954; six were released after the mean date.

Many of the ninety-eight former patients who were located had migrated such distances from Pacific State Hospital that the cost of an attempt to contact them all personally would have been prohibitive. Hence, a fifty-mile radius from Pacific State Hospital was designated as an arbitrary geographical area within which intensive study would be undertaken. This area included most of Los Angeles County as well as the cities of San Bernardino and Riverside to the east and Long Beach to the south. Fifty-three of the located members of the cohort were present within this fifty-mile radius study area, but forty-five were outside the area. The mobility of many of

Table 3 *Locations of 45 Cohort Members who were Outside the 50-mile Study Area*

Location	Male	Female	Total
California, outside 50-mile radius	4	12	16
In prisons in California	6	1	7
In hospitals in California	4	2	6
Out of state[a] (not institutionalized)	10	3	13
Deceased	2	1	3
Total	26	19	45

[a](Arizona, Illinois, Iowa, Michigan, Mississippi, Nebraska, New Jersey, New York (2), Oklahoma, Oregon, Utah, Washington.)

these former patients, all of whom entered the hospital from the Southern California area, is striking. But it is consistent with the findings of other studies.[6] Table 3 indicates the whereabouts of the 45 located members of the cohort who were excluded from the study.

Comparison of the basic descriptive data concerning members of the cohort indicates that other than mobility there were no major differences between the persons inside the fifty-mile radius study area and those who were located outside this area. This comparison is shown in Table 4.

One possible point of contrast is the relative percentage of males and females in the two groups (58 percent females in study area and only 42 percent outside of it) but this is hardly a major differential. This difference aside, the former patients located outside the study area were similar in age, IQ, and date of discharge to those within the study area. Thus while the exclusion of nearly 50 percent of the cohort from intensive study admittedly lessens the general applicability of the findings, there is some reason to believe that the population studied is not atypical of the cohort as a whole.

DATA COLLECTION

Personal contacts were made with all of the fifty-three former patients who were located within the fifty-mile radius study area. In fifty-one of these cases, repeated contact was made; in two

6. For example, see the studies of Baller (1936) and Charles (1953) concerning the mobility of mental retardates over a fifteen-year period in Nebraska.

Table 4 *Comparison of Cohort Members Inside the 50-Mile Study Area with Those Outside the Study Area*

				Race						
Location	*Total*	*Male*	*Female*	*White*	*Negro*	*Mexican-American*	*Other*	*Mean age*	*Mean IQ*	*Mean date of discharge*
In study area	53	25	28	42	3	8	0	34.3	65.3	1954.6
Outside the study area	45	26	19	33	2	10	0	32.8	65.1	1954.9
Not located	12	4	8	6	0	4	2	34.1	60.6	1954.1
Total or mean	110	55	55	81	5	22	2	34.6	64.7	1954.7

cases, the initial contact was met with refusal to be interviewed again. In both cases, the refusal was made by a "normal" person—in one case a husband and, in the other, an adoptive "mother." Detailed information was collected for fifty-one of the ex-patients; in three instances, although several contacts were made, the data collected were not considered to be sufficiently complete. These three cases were excluded from this report. Thus, the total number of ex-patients for whom detailed data are reported is forty-eight.

The research staff—all of whom interviewed and did participant-observation—consisted of three senior students (one in sociology, one in anthropology, and one in psychology), two experienced secondary-school teachers, a graduate student in sociology, and the author. In all, there were four men and three women.

DATA COLLECTION PROCEDURES

Initial contact was made in person by one or more of the interviewers who introduced himself (or herself) as an employee of the research department of Pacific State Hospital. The former patient was immediately relieved of any suspicion that this research visit portended any action that might cause him or her to be reinstitutionalized. Assurance was given that the reason for the visit was simply an interest in how the former patient "was getting along." It was added that we wanted to learn about the experiences of patients discharged from the hospital in order that we might improve the hospital's program and better counsel patients who would be discharged in the future. The patients were asked to discuss their feelings about their lives in the hospital as well as their experiences after being discharged. The emphasis was always upon a friendly and interested conversational approach. The former patients were encouraged to speak at length about any subject they chose. Only after this most informal introductory period was an attempt made to follow an interview schedule.

Since this research was dedicated to learning about the problems of mental retardates in the community by observing and participating in the lives of such persons and by permitting them to present their own lives in their own words, the interview schedule, though focused upon certain information areas, was very loosely structured. The interviewers were instructed to lead the respondent into a discussion of certain areas of interest by nondirective questioning. The areas of interest were focused in general upon (1) where and how the ex-patients lived, (2) making a living, (3) relations with others in the community, (4) sex, marriage, and children, (5) "spare time" activities, (6) their perception and presentation of self, and (7) their practical problems in maintaining themselves in the community.

Conjointly with these friendly and informal interviews, as much participant-observation as possible in the lives of the former patients was undertaken. This included trips to recreational areas, grocery shopping, shopping excursions in department stores, sight-seeing drives, social visits in their homes, invitations to restaurants, participation in housework, financial planning, parties, and visits to the homes of friends and relatives. Notes were never taken in the presence of the former patient although, with the ex-patients' knowledge, some sessions were tape-recorded on inconspicious portable machines after rapport had been established.

Further, whenever it was possible, friends, relatives, neighbors, and employers were also interviewed. This approach was exceedingly delicate as great care had to be taken never to expose the private past of the ex-patients to someone who did not know of the period of institutionalization for mental retardation. Often, however, in the course of establishing contact with a former patient, it was discovered that other persons already knew of the ex-patient's past. In these circumstances, the interested and knowledgeable parties were interviewed at length about the former patient's life and their involvement in it. But where the ex-patient had concealed the past, nothing was ever done to disclose his secret.

The field-workers were rotated so that the former patients were seen by two or more field-workers, usually both a male and a female. The contacts with the ex-patients were long and repeated, as seen by the fact that the mean number of hours of contact per respondent was seventeen. No one was seen for fewer than five hours and some ex-patients received over ninety hours of contact.

The ease with which contacts were made and maintained was extraordinary. Literally from the first ring of the doorbell, the lives of these former patients were open to us. There was virtually no resistance or reticence, and except for the two previously mentioned cases, there were no refusals to cooperate. Typically, once the field workers had completed their introductions, they were welcomed from the outset, and treated as confidants and friends. Response was both voluble and free. The reasons for this phenomenal degree of acceptance are not entirely clear, but in large part they reflect the attitude of these former patients that "people from the hospital" were not to be lied to—"They've got everything written down, they know all about us." And, in part, this acceptance indicates the loneliness of many of these people and their eagerness to attach themselves to anyone who would listen to their life stories and problems with polite interest.

In five or six instances, our rapport diminished after the first few contacts, but in each of these cases the disaffection could be traced to the intervention of another, "normal," member of the community, who had become suspicious of our activities and had advised the former patient to avoid further association with us. Overwhelmingly, however, we enjoyed a uniquely complete acceptance and welcome. Our problem was not in the establishment of rapport but rather in terminating the relationship when the research had been completed, without engendering undue disappointment. As a consequence, the information acquired appears to be an accurate reflection of the everyday lives of these retarded persons.

CHAPTER TWO

Detailed Portraits
of Selected Persons

This chapter will provide extended portraits of certain of the ex-patients who have been selected to represent typical modes of living. True typicality is largely fiction, of course, but these people are, insofar as possible, representative of their fellows who live in like circumstances. These persons were chosen for intensive description because their lives provide a sense of the range of competence which the ex-patients in this research cohort possess, as well as the variety of the problems they face in their everyday lives. Furthermore, they are persons about whom there was a mass of detailed knowledge sufficient to permit an extensive and objective account of their lives.

Four cases will be presented. Case A is a retarded man married to a retarded woman; their life together is filled with stress, but at times both persons display considerable competence. Case B is a single man who represents a relatively high degree of competence and a complex mode of life. Case C is a single woman whose competence is minimal and whose life is miserable. Her plight is not unusual for single women. Case D is a woman married to a normal man. Her competence is in the lower middle range, compared with the other ex-patients, and her marriage is in many ways typical of the relationship between retarded women and their normal husbands.

The term "normal," as employed throughout, refers to any person who has never been in an institution for the mentally retarded and who gives no good reason for suspicion that his intelligence is below the normal range. Normal, then, refers only to apparent intelligence and nothing more. The term is in many ways unfortunate, but it will be used because it is less cumbrous than the alternatives.

The detailed vignettes in this chapter are intended to present an immediate and vivid introduction to the lives and capabilities of these retarded persons. For this reason, the present tense is often used, although the present is, in reality, the time of research contact. Although personal names have been changed to assure anonymity, the places and events in the lives of these persons remain unaltered.

Case A. Hank and May: Ex-Patients Who Married Each Other

LIFE BEFORE PACIFIC: HANK SCOTT

Hank's father was an illiterate Englishman who came to the United States in 1889 and, at the age of thirteen, settled in California, where he worked as a cattle feeder on a large ranch. He did not marry until 1924, when he and the luetic daughter of a transient farm worker settled down together. She had no education, was considered to be "nervous" and was thought by some to be of subnormal mentality.

Their first child, June, was born the following year; two years later, Hank was born. Hank appeared to be normal at birth and he began walking and talking at the age of one. However, both parents soon concluded that his speech was indistinct and sometimes incoherent. At two, Hank had pneumonia, and throughout these early years was badly malnourished and rachitic.

Hank and his sister competed for the attention of their father, and after a bitter struggle, Hank won. Hank tried never to leave his father's side; before Hank was three years old, he went to work with his father, and followed him everywhere around the house. June was ignored and she was intensely jealous.

In 1932, when Hank was only five, his father died. Hank was inconsolable, and his mother, who had always resented the boy's exclusive affection for his father, was both unable and unwilling to help him. June, on the other hand, was triumphant. A third baby, William, was born a few months after his father's death. Hank's mother was unable to support her three children in these depression years, and a few months later, she placed Hank and June in separate orphanages. She kept her favorite, the baby William, with her.

During the next seven years, Hank was shuttled from orphanage to orphanage. He was terribly unhappy and mourned for his father. Also, he became increasingly disturbed, with episodes of dangerously aggressive behavior. For example, at the age of eight, he strangled another little boy and only artificial respiration saved the victim's life. During these years, he attended school only two years, and then haphazardly. He was considered to be poor in all subjects. He was regularly reported to be a behavior problem for fighting, masturbation, and voyeurism, and eventually his behavior became completely unacceptable. At this point, the orphanage complained to Hank's mother and she turned to Pacific State Hospital. In 1939, at the age of twelve, Hank was placed in Pacific.

LIFE IN PACIFIC

Hank entered Pacific with profound hostility toward his mother, whom he accused of abandoning, and indeed hating, him. In truth, Hank's mother was completely rejecting and unwilling to do anything for Hank or his sister. She made it very clear that both children were incompetent and unworthy, and insisted that neither child should ever be permitted to leave Pacific. She often wrote letters to the superintendent at Pacific repeating her conviction that "if they died it would be a mercy."

Hank's IQ at admission was 65, but by 1956 it had risen to 77. Hank went to school at Pacific and did as well as most patients at the school. His vocational training included jobs in the laundry and the cafeteria and clean-up work on the nursery wards. Hank was an able but erratic worker. He worked best alone and would not tolerate close supervision, against which he repeatedly reacted with explosive anger. Still, he became known as a good worker and within five years was considered to be one of the very best workers in Pacific.

His relations with employees in the hospital were acceptable, but he was known as a "loner" among the patients. He had few friends, and the girls thought him withdrawn and aloof. He was not considered to be a problem patient, although he was occasionally in trouble because of his temper. He was sterilized in 1946 at the age of nineteen. His mother remarked in signing the consent papers that her son's sterilization was "a damn good thing. We don't need no more around like him."

Hank detested his loss of freedom in Pacific and felt debased by his enforced association with so many, as he put it, "handicapped" people. He was always eager to leave the hospital and in 1949 his good work-record was rewarded with an indefinite leave to work on a nearby cattle ranch. Hank was satisfied in this work, which duplicated his early childhood experiences. He worked well in this sheltered atmosphere for a full year, only to be returned to Pacific abruptly under unclear circumstances. Hank resented his return to Pacific and demanded that he be sent out on another work assignment. But it was only after two more years of confinement, during which time Hank was sullen and resentful, that he was given another job, this time doing general clean-up work in a sanitarium. With the exception of occasional short returns for medical care, Hank was never again sent back to the hospital.

However, his years on leave from Pacific were anything but tranquil and completely successful. Hank had four separate work placements, and in each of these he had serious problems with his employer and his co-workers. The pattern was always the same: unwillingness to "take orders" from a "boss," great difficulties managing money, a tendency to work only when he felt like it, and temper outbursts at the least opportune moments.

Hank's experience with girls had been very limited in the hospital but one of the girls he had known slightly was May Hatfield. When Hank and May met on "work leave" in June, 1955, Hank began a whirlwind courtship that ended in marriage three months later. After two and one-half years of marriage, Hank was discharged in March, 1958.

LIFE BEFORE PACIFIC: MAY HATFIELD

May's father was born in Chicago in 1900. He completed only a fifth-grade education before he went to work as a manual laborer. He served as a cook in the Navy for four months at the end of the First World War, but for unknown reasons he spent the year after the war in a mental hospital, diagnosed simply as "insane." After one year he escaped from the hospital and made his way west to Utah. In 1922 he married, but after several months of conflict his wife left him. In 1924 he was remarried, this time to May's mother.

She was a Mormon girl, born and raised in Utah. She completed an eighth-grade education but "had trouble" with her parents and "ran off" to marry at the age of seventeen. When this husband deserted her after a few months, she took another husband in common law. He too left her. Her third husband, whom she married in 1924, was May's father.

May was their first child. She was born two months prematurely and weighed only two and one-half pounds. Her eyes were crossed from birth, but she showed surprising vigor and health and was able to walk and talk at eighteen months. For her first eight years she traveled with her parents. Her father had become a roustabout with a circus and the family was continually on the move. For these first eight years May received no schooling whatever. When May was eight, her father was in a serious automobile accident, and while he was recovering he was transferred to a mental hospital, where he was confined as a "psychopathic personality," a "moron" with a mental age of 12.6 years, and a "syphilitic." He is still alive in this State hospital.

After her husband was injured and then institutionalized, May's mother no longer felt able to care for May and her younger brother (this brother is of borderline intelligence and has been arrested on charges of drunk driving, possession of marijuana, and bigamy). She consequently placed both children in foster homes and had little further contact with either of them before her death in 1951 (she committed suicide by eating ant poison).

May bounced between several foster homes only to be placed in a Catholic home for "wayward" girls at the age of thirteen when her enuresis allegedly became unmanageable in her last foster home. In May, 1941, at the age of sixteen, she was placed in Pacific by county authorities. Her IQ was measured at 65.

LIFE IN PACIFIC

May remembers her life in the hospital as being not too unpleasant: "In some ways it was better than being outside." She worked on wards for children, and she did housework for the doctors' families. She did not always get along with the other patients, who felt that she was "stuck up" and "snotty." She had many fights with other girls her age but she was popular with the boys, who found her attractive. While in the hospital, her epilepsy became manifest and she experienced *grand mal* seizures.

After eleven years in the hospital May was officially considered to be a "good worker" and she was finally sent out on "work leave" in 1952. She was terrified at the prospect of "making it on my own on the outside," but after it was pointed out that she would still be helped, supervised, and protected by the hospital, she agreed to try. Between 1952 and 1956 she had eight different work placements— seven were in sanitariums and one was doing general housework for a private family. Her response to these jobs was always the same: for some months she would work well enough to be given added trust and responsibility; she would then become frightened at the thought of failure and would develop gross somatic complaints, repeated sei- zures, and some bizarre delusions and actions; eventually she would quit, "for my health." Each time, following a period of illness and complete dependency, her social worker would give her another chance. Finally, when she did well on one job for two full years, she was discharged.

During her years on work leave May dated several patients who were similarly "out" on leave. After an off-and-on courtship she ob- tained her social worker's permission to marry Hank in 1955. Al- though Hank and May were separated several times, full discharge was granted to May in 1958 with the formal prediction that both she and Hank were "capable of self-support and successful marriage."

LIFE AFTER DISCHARGE: HANK AND MAY

When located in the summer and fall of 1960, Hank was a tall, gaunt man of thirty-three. Although he weighs less than 140 pounds and is six feet tall, Hank has a "wiry" muscular body. His hair is lank and uncombed, and his beard is only occasionally and partially shaved, so that he presents a thoroughly disreputable appearance. Hank seldom washes either himself or his clothing; his face is splotched with dirt, his hands are grease-encrusted, his fingernails are black, his shirts are badly sweat-stained, his pants ap- pear never to have been washed, and his old black shoes manage to be both muddy and dusty. His speech is clear and articulate and his vocabulary surprisingly good when he is calm and self-possessed. However, under stress, as when speaking to strangers or when angry or frightened, Hank stutters, stammers, and becomes quite inarticulate. The general impression is of a sullen, suspicious, rustic man, but not necessarily a retarded one.

At the time of contact, May was thirty-five years old. She is a short, pudgy woman whose fatness is most noticeable in her puffy face, ankles, wrists, and elbows. Her light brown hair is in perpetual disarray and she often tries to brush it out of her face with a nervous, ineffectual gesture. Her eyes dominate her face, for she suffers from severe strabismus and one eye is continually wandering off, away from the gaze of the other. May's teeth also command attention as they are very yellow and crooked. Furthermore, most of May's small wardrobe is too small for her, accentuating her excessive weight. She dresses cheaply, mostly in worn, simple clothes and sandals. She seldom uses lipstick or any other cosmetic and owns only a few pieces of costume jewelry, which she almost never wears. Her fingernails are generally quite dirty. By repeated complaints, whimpers, and tears she conveys a picture of abject suffering at all times.

NEIGHBORHOOD, HOME, POSSESSIONS

Since their marriage five years ago, Hank and May have moved many times, sometimes because they have lost a job, other times because they have failed to pay the rent or have antagonized the landlord. They have lived in quarters provided by sanitariums; they have rented their own house; and they have had a number of apartments, furnished and unfurnished.

At the time of contact, they occupied a tiny run-down apartment on the back lot of a private home. The neighborhood is a middle- to upper-middle-income residential area in the San Fernando Valley. The main house is large and looks expensive. The front yard is professionally landscaped and cared for. The large backyard is planted in vegetables and fruit trees. The owner has built two small "guest house" apartments on this back lot, far from the main house. The larger of these apartments is attractive and fully equipped. The smaller one is far less appealing. It consists of a small room that serves as sitting room and bedroom, a tiny adjoining kitchen, and an equally small bathroom. It is intended to be a bachelor apartment but it is unfinished, with still incomplete wood paneling, painting, and furnishings. It was here that Hank and May were living.

Their present reduced circumstances are due in part to earlier problems. For one thing, when Hank and May were first married they not only rented a six-room house but also purchased a large amount of new furniture at a department store. The rent and the furniture payments were far beyond their financial resources. Hank and May were unable to pay the rent and they went heavily in debt for the furniture. This failure left them in serious financial trouble for several years. But as the debt was slowly paid off, their circumstances improved, and just before the time of research contact they were living in a relatively nice furnished apartment for which they were able to pay seventy dollars a month. Then, May suffered an epileptic seizure in the home where she was working as a housekeeper; following the seizure she apparently demolished much of the furniture in the house and assaulted the unfortunate woman who employed her with a leg broken off a chair. When the police restored order, May was taken in for observation and was judged to be in need of psychiatric treatment. She was admitted to a State mental hospital with a diagnosis of "chronic brain syndrome associated with convulsive disorder with psychotic reaction." While May was in the hospital, Hank neglected to pay the rent (or any other bills). Three months later, when May was released from the mental hospital, their financial condition was again deplorable.

Hank found the current apartment by answering an ad in the paper and in doing so he found unexpected good fortune. The landlady was extremely sympathetic and provided the small apartment at minimal rent, gave them both odd jobs, donated food, and generally did a great deal to help them.

Hank and May have almost no possessions of their own. He has very little clothing; his wardrobe consists of a few work clothes that are inexpensive and old, and one old-fashioned, double-breasted suit coat. May has a few clothes—most of them are old and simple cotton dresses—but she keeps them all packed in a few cardboard cartons. Their only other possessions are a few magazines of his and a few cookbooks of hers. They owe more money ($160) than all their worldly possessions are worth.

MAKING A LIVING

When Hank and May were first married she was by far the more successful of the two as a wage earner—not only was she able to hold a job better than he but she earned more money. May worked in a sanitarium as a "nurse's aide" and cleaning woman, and she also did live-in housekeeping in a private home. While May was working with relative success, Hank was having problems; he lost several jobs and was able to earn little money (never over seventy-five cents an hour). He explains that his problems were due to his stubbornness: "You know I always say they don't teach you how to work in the hole (Pacific). I always say, 'easy in ain't easy out.' You gotta learn how to work and how to take orders. I used to balk back, but I learned to control myself when I get to feeling ornery. Like once when I was pearl-diving (washing dishes) at this restaurant, the boss said I was working too slow, so I balked back and just walked out. Left him just standing there."

For the last five years, on and off, Hank has worked at a factory that hires "handicapped persons" to refinish used furniture and clothing. When Hank went so deeply into debt in his disastrous purchase of new furniture, this organization assumed his debt and has deducted small sums from his salary for the last five years. He has left this job on several occasions but has always been accepted back when he returned. He started at sixty cents an hour and now earns a dollar an hour. His duties consist of loading and unloading trucks, moving crates, cleaning up, and scraping paint off used furniture. He is proud of the fact that he walks two miles each way to work.

Hank's hatred for work of any kind knows no bounds. He especially detests "dirty" work, claiming that he always "gets stuck" with the difficult and dirty jobs. When he has been given such a "dirty" job, like scraping paint off old chairs, he will not come to work for several days. When he fails to show up for work, he receives no pay, but he says, "There's times when I get the itchy foot, I guess it's just the gypsy in me. I just gotta get away. All I've ever done is work. I've been working since I was a little kid and I just gotta balk back sometimes."

Occasionally Hank will boast of his ability to work, saying that nothing is too hard for him to do nor too heavy for him to lift because he has such great "strength," but for the most part he complains bitterly about having to do *any* work.

The most Hank ever makes per week is $40; with his debts, this is usually reduced by 25 percent. May has been unable to work regularly for the last two years, but she used to receive public welfare assistance in the amount of $106 per month. While she was receiving this and Hank was earning roughly $160 a month, they were able to meet their expenses and reduce their debts somewhat. But following an episode in which her "closest friend" (a normal girl who lived in the same apartment) "borrowed" her welfare check, she was thought guilty of wrongdoing and, following a review of her case, was found to be well enough to go back to work. Not only did her work pay less than her Bureau of Public Assistance aid had, but she was unable to work regularly and eventually became so "nervous" that she had to quit altogether. She had just returned to work when she suffered the psychotic episode that took her to the hospital.

While she was in the hospital, Hank spent all the money he earned on beer and a girlfriend. He even visited May in the hospital twice in an effort to borrow money from her. The bills and the rent went unpaid. At the time of research contact Hank and May had almost no money and were sometimes forced to go hungry.

SEX, MARRIAGE, AND CHILDREN

When May left the hospital on work leave, she dated modestly and conservatively, seeing one or another fellow work-leave patient for an occasional quiet date at a movie. One of the boys she dated "once in a while" was Hank, but she did not particularly like him. Hank says, in fact, that "at first she hated my guts." At this same time Hank was conducting himself with less restraint. He often visited "sexy" movies and burlesque shows on "skid row," drank heavily, and then spent his earnings on a B-girl or prostitute. It was only after he was rolled by a B-girl that he began to avoid this area and confined his romantic interests to girls from Pacific also out on work leave. One of these latter so entranced him that he had her name tattooed on his arm.

After about a year, May was "going steady" with a work-leave patient who worked at the sanitarium where Hank worked. Hank still had some interest in May (who was then slim and fairly attractive) and he delighted in tormenting her ineffectual boyfriend by telling how he could take May away from him "any time I want." One day he did just this by taking May on a date and seducing her. He recalls the experience by saying, "I just couldn't wait to sink my hooks in her." Hank still had no desire to marry May but he did delight in flaunting his conquest before May's "steady" boyfriend, who had to be returned to Pacific in an acute anxiety state.

But at this point an event occurred that changed everything.

Hank's sister, June, got married. She too was out of Pacific (a cohort member) on work leave and, as always, she and Hank were competing strenuously. June was determined to marry not simply a normal man but a successful one, and she married an engineer at an aircraft plant. When Hank heard that she had married "an outside guy" who was an "important" and "rich" man, he was beside himself with envy.

Hank immediately decided that he too would marry to show June that "she was no better than I was." He chose May. May still was highly ambivalent in her feelings toward Hank, but she had become so guilty about having sexual relations with him that she decided she "had" to marry him. Hank and May immediately asked their respective social workers for permission to marry, and received reluctant approval one month later. Hank was no sooner married than he made the extravagant purchase of furniture for his newly rented house. This too was done to "show" June that he was as "good" as she was. The debt Hank incurred was an embarrassment to the social workers involved, who were in the uncomfortable position of having sanctioned a marriage that was motivated by jealousy and begun with high irresponsibility. The social workers responded by separating the couple.

In fact, in the next eighteen months May's social worker three times interceded to separate the couple, but each time Hank was able to win back May's affection and overcome her social worker's reservations (sometimes with the assistance of his own social worker). The last time they were reunited, their marriage and economic situation appeared to have improved sufficiently for them to be granted final discharge. Once this discharge was received, there were no formal separations, but their relationship continued to be uneasy.

Both Hank and May recognize in retrospect that they were not prepared for marriage. As Hank puts it: "That hospital sure didn't teach nothing about marriage life." He explained that the patients did not learn about the practical matters essential to getting and holding a job, about managing money, about shopping, "or nothing important about life on the outs." And, he lamented, "They sure don't teach you about the bees and the . . . " (he couldn't remember what went with the bees in the phrase). Both he and May were agreed that they didn't understand "about the bees" and had to learn "the hard way."

One thing they did not understand was the efficiency and permanency of the surgical sterilization performed at Pacific. May desperately wanted to have children, and four times she announced to Hank that she was pregnant. Each time Hank responded with anger and reiterated his hatred for children, saying, "The last thing I wanted on earth was to have any 'damn kids.' " In each instance of presumed pregnancy May glowed with anticipation and elaborated her dreams of motherhood; but all four times there was a "miscarriage" and the phantom pregnancy was terminated. Hank gloats over her "miscarriages," saying, "She came across four times but she couldn't make it." May deeply resented his attitude and struck back by accusing him of fathering a child out of wedlock, at the same time that he refused her the child she had "a right to." Both Hank and May are infertile.

As time passed in their marriage and as May "lost child after child," her health worsened and she frequently lay in bed for days. Her health was not improved by Hank's extramarital affairs, which became more frequent and more blatant. Everyone, including May, had to know what was going on. For example, while Hank and May were living in a cooperative apartment house, Hank began to extend his unique view of cooperation to his next-door neighbor's wife. His romance next door was known to everyone in the building, and finally the cuckolded husband sued for divorce, naming Hank as a correspondent. It is in this affair that May accuses Hank of paternity. But this was simply one of many times that Hank had sexual relations with other women. At the time of this study Hank was spending virtually all his money and spare time with a woman he met at work, again with no attempt at concealment. This woman owned a car (which in Hank's explanation was her principal virtue) and drove Hank "all over." She was a three-times divorced woman of about thirty, short and quite fat, with a prominent speech impediment. The other men at the factory described her as "real trouble, wildfire," and indicated that "only a damn fool would have anything to do with that one."

This affair became so serious that Hank considered divorcing May in order to marry his girlfriend. It was by no means the first time he had considered divorcing May, but it was the first time that he actually took some action and the first time that he had someone else in mind to marry. He says that he made up his mind to divorce May before she entered the mental hospital. While she was in the hospital he wrote to her doctor (with his girlfriend's help) as follows: "I have made a decision regarding May and that is that it is better for both of us if we do not live together again. I do not have any place for her to live and I do not make enough money to help her also we do not get along and we upset each other when we are together. I hope that you can help her." Thanks to the psychiatrist's discretion, the letter was never shown to May.

When Hank learned that divorce proceedings would be difficult if not impossible while May remained in the hospital, he drove to the hospital (with his girlfriend) and indicated that he didn't want to leave May after all. On the contrary, he insisted that his earlier letter was a mistake, and he wanted her to come home with him. Two weeks later May was granted indefinite leave to go home to Hank. She had no sooner returned than Hank informed her of his intention to get a divorce as soon as possible. "My stubborn mind's made up," he announced. Later he admitted to a research worker that he had arranged matters this way because "I knew I couldn't divorce her while she was in no hospital."

Faced with such a stunning ultimatum, May sought help from all her former friends. She asked advice and protection because, she said, Hank had threatened her if she "didn't go along." Hank admits that he sometimes "gets ornery," especially after he has "killed a few beers," but there is no evidence that he has ever struck May. There is plenty of evidence, however, that he abused her verbally and that they had bitter quarrels. As this conflict grew, May became more terrified of Hank yet more afraid of losing him. But two factors combined to "save me," as May put it. The landlady interceded on May's behalf and threatened Hank with a series of unpleasantries if he persisted. These included legal support for May, eviction for Hank, and legal action against him for debts past due. At the same time, for reasons that are unknown, Hank's girlfriend became angry and, as he said, "called the whole deal off." Hank then repented, agreed to try to pay his bills to his landlady, and returned to May. Although the conversation between them was barely civil, the tension was reduced, they were speaking to each other, and they were once again making plans for the future—together.

FRIENDS, FAMILY, AND THE COMMUNITY

May has but one living relative and he (her younger brother) is currently in jail in northern California. They have no contact. As has been noted already, Hank's competitive relations with his sister June have been of immense importance to him from his earliest years. He still feels that it is absolutely essential for him to be conspicuously more successful "on the outs" than she is. She shares this competitive and hostile feeling and believes her own success in life to be so complete that she will "not have anything to do with someone like Hank." In fact, she refuses to see or to aid Hank or May, even though May (not Hank) has sought her advice and assistance on several occasions. Hank's mother is still alive in a hospital in central California, where she has been an invalid for many years. Hank has not seen her since 1955 on the grounds that "I get too twisted up when I see her." This comment reflects his anger toward his mother far more than it does any affection. He says that he hates his mother, and everything he does would confirm that this hate exists with very little ambivalence on his part. Thus, for May and for Hank, neither kindness nor assistance has ever been available from their relatives.

Their relations with friends are little better. Neither one was popular with other patients while in Pacific and neither has made lasting friendships after leaving the hospital. Hank has never established any friendships with other men, and although he has had a number of girlfriends, these relationships seem to be entirely sexual in character and have never lasted for any length of time. This is not too surprising in view of his firm conviction that "you shouldn't get too close to people—you can't trust anyone in this world." May claims to have many friends, but upon investigation, none of these alleged friends would admit to being anything more than a casual acquaintance. For example, one of these "good friends" of May is the girl who borrowed or stole her relief checks. On one occasion it was possible to observe the couple described by May as her "best friends," in a demonstration of their friendship. May had often mentioned this girl and her husband, emphasizing their friendship for her. On this occasion, May had been afraid to stay at home alone because Hank had argued with her and had then gone out to drink and she was afraid that he would be "ornery" when he returned. So she asked one of the researchers to drive her to her friend's place, where she would spend the night. Even though the researcher was present throughout, these friends not only declined to have May spend the night but were unfriendly, even hostile toward her. When asked later to reconcile their behavior with their supposed friendship, May said only that she "guessed" that they didn't "have room" for her that night. In fact, neither Hank nor May has any friends that can be relied upon for affection or assistance.

On the other hand, Hank or May do have excellent knowledge of the community. They have traveled rather extensively in the Los Angeles area, and they know their own neighborhood quite well. They know the stores and restaurants and their prices. They know where they can get bargains in markets, cafes, and bars. They know the bus schedules, and Hank in particular is fully capable of long walks when buses are unavailable. They also know what community resources are available to them.

Their knowledge derives in part from the extraordinary intercession of others in their lives. For the first two years of their marriage, they were under the formal supervision of social workers affiliated with Pacific. As has already been mentioned, these social workers took an active role in the marriage. But after marriage, when formal supervision ceased, informal supervision and intervention continued. May's social worker in particular retained an active interest in her welfare. He has sometimes telephoned or visited her and he was always ready to offer advice or, if need be, to take action if May called him. Many times, it was only the threat of the social worker's intervention that gave May any ability to contend with Hank. He also provided vital knowledge of community resources that might be available and repeatedly interceded on the couple's behalf with employers, aggrieved landlords, cuckolded husbands, and others who were in need of mollification. When he transferred to another area some six months before the time of research contact, a terrible void in May's life was created.

Hank's social worker was far less involved either officially or unofficially on behalf of her charge. Nonetheless, on several occasions she did defend him against May's social worker, and recently has lent him small sums of money, given him advice on divorce and legal matters, and even supported him in many of his schemes.

When May's social worker left her life, another benefactor appeared, in the form of the landlady. This woman, who had originally befriended Hank, soon transferred her protection to May. She gave May the promise of every assistance and provided small household tasks for spending money. Perhaps most important of all, she gave May essential emotional support and encouragement. At the time of the couple's crisis over divorce, she moved into their life with an active authoritarianism that May welcomed and Hank was forced to accept.

At no time since their marriage have Hank and May been free of outside supervision, and at least the threat of intervention in their affairs has always been present. Neither have they ever been at a loss for advice or assistance on the many occasions that they have needed it.

SPARE TIME

Hank and May seldom enjoy their spare time together. Hank hates to "talk," doesn't "know anything about sports," doesn't care for music, and loathes TV "because of all that kid stuff and cowboys." When he and May are together they usually sit while May attempts conversation and Hank replies laconically or simply ignores her. More frequently, Hank spends his leisure time elsewhere: with a girlfriend, in a bar, or in a "sexy" movie. His greatest pleasure is in "raising the roof," or "raising hell," which means drinking beer, then driving into the nearby hills that overlook Los Angeles. He loves to sit, drunkenly admiring the lights of the city, or lie down and stare at the stars, dreaming of "getting away from it all." While "raising hell" he also likes "you know, to get together with a girl," whenever he can.

May necessarily spends her leisure alone. She once enjoyed cooking and even bought several cookbooks, which she still has but admits she has never read. Sometimes she listens to a radio but she seldom enjoys this. She likes to look at picture magazines when she has them available, but what she enjoys most is conversation "with some nice person." Indeed, her energies seem to be focused upon locating a likely target for such a conversation which, when it takes place, inevitably consists of a lengthy and pathetic recital of her problems, the injustices she has suffered, and the hideous acts of Hank, both in the past and those that she is certain he will shortly commit. The flavor of her conversation is by no means simply paranoid; she is also infinitely gossipy, honestly pathetic, and continually groping for some shred of encouragement against her feelings of depression and worthlessness.

SELF-PERCEPTION

Hank is fairly competent in the conduct of everyday matters. Unless he is confronted with an unusual situation and becomes highly emotional, he performs relatively well. He speaks well, with a good vocabulary. He can read a little and write enough to get along in most situations. But he does have limitations. Unusual requests or circumstances (such as ordering a meal from a menu in a restaurant) sometimes fluster him badly. His unkempt appearance puts him at an immediate disadvantage in most interpersonal encounters. There also seem to be limitations to his ability to learn specific tasks. For example, he enrolled in a "special" adult education "basic reading" course in a nearby high school. Here he was competing with persons who were either "handicapped" or did not know English at all well. He did very badly and dropped out. Also, one of his girlfriends attempted to teach him to drive her manual-shift car, but he complained that "three pedals is too much but I think I could handle a two-pedal car." It is reported that his efforts to learn to drive were a total failure. For one thing, he never learned to distinguish the clutch pedal from the brake pedal, with predictably frightening consequences.

Hank's view of himself is expressed repeatedly and clearly. He insists—and believes—that he is physically strong and has great endurance. His ability to lift heavy objects, to walk great distances, and to work long hours is an important source of his self-esteem. He likes to refer to himself as "a jack of all trades with a back like a mule." Most of all, he strives to avoid any suggestion that he is retarded. He knows that he was regarded as a mental retardate at the time he was in Pacific, but it is doubtful that he has ever accepted this verdict. At any rate, he is diligent about hiding his past and denying that he is retarded. He has told no one that he was at Pacific, and he was horrified lest the research investigators somehow let slip something about his past. He is always eager to validate his competence by an assertion such as "I've lived long years alone here on the outs and I guess I've showed everyone I can take care of myself." He is equally prepared to explain the reason for his "problems": "My only handicap is a lack of schooling." He argues strongly that were it not for his neglected education he would be as "rich and famous" as anyone else. These explanations never vary. Hank has them well worked out.

Hank's vision of his future is equally clear. He wants to be "free," to have "a fresh start." He continually dreams and talks of becoming a gypsy, of being free to go and do what he pleases. He speaks of living alone on top of a high hill, saying, "The only roof I want over my head is the blue, blue sky." He realizes that he has made mistakes, particularly in falling so deeply in debt, and admits that it is wrong to "shoot for the moon." But he wants to be free of these debts, of his responsibilities, of long and hard work, of May, and of all supervision. He talks endlessly of getting "out from under the State," saying that the "State" has always been "over" him, telling him what to do. His practical procedures for achieving his needs include "getting hold of some money," "getting me a car," and then using this money and mobility to find a job as a male nurse at some distant sanitarium where "nobody knows about me."

May's ability to deal with everyday matters is, at its best, greater than Hank's. Her verbal ability is excellent; she can carry on a conversation in an articulate and appropriate fashion. She has an excellent memory for names and places and seems to behave appropriately in almost any situation, including unfamiliar ones. She also has demonstrated that she can learn quickly and work well under certain circumstances. Her outstanding deficit is her inability to tolerate emotional stress and her recurrent epileptic seizures. As a result she is often unable to deal with even the least demanding aspects of life. Her appearance has progressively deteriorated until she is now so unattractive that she is greatly handicapped in most interpersonal relations.

Unlike Hank whose public performance exudes self-confidence, May is extremely self-effacing. For example, at the height of the election campaign of 1960, neither Hank nor May had ever heard of Kennedy or Nixon. Both thought Truman was President. When this misconception was pointed out to them, May was embarrassed and apologetic for her ignorance, but Hank shrugged it off as nothing, the kind of mistake anyone could make. May deprecates herself continually. When asked if she were going to vote in the 1960 presidential election, she said that "all that voting business" was simply "too complicated" and "I couldn't trouble my small brain about that." Hank merely said that he didn't want to vote for "those crooks." May also is sometimes "too nervous to think," but even at the best of times she manages to appear less competent than she is. For example, she makes very few errors in the use of language, but those few (e.g., "repaired" for "compared," and "voulevard" for "boulevard") stand out and emphasize her incompetence far out of proportion to their frequency or seriousness.

Like Hank, May would like to be able to think of herself, and to be thought of by others, as not retarded. Unlike Hank, she readily admits to some incompetence. But she has an excuse. For example, "I was a bright child but I was hit on the head with something. It was all my father's fault. Now there's something wrong with my head. I'm sick; I'm epileptic. Sometimes I have trouble thinking right. But Hank, he's not sick. He was in Pacific because he is dumb, but he won't ever admit it."

She tries to deny that she is retarded and that she belonged either in Pacific or in the mental hospital. But she is far from being convincing. She sees herself as "poor May," the pathetic victim of circumstances. Often her reaction is depression, sometimes suicidal depression, for she seems to be convinced of her own worthlessness. She is usually bitterly resentful of Hank's misbehavior, but her evaluation of herself is perhaps best expressed in her own words: "I'm the weak one, I always get sick."

Her hopes for the future are evident in what she calls her "dream." She wants a home of her own, her own furniture and children. She also wants self-respect and better "health," but most of her "dreams" center upon children: "I want to have kids and I want to be nice to them and never treat them mean. I want them to be happy like I never was."

THE OUTLOOK

As the research contact was terminated early in 1961, Hank made another attempt to gain his freedom. He had saved a few dollars and was planning to run away, leaving May behind. He intended to leave no forwarding address and pay none of his bills. He planned to go to San Diego, where he would be unknown and could "start over" without the "State" or any debts to worry about. For unknown reasons he told May about his plan, warning her not to tell anyone what he intended. May immediately told the landlady, who stepped in to warn Hank about what would happen if he deserted May and defaulted on the bills he owed her for rent and groceries; she also threatened to inform his employers of his intention to leave without paying the remainder of his furniture debt. Hank surrendered meekly, insisted he had never meant to do such a thing, and returned to May and the tiny apartment. May was triumphant. She announced gleefully that "Hank left me in the lurch but poor May made out OK." She also said that it was clear that while she did not need to be shocked (she received electroshock therapy at the mental hospital), Hank needed exactly that to "shock his brain and make him forget all his bad ideas."

Five months later another brief research contact was made to ascertain any possible changes in the relationship between Hank and May. Surprisingly, they were still together, living in the same tiny apartment. Hank and May were still at odds but her health was better, she was fully discharged from the mental hospital, and she was better able to assert and defend herself against Hank's dominance. Hank was working fairly regularly and trying to pay his debts. May stayed home but did odd jobs for her landlady, who still supervised the couple and protected May. But Hank was again planning to run away to San Diego "as soon as I get some money saved up."

Apparently, Hank and May will continue to live as always—a life of hostility, conflict, and constant crisis. Intervention in their life by some interested normal person seems to be an invariant aspect of their marriage. Despite everything, at last contact, Hank was still hopeful that he would find his freedom, and May was again dreaming of a peaceful home and happy children.

Postscript—1992

Hank and May typify many of the people who come to be labeled as persons with mild mental retardation. Their parents had little education, were emotionally disturbed, and apparently were thought by others to possess limited intelligence. As children, they lived in a violent and chaotic environment, neither child received even minimal acceptance or affection, and their formal schooling was at best perfunctory. One could hardly invent circumstances more likely to lead to impaired cognitive development. And, indeed, both Hank and May were not only visibly limited in a variety of cognitive skills—reading, writing, understanding time, money, and a variety of other quantitive relationships—they also had difficulty solving everyday social problems and they were emotionally disturbed as well. Their marriage, like their early lives, was tumultuous and tragic.

After 1962, still obsessed by his dreams of freedom, Hank continued to bounce from one odd job to another, and he often left May, frequently threatening to divorce her. In 1964, his inability to hold a job became so critical that he applied for and was awarded Aid To The Totally Disabled (ATD); his welfare allotment was $131 per month. For the next four years, he did not work, living solely on his ATD check. He became increasingly delusional, often imagining that he was another person living in another place, always a place where he was "free." In 1968, his delusions became so bizarre that his ATD social worker recommended that he be admitted to a state hospital for the mentally ill. Diagnosed as suffering from schizophrenia and as being a "high-grade moron," he was placed on phenothiazines. After two years as an inpatient, he was released to a board and care facility under the supervision of a social worker.

After that time, 1970, nothing of substance is known about his life until fifteen months later when he died of sunstroke while sunbathing. He was forty-four years old. His medical records said that he "never married." May must often have felt this way herself because after 1962, she and Hank seldom saw one another. Early in 1964, Hank announced to May that he was leaving her in Los Angeles while he went to San Diego in an attempt to find work. When May implored him to stay, there was an argument and Hank left, apparently telling her that he would divorce her. The next day, May took an overdose of phenobarbitol. Found still alive but in a coma by her landlady, she was rushed to an emergency room. Soon after, she was admitted to a state hospital for the mentally ill.

This was not the first time that May had attempted to kill herself. During the previous two years she had been living on $140 a month provided by ATD and by the little income that Hank contributed before he too relied on ATD. On several previous occasions Hank and May had fought, usually about his demands for a divorce, and she had attempted suicide, always by taking an overdose of pills. After May was hospitalized, Hank mournfully accepted his social worker's opinion that he could not divorce her until she was discharged. It is probably that Hank and May never saw one another after this. We know that May was never notified of Hank's death.

May had dreamed of a happy home and children of her own. She was to have neither. She often referred to herself as "poor May," saying that she was "the weak one." Released from the state hospital in the early 1970s during the deinstitutionalization movement of that time, she was placed in a board and care facility. Soon after, she was found dead in her room of head injuries apparently received in a fall associated with an epileptic seizure.

Case B. Fred: A Single Man

LIFE BEFORE PACIFIC

Fred Barnett was born in Los Angeles in 1928. The birth was normal, after three hours of labor. Fred walked at seventeen months but he was slow to talk and his speech was unclear and "stammering." Fred's mother thought he was a normal child but "a little slow." It was only at about age five, when his slowness to learn and his verbal inadequacy became obvious, that she began to worry seriously about him.

Fred's father was a cabinetmaker, born and raised in Idaho. He had an eighth-grade education and worked only periodically, but he was generally able to support himself and his wife. Little is known of him beyond his wife's later recollection that he was "very nervous and irritable." Fred's mother was also from Idaho, where she met and married Fred's father. She completed an eleventh-grade education before marrying at the age of twenty-two.

While Fred's mother was still pregnant, she divorced his father because of his "terrible disposition" and moved to California. Shortly after Fred's birth she married a man from Los Angeles and they subsequently had two children, a boy and a girl.

When Fred was six he was struck by an automobile and seriously injured. His skull was fractured and he was unconscious for five days. His hospital records state that he may also have suffered "slight" neurological injury. His mother, however, attributed all Fred's problems to this accident: "After the injury he had a very poor memory and just seemed stupid." Whatever the reason, Fred was unable to keep up in school, where he earned no promotions. He also fell more and more into conflict with his younger brother and sister. At the age of ten he dropped out of school and remained at home. For four years his mother and stepfather attempted to resolve the problem that his constant conflict with his siblings caused but they finally concluded that Fred's effect upon the younger children was simply too deleterious. In June, 1942, when Fred was fourteen years old, he entered Pacific.

LIFE IN PACIFIC

Fred had taken several IQ tests, beginning at the age of seven. These tests repeatedly placed his IQ in the middle or lower 50's. He was tested upon admission to Pacific and again his IQ was in this range—52. The psychologist who examined him at Pacific commented that when Fred was unable to answer a question he pretended to be bored, and that Fred was much intent upon "maintaining a façade of normalcy despite his very limited intellectual capacity."

Fred was seldom in trouble in Pacific. He worked on the wards and in the kitchen and sometimes as a messenger. Fred's comments about his stay in Pacific concentrate almost exclusively upon food and sex. Regarding food: "When I was out there the food was very bad. The food wasn't even fit for a dog to eat. I'd keep telling the doctors up there that this food, it's got something wrong with it. I'd find match sticks in it, I'd find pins in it, I'd find rocks in the stew and the beans. What are you gonna do? You can't talk to the head doctor, that's tiresome. They wouldn't even let you in to interview him."

Or the following highly fanciful story about sex: "When I was there it was lonesome. You didn't know what the hell to do with yourself when I was up there. There was only one thing to think about. I used to sit outside and think and talk about it (sex), you know. Lots of stuff goes on up there, they don't even know what goes on up there. I used to see them girls up there on a side street— I didn't know what was going to happen so I didn't ever worry. Them girls got to have something to do to enjoy themselves so the hell with it. Before a guy could get to the front office he didn't hardly have any clothes on at all, 'cause the girls up there would rape 'em. You know, some of them hot girls. And some of the guys would let 'em do it. I knew they was gonna do it, so I'd just walk down the street natural like—you can't fight it. It happened quite a few times when I was up there. I didn't have it too bad up there."

Fred was released on leave in 1945, three years after he entered the hospital. But in Fred's recollection of the elapsed time we have a good insight into his typical mode of thought and speech: "I was only there a year and a half. I went there about 1941 and it was about 1943 when I came out. I was discharged in 1943, but it might have been 1942—I know it was either 1941 or 1942—I was only there a year and a half. Hell, you guys know more about when I went in than I do."

After Fred's release in 1945 he was under almost continual supervision by his employers and his social workers, yet he managed to stay in fairly continuous trouble. He worked in several sanitariums and in restaurants as a dishwasher, and in all these places he earned a reputation for temper, aggressiveness, profanity, and boorishness. Still he was also capable of charm, and his conduct was seldom bad enough to cause him to be fired. He was also in several minor difficulties with the police; for example, he was picked up for vagrancy on three separate occasions but was always released when his social worker intervened. On one occasion his misbehavior was more serious. He took his employers' car without permission and drove it recklessly, almost running over a child. Despite this and his lack of a driver's license, he escaped with nothing worse than assignment to a probation officer, thanks to the efforts of his sympathetic employer and social worker.

In 1948 he became infected with syphilis and had to be returned to the hospital for treatment. When he returned to a job in the community, provided by the hospital, he resumed his usual pattern—periods of responsible work and personal charm followed by moods of recklessness and anger. At times he would become a transient and would subsist by selling his blood at twelve dollars a pint. At other times he would work hard and well, ingratiating himself with everyone.

With time, his conduct became more competent and his emotions more stable. Beginning in 1951, his social workers several times offered to discharge him completely, but on each occasion he refused. The following statement by Fred's social worker characterizes him and the problem:

"The patient has been on leave of absence for six years, is of questionable mental deficiency, and is able to manage his life although probably in a marginal fashion. However, he regards the Department of Mental Hygiene almost as a family and is most reluctant to be discharged."

Finally, after many years of indecision, Fred agreed to accept discharge. In 1957 he began life without the formal supervision of Pacific.

LIFE AFTER DISCHARGE

In the summer of 1960 Fred was a robust-appearing man of thirty-two. Heavyset and fleshy-faced, with a cigar perpetually in his mouth, and a careless good humor, Fred gives every appearance of being a happy-go-lucky, easygoing, altogether happy man. There is nothing in his appearance to suggest that he is anything less than a normal man, and his speech is likewise unexceptionable. Fred usually dresses in a sports shirt which, although it is moderately clean, is faded, frayed, and stained around the neck. His trousers are always soiled and worn, with a very dirty and shiny seat. His shoes are usually quite dirty but he does sometimes polish them. His face generally is clean-shaven and liberally covered with talcum powder.

It is only upon much closer inspection that Fred's intellectual deficit becomes apparent. To the casual observer, he is an ordinary man, competent to live within the not-too-demanding constraints of his life circumstances.

NEIGHBORHOOD, HOME, POSSESSIONS

Fred's domicile is in a small trailer, illegally parked behind the all-night skid-row cafe and bar where he works. This area of Fred's residence is two blocks removed from the central street where "winos" and "B-girls," cheap bars and "strip-shows" predominate in a classic stereotype of every city's skid row. The area consists of deteriorated housing, empty warehouses, and rooming houses for single men, who are typically poor, elderly, and transient. The cafe where Fred works—"Bill's Bowery"—features cheap whiskey, cheaper muscatel wine, beer, and twenty-cent hamburgers. Despite the lack of a city permit to park a house trailer in the alley behind his cafe, the owner lets Fred occupy the trailer as a condition of his employment.

The trailer is an elderly plywood model, about twenty feet in length and in delapidated condition, with several broken windows. However, it is reasonably waterproof. The trailer contains a small refrigerator, a stove and sink, two closets, several small cabinets, a double bed, a table, and a couch. However, the refrigerator, stove, and plumbing do not work, and the interior is a dusty, littered jumble of personal possessions. For example, on the stove rests Fred's old record player, surrounded by some two dozen long-playing records, of obscure vocalists, dance bands, and jazz concerts. Fred explains that they were "bargains." Cabinets, closets, drawers, and open surfaces are filled with an array of miscellaneous objects such as old electrical plugs, can openers (several dozen), odd pieces of wood, strips of scrap metal, pieces of wire and string, assorted nuts and bolts, and stubs of old pencils. Bottles of pills and patent medicines fill drawers, stand on the floor, and are piled in closets. Some of these bottles are half full but most are empty, or nearly so. Fred has the walls of the trailer decorated with nude photographs, and magazines containing such pictures are stored in a large cabinet. But the most striking aspect of his living quarters is the litter of clothing, both Fred's and those of the woman and her month-old infant who live with him.

This woman is a German immigrant who began to share Fred's quarters about a month ago after the birth of her child. The addition of the woman and child makes the small living area extremely cramped, but Fred works at night while the woman and child sleep, and they generally leave during the morning when Fred sleeps. Fred's trailer was exceptionally messy even when he was living alone, but with the added paraphernalia of a woman and infant, the interior of the trailer is truly chaotic.

MAKING A LIVING

Before beginning his present job Fred had a varied and moderately successful work career. After leaving Pacific, he held a number of jobs in sanitariums, involving the usual kitchen and janitorial work. He also scrubbed and waxed floors, something which he says he did well. He held one of these jobs for close to six years and was a reasonably adequate worker on the others. As Fred puts it: "Well, sometimes you get tired of the same thing and you want to get something else. You quit, or you keep looking until you find a place you like. My problem has been quitting jobs. They don't fire me. You can see my record. I got a good record behind me." In general, what Fred says is true: he quits jobs; he is not fired. He has also worked as a dishwasher in several downtown slum-area or skid-row restaurants. But for the two years prior to his present job, Fred's employment consisted only of odd jobs for persons who had befriended him.

One friend whom Fred describes as a "big shot with a great big house" offered him occasional jobs of gardening, as did his former social worker, who has kept in touch with him throughout the years. Every weekend Fred would get on a bus downtown and ride to the homes of these "friends" in the suburbs. His former social worker would pay his bus fare and give him five dollars for an afternoon's work of painting, cleaning up, or gardening. She also gave Fred all he could eat for lunch, then paid his bus fare back. When she had no work for Fred, she would try to find him a day's work with a neighbor. In this fashion, Fred would usually make ten dollars each weekend and he also collected an "unemployment" check part of the time.

After some time, however, the odd jobs were available less often and Fred was tired of the long bus rides. Five months ago, as Fred was drinking coffee in "Bill's Bowery," the owner, Bill, approached him about replacing an employee who had just "skipped town." Bill offered him a dollar an hour for four hours work each night. Fred agreed, saying, "Four dollars is four dollars." Fred works every night from 2 a.m. to 6 a.m. In addition to the pay of a dollar an hour, Fred receives the use of the trailer and three meals a day in the cafe. In Fred's words:

"I go to bed about eight or nine and get up at 1 a.m. I go in the cafe and eat all I want, then the bar closes and I clean it up, fill the icebox full of beer, then I sweep everything and mop up. Then I go in the restroom and clean that up. I fill the icebox up with cold drinks. Then I go through the halls and get all the empty beer cases and take them out on the back porch. Then I go to the cafe counter and clean all that up."

Actually Fred works hard only from about 2 to 4 a.m., when he cleans up the bar and restroom. When the bar closes at two, the cafe is quiet, except for a few coffee drinkers, until people begin to come in for breakfast. Fred sometimes talks with these late coffee drinkers but usually he talks with Bill and does whatever tasks Bill requires during the night. The work is not demanding. As Fred puts it: "Sometimes I take my own time, sometimes I'm late getting to work and the boss don't say nothing. I'm my own boss, do my work my own way."

RELATIONS WITH OTHERS

Fred's stepfather and stepbrother both live in a nearby slum area, but Fred never sees either of them. He says, "Naw, I don't bother. I don't care one way or the other." However, his relationships with others in the community are numerous. Fred's community contacts are facilitated by his exceptional mobility; he rides buses without notable difficulty, he hitchhikes (with indifferent success), he also walks a great deal, often for considerable distances. Almost every day, Fred goes for a walk, usually stopping to window shop as he goes along, and always stopping to have lunch in some place that intrigues him. The fact that he has just eaten lunch at the cafe seldom prevents the ingestion of a second meal. He maintains an impressive knowledge of coffee shops and cafeterias in the downtown area, and he can recite (with some accuracy) the locations of sales on men's clothing, phonograph records, various toilet articles, and all manner of vitamins and patent medicines. He seldom buys anything, but he window shops in the manner of an experienced and wary shopper.

One day, in strolling through the downtown area, Fred was pointing out areas where winos slept, alleys where there was danger of being rolled late at night, and small cafes where there "was lots of good cheap food." When Fred passed by a store, he would glance in each window, and sometimes he would stop to comment at length upon the quality of the goods or the exorbitant prices. In one "Army and Navy" store featuring a miscellany of goods, Fred said that he was thinking of buying a pair of binoculars and had been bargaining with the owner for some time now. Fred entered the store and was met by the "owner." This man showed no recognition of Fred, nor memory of his interest in binoculars. However, Fred did know where the binoculars were located and what their prices were. He looked through the binoculars, adjusted them and commented: "By God, when I get these I'll be able to see everything." The glasses were used, of Japanese manufacture, and appeared to be in good condition. I asked Fred what the "7 × 35" on the glasses meant and he said he didn't know but that it probably was the price "in Jap money." I asked him for the price in American money and he said it was "about twelve ninety-nine" but that he was "working on that" and would "get it down OK" before he made the purchase.

Although Fred can eat "for nothing" at the cafe where he works, he usually prefers to eat lunch somewhere downtown. "I like to eat downtown, you know. I eat all I want to eat. I got plenty of money. I usually go to places like (a well-known cafeteria, exotically decorated, that does an excellent tourist business), or other big places, mostly where they do a lot of business. You get more for your money, which pays. I like cake and pie and I like chicken. I think you've heard of (the cafeteria)? Their food is cheap, see. See, they make it themselves so's you can get more than what you pay for. You go to a whole lot of places to eat and you don't get that much. It costs you maybe a dollar or one-fifty or two-fifty and you still don't get a good amount. That's why I usually go to (the cafeteria) or to the doughnut shop or something."

Fred knows the bus routes and the numbers of the buses that will take him to the places he generally visits. There are four buses he takes often and he knows their numbers, although he admits that once in a while he makes a mistake. He has never owned a car, however, he is interested in them. He sometimes asks the prices of cars, but he usually concludes: "That's too much dough, I can get around OK. I got everything I want right now."

Fred's relations with people take three characteristic forms. With other former patients, Fred assumes a domineering, even arrogant role. He maintains contact with several former patients and he also makes regular visits to a social club where many such "handicapped" persons meet. In all these contacts, he adopts a superior, almost imperious, air and becomes domineering to the extent of issuing commands which he expects to be obeyed. When his commands are ignored, he exclaims bitterly about the "low intelligence" of the person involved and then he becomes very distant and aloof: "I try to help these people and they don't listen, so I just don't want nothing to do with them. Hell, I got to tell half of these people what bus to take. They can't even find their own way around. They don't appreciate nothing." In this role Fred affects a dignified and busy manner. He recites lists of his current accomplishments along with his present obligations, then gives direct advice in a highly peremptory fashion. As the other person has almost never asked for advice, he or she usually ignores Fred or makes some rude comment. Nevertheless, Fred continues to seek out contacts of this sort and attempts to establish his domain over former patients. When asked about his conduct at these times, Fred will not admit any desire to dominate and will say only, "Those people come to me for help so I try to help them out." In fact, Fred is very unpopular with former patients, most of whom go to some lengths to avoid him.

A second role is one of happy, carefree competence; this role is used in the presence of most normal persons. Here Fred appears as he would most often be seen: easygoing, pleasant, able to care for his own needs, outgoing but never aggressively so, and happy, always happy with his place in life. This view of Fred will be discussed in detail later.

The third role which Fred regularly adopts occurs vis-à-vis "important" or "big" people who have befriended and protected him. With such persons—his "big shot," his former social worker, his boss —he is passive, deferential, almost reverential. He depends upon the beneficence of these persons with complete trust: they have helped him in the past, they can always be depended upon to rescue him in any future difficulty. Fred has strong feelings about his "freedom" and independence, but he is also able to be dependent upon benefactors and social agencies without any apparent sense of conflict or discomfort.

For example, Fred is speaking about his job history: "Mostly I didn't find none of my old jobs. Old Mrs.—, the social worker, she found them for me. Hell, she got me the job at (a sanitarium). I didn't know nothing about the place. She picked me up and took me out there. She got me another job later, too."

Or, about paying the bills: "When I was working over at (a restaurant), I got sick and was in the hospital, and it cost a lot of money and I didn't have the money to pay it. I guess the State paid it or something. Somebody paid it anyhow."

Or, his view of the future: "I'm working out OK—I'm my own boss, I do what I want. But if I get in some troubles I'll be OK. I just gotta see Mrs. (the social worker)—she'll take care of me."

SEX, MARRIAGE, AND CHILDREN

Fred has never married but he has apparently always had girlfriends. He still does. Fred is not sterilized and is very pleased that he is not. "You know that operation makes you weak, you can't lift heavy things and you're always tired. It might be OK for some people, but not for me. When you're like that you can't please no woman—no woman wants a weak man." Continuing with his interest in girls, Fred says that he used to be very interested in a girl called Cookie. "You know, she was the short, fat one I told you about. We liked each other real good but she was way out in the Valley (some twenty miles away) and it was too far to go all the time."

Fred continues: "You know, all the girls around here are after me.

They know I'm not weak. But they all want to go out somewhere and that costs too much. Mostly I don't go out with them. I usually go see my friend (a former patient from Pacific). She lives on top of Bunker Hill (downtown area). She's all right. She don't want to do nothing but—well you know, play around, get her kicks. She's all right. She don't want to go out."

Fred also visits prostitutes occasionally but has become somewhat timid about doing so since he was relieved of all his money while visiting one about two years ago. Fred says that he visits a prostitute (usually a skid-row B-girl) about once a month but that he doesn't have to pay because "they like me. I'm not weak so they like me." Fred also goes to burlesque shows or "adults only" movies about once a week. It was impossible to determine the actual extent of Fred's illicit amorous activities, as he was most reluctant to speak openly of such matters. It was learned from his employer that Fred has been less active in recent years, perhaps because his unhappy experience of losing his money was accompanied by the acquisition of a venereal infection.

Fred still has hopes of finding marriage "with the right girl." But there are problems as Fred sees it, most of which relate to living in a downtown skid-row area:

"You know one thing, I haven't been able to find any nice girl who lives around here close. I had one up to the hospital, but I can't think of her name right now. She went there after I came out. I been trying to find out what her name is, but I could never find out. I been trying to find out from Mrs. (the social worker), but she won't tell me. There just ain't no nice girls around where I live.

"I wish there was someone around close who I could take a walk with or go to the show or something. I don't know too many girls up there at the hospital (Pacific). This colored guy who stole this car about a month ago, he just came out. They had a girl out at the North Hollywood Club. I was up there once and they were there having a party out there and I met a nice girl. But I haven't seen her no more.

"Most of the girls at the Club (a social club for the "handicapped") are going with somebody. Either going with somebody there, or some of 'em are married. Me, I never can find anybody I can get married to. Can't find nobody that's close enough where you can come see 'em. Nobody close."

This, then, is the quality of Fred's matrimonial concerns: strong feelings about girls he saw once or whose names he cannot remember; wishes for a "nice" girl to do "nice" things with; vague desires for someone "nice" to be "my girl."

But at the time of the research contact, Fred's interests and energies were taken up by the woman who was sharing his trailer. This woman was a rather plump but attractively dressed West German of about thirty years. Her story (as confirmed by others) is that she came to this country after marrying a U.S. serviceman during the Korean War. This man left her after fathering two children, whereupon she put the children up for adoption. She then began to live with another man in a cheap downtown hotel, but when she became pregnant, he too left her. After delivering this child she had no money and no place to stay. She said that she felt guilty about relinquishing the other children, and wanted to keep this child, so when she met Fred in the cafe she accepted his offer of a rent-free place to stay until "her lawyer works things out."

The story (not by any means confirmed) continues in Fred's words to the effect that she needs to remain in this area because her "husband" lives just across the street in a hotel and she needs "to keep an eye on him so's he don't run out before she can get him to court" to pay for child support.

The whole truth of the story is not available. What is clear is that Fred and the woman are friendly, are co-residing, and the arrangement seems to please them both. Fred admires the woman's intelligence and tells extravagant tales of her past achievements. For example, he insists that she has gone to "many" schools and was "famous" in Germany. She speaks fondly, if condescendingly, about him but says she will leave as soon as the baby is old enough for her to get "a nice apartment."

SPARE TIME

In Fred's current circumstances, most of his time is spare time. He prefers it that way. He travels to the social club for the handicapped at least every fortnight and sometimes more often. He goes to movies, especially "adults only" films on skid row, every week or so. He also watches TV in the lobby of a nearby hotel where he used to live. For twenty-five cents he can watch the coin-operated TV, "for twenty minutes, half-hour, or something like that." His major interest on TV is baseball games and Western movies. Fred also enjoys some drinking, but this is usually confined to beer, occurs infrequently, and almost always stops well short of drunkenness. And Fred often travels, either by bus or on foot, for substantial distances, "just to see the sights." He will walk several miles or ride the bus to the end of the line and back "just sightseeing."

Of somewhat greater interest for Fred are sports, music, and sleeping. Fred is a baseball fan who follows the fortunes of the Los Angeles Dodgers with interest if not with any expert knowledge. He goes to games in person, watches TV, and listens on the radio "almost every day," yet in response to direct questions he could name but six members of the team's twenty-five-man roster. He is also interested in football and becomes excited about games he watches, but again he knows little about the players or the details of the game.

About music, on the other hand, Fred does have some specific knowledge. He is a fan of "swing": "I like to buy records; I see some records I want and I buy 'em. I know all the records and play 'em all the time. I got my own record player. Mostly I play good swing music; reminds me of the old times. Artie Shaw, Benny Goodman, all them good swing music bands. I keep a pretty good tag on new records. You can get 'em pretty cheap. I just keep track of something new I hear on the radio. I go down and get it and if it costs three dollars or something like that I go down and buy it."

A competing interest for Fred is sleep. He devotes much time to talking about sleep and still more to actually sleeping. Fred explains his concern this way: "I got to get my rest. Lotta times I go to bed in the afternoon to rest up—sometimes I listen to a ball game but mostly I just sleep. I sleep good at night too. I got these pills that put me to sleep so I just get in bed about eight or so and take a pill. When I get off work in the morning I take another pill and go to bed and sleep till about noon usually. If you're gonna feel strong you gotta sleep. Next to eating, sleeping is the best thing for you."

But Fred's fundamental interest in life is food. By far the greatest part of his working energy is devoted to some aspect of food: its gustatory delights, its importance for health, its cost, where it can best be acquired, how to eat yet not grow fat, and how to lose weight if one is already too heavy. Fred discusses food:

"I love to eat. I eat a lot, that's one of my problems, not eating. You know, when I eat, I eat the right kind of foods; it's just that I put more weight on anyhow. I like to eat a lot of meat and stuff, salads, steaks, sandwiches. See, I eat the right kind of food. I can get anything what I want, candy, ice cream. By eating the right kind of stuff I can keep my weight where I want it. Then I go down and take some medicine that makes you lose weight—you take it just before you eat. Then you can eat all you want. It costs me four something—four eighty-five. Sometimes I get pills and take 'em every day. I take some when I go to bed at night; they don't always make me sleep good. Then I get nervous. Then I take another little old brown pill about a half-hour after I get up. That way I keep my weight OK."

In spite of his "dieting" Fred is actually twenty or more pounds overweight. But even this amount is minimal when Fred's phenomenal intake of food is considered. Fred does not simply talk about food, he eats, and most of the time. In addition to four major meals each day, he nibbles constantly on whatever he can remove from the refrigerator at the cafe. Much of Fred's mammoth collection of pills, potions, and nostrums is devoted to weight control. He consumes many pills and fluids that are advertised to permit the user to eat as much as he wishes yet not gain weight. Fred also experimented with Metrecal as a dietetic device until he discovered that the product was meant to replace other foods, and not to be eaten in addition to everything else. As Fred put it, disappointedly "What the hell, a man's got to eat."

He sums up his daily routine as follows: "When I wake up in the morning I don't even think what I'm gonna do. I get up, wash, dress, and go downtown and eat. Then I walk around to kill time, go home and rest for a little while, then maybe go downtown and go to a show. Then I go to bed and maybe eat some more."

SELF-PERCEPTION

Fred presents himself to his world with bravado. He wants to appear to be a conspicuously competent man, and he does possess a certain hail-fellow-well-met charm, as well as a good command of the language. In fact, his competence is sufficient—if barely so—for his world, because Fred's world includes several dependable benefactors.

Fred's concern with demonstrating his own competence is displayed in most aspects of his life—in his ability to ride buses, in his capacity to use money, in his arrogant dominance over his fellows, and in his general mastery over the demands of his everyday life. He also stresses his autonomy, his freedom and independence. This focus forms an almost continual refrain in his speech. Again and again he emphasizes his freedom to do what he likes, to go where he wishes, to eat where and what he likes, to work or not to work, to be free of the control of any other person. "Nobody tells me what to do. I run my own life; I'm my own boss." For Fred this is the essence of the matter.

Fred also makes much of his strength and of his sexual prowess, but both are diffused into his more general concern with health: his sleep and food and weight. He wants to be seen by others as strong and masculine, but he is more concerned with his own satisfaction that he is properly fed and rested, perhaps because these things represent to him his own ability to care for himself. As he says, "A man's gotta take care of hisself. You gotta eat and sleep good. Nobody else is gonna help you eat or sleep."

Perhaps most important of all is Fred's ability to combine a belligerent, "I'm all right, Jack" (a phrase he often uses), independence with a complete willingness to accept the assistance of his benefactors when times are difficult. He sees no contradiction here and moves between periods of relative independence and dependence without signs of emotional distress. He admits that he could not have "made good outside" without the regular help of his benefactors, but somehow he takes this help as simply given, as his natural right, and always insists: "Don't worry about me, I can take care of myself."

THE OUTLOOK

Six months later, Fred's circumstances had altered. Fred no longer had his job at "Bill's Bowery." He had, he explained, become tired of the work and had quit about a month earlier (his former employer agreed that this story was correct). Fred was living in a cheap "flop-house" hotel only two blocks away from the alley where he had formerly lived in the trailer. The German woman and her child were gone, for reasons and to places that Fred could not or would not specify. Fred was once again under the protective wing of his former social worker, who was providing him with odd jobs in the old pattern. She was also attempting to find him a better place to live.

Still Fred had lost none of his old bravado and had no complaints about his changed circumstances. The basic aspects of his way of life were unchanged. He was making some money working for the social worker and he still had several weeks of unemployment compensation to collect. As Fred put it, "When that runs out, I guess I'll get me another job. I got this friend who's a big shot . . . "

Postscript—1992

Fred (who has since asked to be referred to by his real name, Ted Barrett) still lives in the same run-down area of downtown Los Angeles. The part of the city has progressively deteriorated over the years with an influx of illegal Latin American immigrants, homeless people, drug dealers, prostitutes, and violent criminals. Ted has been robbed, mugged, and burglarized on several occasions, but for the most part he has managed to avoid trouble largely because he is remarkably alert to potential danger. His impressive size may also help to deter some criminals and so, according to Ted, does the feigned psychotic behavior he calls forth (his "crazy-man act") when he senses danger.

Ted's neighborhood has changed but he is very much the same today as he was thirty years ago. Until recently when he qualified for SSI, Ted has supported himself by working one or more low-salaried jobs cleaning or maintaining liquor stores or laundromats at night, and working hard has always been central to him. He often says, with characteristic exaggeration, that all he does is work, sleep, and eat. But it is true that he has worked long hours and that he enjoys eating, usually at a neighborhood coffee shop; moreover he has many interests including his collection of swing and big band records, watching television, and chatting with the many friends and acquaintances he has made while wandering around the neighborhood. He also enjoys an occasional bus ride to distant parts of the city. And he still has his vast collection of pills and nostrums to control his weight and increase his sexual potency.

Ted has always talked about sex a great deal, sometimes boasting about his powers with women and sometimes complaining about impotence. As the years have passed, complaints about his loss of sexual potency have become an everyday topic of conversation with virtually everyone he meets. Whatever the truth about his past or present sexual capacities, Ted has had several girlfriends and sexual partners. He was in love once, and may even have considered marriage (something he has always sworn to avoid), but the woman moved away. He has also had many relations with prostitutes, some of whom are intravenous drug users. Fortunately, he is HIV negative. Ted banters happily with these women and sometimes gives them money with no expectation of sexual services.

Ted's health has been good over the years but in late 1991 he suffered a mild heart attack. Angioplasty failed to open his clogged arteries and bypass surgery was required. As this is written, his recovery is excellent. Ted used to boast about the "big shots" he knew who would help him if the need arose. In reality, there have been no "big shots" in his life for thirty years. But he does have a large circle of friends who truly like him and sometimes help him. In return, Ted helps them with money, advice, and his irresistible good humor. He is a charming, charismatic person who can be tender, sympathetic, and sensible. Ted still cannot read or write and his intellectual limits are apparent to those who know him well, but he is truly a good, kind, and wise man who continues to enrich the lives of his many friends.

Case C. Martha: A Single Woman

LIFE BEFORE PACIFIC

Martha was born in Los Angeles in 1921 to a fifteen-year-old unmarried girl who had fled her home in North Carolina when she learned that she was pregnant. Martha's father was unknown and her mother knew only that she was unwelcome to remain at home in her condition. It is not known how Martha's mother got to Los Angeles, but shortly after the birth of Martha (about which we have no details) she was out of money and consequently gave Martha to an adoption agency. Neither Martha nor the agency ever heard from the young mother again.

Although Martha was slow to walk and talk, she was considered to be a normal baby when she was adopted at the age of two by a family that took her back to New York. Only a few months after the adoption, Martha was deposited with "friends" and her adoptive parents vanished. Friends cared for Martha for over a year but, as the adoptive parents had still not returned to claim her, Martha was taken to an orphanage. She was transferred from orphanage to foster home until, as a result of some legal intervention, she was returned to her birthplace in Los Angeles. There she remained in foster homes until the age of fourteen. Although she reached the fourth grade in school, her school performance was poor, she was highly irritable, and "didn't get along" with other children. In various foster homes she was a problem because of her temper, her frequent bed-wetting, and what is referred to as "open masturbation." However, several serious episodes of menorrhagia were the immediate reason for her commitment to Pacific for "vocational training." She entered the hospital in 1935 with an IQ of 67. Martha recalls her admission this way: "It was a rotten deal. I had my freedom taken away and was put behind bars like a criminal just because I didn't have a family and the State was tired of taking care of me."

LIFE IN PACIFIC

Martha spent over eighteen years in the hospital. She worked in many jobs but primarily in the clothes room of a ward for the profoundly retarded. She had few friends and few enemies. She was seldom in trouble, although ward notes refer to infrequent "blowups," but neither was she a model patient; her anxiety and emotional lability made her mildly unpopular with patients and staff alike. For one thing she pulled her hair out in great bunches and then ate it, to the horror of all witnesses. All the while, Martha protested that she was wrongfully placed in the hospital, because she was "just as good as anybody on the outside."

Martha recalls her stay at Pacific as one of unrelieved misery. In the first place, she felt exploited: "Nobody paid me anything. I did all that work every day and never got one cent. They just kept us smarter patients there because if it wasn't for us who'd do the work? The employees wouldn't do it. They just stand around and make the patients work."

But she also felt fear and the loss of freedom: "I was just like an animal in a cage. Bars and all. And anytime you did something they didn't like they'd threaten you with punishment like being locked up in a side room all alone. That's what they'd do, you know. They'd drug me with narcotics, like amdol (amytal), then put me in a room all alone. How is a person going to live right when they're full of narcotics?"

Most of all, Martha felt humiliated: "I never belonged there in the first place, and then they made me stay eighteen years with all those crazy people and people that had to be taken care of. It was terrible, it was like they thought there was something like that wrong with me!"

In 1953, after eighteen years in the hospital, Martha was placed on work leave in a motel in the community. Reports of her "adjustment" in the ensuing months were generally favorable although it was noted that she always cried when her employer corrected her, and that her living quarters and "personal habits" were "slovenly." Thanks largely to a laudatory report from her employer she was discharged two and a half years later. So complete was the control of her employer at that time that Martha did not even know she had been discharged. Indeed, it was not until 1960, when a research worker told her, that Martha knew that she had been discharged by the hospital authorities in 1956.

When located in the summer of 1960, Martha was thirty-nine years old. Her height and stature are ordinary but her appearance is not. Martha's yellowed, protruding teeth are very prominent despite her efforts to hide them by keeping her mouth closed whenever possible and by trying to cover them with her tongue or her hand when she speaks. She is often highly agitated—she cries, wrings her hands, picks at the skin of her arms and legs, and has difficulty sitting or standing still. Her eyes are crossed, and because of her poor vision she accentuates the condition by peering intently at persons or objects. Her short hair is uncombed and lends a wild quality to her appearance. She wears cheap cotton dresses, which while clean and ironed, are several sizes too large. In all, she is a pathetically unattractive woman.

NEIGHBORHOOD, HOME, POSSESSIONS

Martha lives in a small apartment in a thirty-unit motel in a partially commercial area, fifty miles east of downtown Los Angeles. Martha receives the motel apartment in return for her services as a part-time maid. She cleans rooms when the regular maid is not available; she does errands and odd jobs; and on Sundays she watches over the front office if the manager is off duty. She has lived and worked in this motel since her discharge from the hospital.

The motel is old and rundown but it still does a profitable business, depending primarily upon guests who stay for a week or more at reduced rates. Martha's apartment consists of a bedroom and separate kitchen. The bedroom is furnished with a large, old double bed, covered by a threadbare bedspread, an old dressing table, two badly worn chairs, and a television set. The worn linoleum floor was covered by a dilapidated rag rug. There is one small picture on the wall of some flowers in a vase. The small kitchen is crowded but Martha usually keeps it clean and orderly. Heat is provided by an unvented gas heater in the bedroom. Martha shares a bathroom with two other apartments in the motel. This arrangement distresses her "because the last tenants I had to share with were drunks—didn't do nothing but drink all the time and they left the bathroom real dirty and smelly—and twice even I woke up in the night with my room full of gas because they fell asleep and turned on the heater without lighting it on. They made me real nervous but they both moved out now and I got the bathroom all to myself until those apartments get rented again."

Martha has few possessions in her room. There is no reading matter at all and there are no visible trinkets or small memorabilia—no letters, pictures, knickknacks, or souvenirs. There is one large panda bear that she keeps on the bed, and inside her dressing table there are a few toilet articles and a half-dozen papers relating to past medical treatment, public welfare assistance, and employment documents. Her major possessions are her small and inexpensive wardrobe purchased from secondhand stores or given to her by various concerned persons, a small television set that seldom operates correctly, and a small radio.

Although her possessions are pitifully few for a woman of thirty-nine—even one who spent over eighteen years in the hospital—Martha does have one major resource that she regards as her treasure and her salvation—her savings account. Since her discharge, the manager of the motel has taken a portion of each of Martha's paychecks and put it into a savings account for her. She had $1,800 in this account at the time of the research. Martha never withdraws any of this money: "It makes me feel good to know that I got all that money for a rainy day. If I didn't have that money, I'd get real nervous."

MAKING A LIVING

For Martha, making a living is a continuing crisis. Her past job failures and her anxiety concerning possible future failures dominate her life interests. Martha's first jobs after release from

Pacific involved baby-sitting and live-in housekeeping. She did badly at both kinds of employment. She explains the problems as follows:

"People just want to make money off their employees. I didn't like those housekeeping jobs where you live there, because you are really working twenty-four hours a day. You get up all night when the baby cries and you have to get up in the morning when the family does. Those people are so hard to please."

Martha was fired from several such positions, usually because of her extreme irritability and unwillingness to follow directions without complaint. Said one former employer: "Anytime you asked her to do something, she thought it was beneath her dignity. I don't know what she thought we were paying her for if she didn't want to do any work."

After two years of failure in jobs of this sort, Martha found a job through a former hospital employee who had befriended her. This job was as a stock clerk at a sheltered workshop for "handicapped" persons, but Martha describes it grandiosely:

"Well, my position with (the workshop) was very responsible. I was cashier for the whole store. I handled all the money and also I did some looking out over some of the other employees. They have some of these handicapped people working there and I had to supervise them. It was an important job. It's just a shame that that old lady lied about me to get me fired." In fact, Martha worked as a stock clerk at the clothing store; her one effort as cashier was a disaster because she rang up $77 instead of 77 cents and then gave $23 change instead of 23 cents.

Martha's dismissal from this job was a great crisis for her, and it was typical of other job crises in her past. She had argued with her supervisor and had become very difficult after she was denied the right to operate the cash register. When she refused to help sweep the floor one night when the regular janitor was ill, her supervisor criticized her, so Martha went to the phone late in the evening and complained to the district supervisor at his home. The on-duty supervisor intercepted the call and asked Martha to leave for the night. When she began to cry hysterically and refused to go, her supervisor threatened to remove her forcibly. In fairness, both Martha and the supervisor seem to have been at fault, but Martha had encountered such problems with other supervisors many times before. She recalls the episode with deep anguish:

"I was doing real good at my job until this old lady came on as supervisor. She just treated me like I was an idiot and she was always making me do work that wasn't my job. This old lady had spies there that would watch me and report things to her. They'd make up lies too. Then this one night she made me sweep the floor and I just wouldn't do it because it wasn't my job to sweep floors or things like that. I only got eighty cents an hour and the janitors got a dollar and besides, she treated me like an idiot. So I went and called my old supervisor and told him how she was making me do the wrong kind of work, but this old lady heard me calling and came and started to call me names and said if I didn't put that phone down she'd 'knock my head off.' So I got out of there, but the next day they wouldn't let me go back to work because all these people had been telling lies about me. Well, Mrs. (her employer at the motel) got me to go downtown and see the big supervisor (district supervisor) and he was real nice and all, but he said that whatever the old lady said was going to stick. He said I could work in a store downtown but I wouldn't do that because, you know, that's where all those handicapped people work, and I just don't want to be around people like that. So you see, they just fired me and that's a real shame because I was doing real good. Well, if they don't think I can do the job after all my experience then I'm not going to try anymore. If they don't like me I'm not going to push myself on them."

Martha responded to losing the job with an anxiety-laden retreat from contact with people. She depended upon the manager of the motel to manage her life for her, yet when this woman made appointments for Martha to see someone for a job interview, Martha simply refused to leave her room. For Martha, the loss of the job was cataclysmically upsetting because it called her competence into question and it threatened her with return to the hospital as someone who could not support herself.

"They've got me so nervous now I just can't think. I'm doing everything I can to find a job (tears), and you must believe me on that (tears) because I just couldn't stand going back behind bars at that institution. But you know that I'm not the only person who can't get—I mean doesn't have a job. There's other people that can't find work either. I run into quite a few of them. In fact, there is a lady that quit at the (workshop) 'cause she wasn't getting enough money, and then I was told she was back there a week or two ago trying to get a job, but they told her they didn't need any help; but they do need some help. They know I need a job, and they need the help, but they're just being spiteful about it; but if they do hire help they'd hire her before they would me. And she's got a husband and an income where I don't have a thing. I'm just as good as anybody else. I've seen plenty of people are worse than me outside that institution. It's just that I've got to get a job so I can be like other people."

But Martha refused to look for a new job. She insisted that she needed a rest and that her poor health would prevent employers from considering her favorably. At her friend's insistence, however, she did agree to seek help from the County Bureau of Public Assistance. "Well, I just wanted to see if there was some way they could help me find a job, and then I wanted some groceries. They help other people with groceries and so forth and I didn't know if I was eligible or not. I hate to ask for charity like that. I guess they treated me all right but they asked me a lot of questions, you know questions I was undoubtfully I didn't know if I should or shouldn't have answered them. (What kinds of questions were they?) Well, 'Was there any security?'—which I had a little money saved in the bank for medical care and my glasses. Well, they'd probably cut me off for something like that. And I work here one day for my room and board and I didn't know if that—I was doubtful what to say about that. I was scared to lie because I know if I tried some of the things some people do I'd be caught right in my footsteps, which others could get by with. They finally made me raise my hand and swear I would pay back the money when I get work. I don't think they would do that to other people."

So Martha remains in her room all day "trying to get hold of myself and not cry so much" so that she can find a job. "I've just got to get a job like other people."

RELATIONS WITH OTHERS

Martha lives in a world of almost total isolation. She has no relatives and no friends, and she feels the lack of both keenly. She has often attempted to make friends but has never known how to do so and feels that people do not like her because she "doesn't look right." Furthermore, she believes that she becomes "all confused" when she tries to converse. She once attempted to make "pen pals" by writing to addresses listed in a Los Angeles newspaper. Only one person answered and this was a woman who was dying of cancer. Martha was depressed by this and did not continue the correspondence.

Martha's search for relatives includes a search for the identity of her mother, and thus, of herself. She says, "How can I ever feel like other people when I don't even know where I was born or who my mother was or anything." Recently, with the help of a concerned social worker, Martha has learned a little of her origins.

"Well, my mother came from West Virginia out here to have me; she wasn't married and was still going to school, and she didn't know what to do because she didn't have any money and she was all alone way out here from West Virginia. I don't know just what orphan home I was put in, but then some people from Manhattan adopted me and left me at a neighbor's house, and they never did come back and get me, and from there the State has taken over with me, and I've been here and there and all over since I was a baby. I was shifted from one place to another and then to the hospital. I never had a chance. I would still like to know more about myself— how I was adopted and all, and if my real mother is still living, which I learned she was, somewhere back in West Virginia. I don't even know her real name, which is my real name. I don't know why I was denied all of my life like that."

Martha still searches for her mother, including in her search letters to the "authorities" in West Virginia from whom she does not receive answers. She also searches for friends, or at least people to talk to. "I love to ride the bus—you can meet people and talk to them that way. They're real nice. They just look at the scenery and talk to you, which I like."

But Martha has never found any relatives, and has never had a friend. Her world has always revolved around a benefactor—some one person who serves as her idol, her protector, and her sole personal relationship. The first person to serve as Martha's benefactor was a former professional employee of the hospital and the owner of the motel. She eased Martha's entry into the outside world and gave her a place to live in the motel. Martha remembers her fondly:

"Mrs.—was a psychiatrist at the hospital and she talked to me and made me feel that I know as much as anybody. She made me feel like a real person. And she took me around with her and showed me how to go places and do things and how to get along, which I needed to know. She got me this job taking care of the motel and she looked after me and helped me work for other people too and got me my bank account. She gave me responsibility and treated me real good. She was like my real mother to me."

This woman also placed Martha under the protection of a woman who had become the manager of the motel. Gradually this woman took over supervision of Martha's affairs. She found jobs for Martha, banked her money, tried to find friends for her, advised her in all aspects of her life, and supported her in all her many emotional crises.

"Mrs. (the manager) is real close for me. She is really my friend. I don't have to be alone for now. I don't have friends, but I like to be like other people and not a burden to anybody, but I don't know how I would get along without her. She's like a mother to me. She's been so good and helped me straighten my problems out. Every time I have a problem come up I always go to her. And she's got her family to take care of too, besides me."

The motel manager once worked in a state hospital in the Midwest and says that she feels "like it's my responsibility to help people like Martha get along in the world."

But Martha is always eager to locate additional benefactors. For example, she attached herself to one of the female research workers, saying "I want to do whatever you do," and "I want to be just like you." The only lasting personal relationships in Martha's life are of this dependent kind—Martha attempts to add new benefactors to her family of protectors. Few persons are willing to serve her in this way, but those who are willing serve her well.

SEX, MARRIAGE, AND CHILDREN

Martha has never had any relationships with men. She does not even have fantasies about men or marriage. Questions about boyfriends or the possibility of marriage cause her to giggle, but such concerns seem scarcely to be within her ken. She is vaguely afraid of men, but she can recall no unpleasant incidents with them, nor any specific reason why she should feel "tense" in their company. She has never been able to imagine herself married to any specific man. In response to a direct question of whether she would someday like to marry, she said, "I just don't think I would work out on a marriage."

Martha is not greatly concerned about being sterilized at Pacific. She speaks of it with, for her, unusual calmness and lack of involvement: "When I first got to the hospital I had a dyserectament at fifteen. (A what?) Dyserec—um—dyserectament at fifteen. (Oh, hysterectomy!) Yes, they said it was unusual for anybody at that age to have that operation. (What did this operation do?) Well, I guess it made me different from others, 'cause like I say, I haven't been able to have children, and children sense you when you don't have children, I think. (Sense you?) Yes, they look at you funny like and then they run away and cry, and that makes me nervous when they do that. (Do you have any men friends?) No, I seem to feel afraid with men. (Have you had a boyfriend in the past?) No, I've never done that kind of thing."

It is impossible even to elicit gossip from her about other people's sexual or marital relations, or to stimulate interest of any kind in such matters. For Martha, relations between men and women not only do not exist in her life, they do not exist at all.

SPARE TIME

There was a drab, empty, sameness about Martha's activities at the time the research was conducted—indeed, there were few enough activities of any kind. However, Martha talks of more variegated days:

"I like to get out and go places. Like when I worked I was able to do that. Now with no money coming in it's hard to do that; I mean to get out of here and talk to people if I can't go somewhere. I love movies. I used to go to movies every week and sometimes two or three times a week. I like TV too, but I usually don't like the hour-long shows unless it would be something like music on ice, which I like to watch—ice-skating. But now my TV isn't working too good so I go and watch TV in an empty room (an unoccupied motel room). I used to like to eat my lunch out—I used to go to this hamburger place not too far away. And I used to like to wait for the paper to come out, 'cause I'm always interested in reading the newspaper, and then I would go to the post office and write two or three letters, which I like. It gives me something to do. And I used to like to take trips on the bus and see things, which was something I really liked, but now I can't afford it."

After losing her job, Martha's time was spent in a daily routine of fixing meals for herself, talking to people around the motel, seeking the company of the motel manager, and at night, watching TV alone in her room. She often cried and felt "awful sad." She said that sometimes she would cry until six in the morning. She felt terribly alone and she sought the company of indifferent strangers around the motel with pathetic eagerness. Martha reveals much of her own feelings when she talks about these guests at the motel:

"You know there are lots of people who come to this motel who just got to Los Angeles and they don't know anybody. I always go up to them to say hello 'cause it makes them feel they have as much right as anybody else to be running around. Elsewise these poor people would just stay indoors and keep to their selves."

If Martha once enjoyed her spare time, she no longer does. Too much time has come to be a tyranny of leisure to which she cannot adapt. Her sole true interest is in demonstrating her competence. To do this she must "work like other people." For Martha, there is no other dimension to life.

SELF-PERCEPTION

Even more than most ex-patients, Martha is vulnerable to onslaught from every direction, and her self-esteem is correspondingly fragile. Her energies are devoted to "passing" with others and denying to herself that she is in any way less than normal. The burden is a heavy one.

She is characteristically extremely anxious, and sometimes she becomes hysterical. Fear of disclosure, of humiliation, of public ridicule, is always with her: "I've got all kinds of imaginations and fears and they make me real nervous. I know I'm too nervous and I cry too much but I'm afraid all the time. I've just got to get out of the habit of going to pieces. It makes people look at me funny, like when I cry so much. Like I went for a job but I went all to pieces when the man asked me questions, and I just know he was thinking there was something wrong with me."

Martha's attempts to pass as normal are a constant feature of her everyday life. Many of her efforts to be seen by others as normal have already been mentioned—she lies about her past, lies about the importance of her jobs, attempts to hide what she regards as unacceptable aspects of her physical appearance, her speech, and her personality. Martha admits that she attempts to manage the course of her life situations in order to present herself as a competent person.

"I don't see why people don't treat me like a normal person, instead of some kind of—well, you know, some kind of crazy person. I try so hard to act like a normal person. I never tell people that I've been in that . . . institution, and I always treat other people right. I talk right and act right. I just can't seem to make people treat me like a normal person. Is it because I don't look normal?"

Martha's realization that she usually fails to pass as a "normal person" has caused her to devote herself to the development of an elaborate excuse to account for her failures and to deny that these failures indicate that she suffers from any sort of "mental ailment." The closest she comes to an admission of incompetence is seen in her occasionally repeated remark that, "I've got a tendency of an ailment, but it isn't what it seems." But, as always, she excuses herself:

"It's all because I was in that institution so long (tears). They shouldn't have kept me as long as they did, that's what I think. I wouldn't have no trouble except for being in that place . . . eighteen years . . . eighteen years . . . that's longer than I deserved. Maybe there was a few things wrong with the way I acted but that was no cause to put me away like . . . some kind of mental person . . . some kind of crazy person. I didn't belong in there, that was obvious. I wasn't like the other people in that place. They were so, well, there are persons that are all right and there are persons that are not— ones that have to be taken care of. I wasn't like them. I'm just as capable of taking care of myself as anyone else. In fact, eighteen years ago I was as capable as I am now. Better even, because I wasn't so nervous—being with all those crazy persons made me terribly nervous. And then when they let me out I seen all these people outside running around loose that was worse than the people inside. I was just as good as anybody that worked in that hospital or anybody running around on the outside. It was a disappointment to come from there and find so many people outside needing institutional care. Lots of patients in that hospital are smarter than the people outside. The problem is that when you have been locked away in there for a long time you get nervous and also you don't learn about how to live outside, so when you get outside you can't act like a normal person—even when you're smarter than outside people. I was in there so long I thought I was going to rot. It's not right. I never belonged there and then they kept me so long that now I'm confused and nervous and can't get a job. All my troubles come from being in that place."

And so the excuse continues, with variation, for as long as anyone will listen. The explanation and the lament serve not simply to convince the listener; it appears that Martha herself is at least partially convinced that her excuse is valid. All the more so, of course, when sympathetic listeners agree that what she says must be true.

Martha's life is also influenced by her conflict over independence. She feels that lack of independence stigmatizes her and she continually expresses her wish to be independent. Her reluctance to be seen as a recipient of public welfare aid is but one example of her feelings. Her protest is repeated almost daily: "I'd rather be working than be independent." That she invariably says "independent" when she means "dependent" makes the refrain all the more memorable. But it could also be taken as a "slip," because Martha's conscious expressions and her fantasies continually reveal her desire to be totally dependent.

Martha's fantasy is to be the completely dependent child in a large, loving family. Her dreams center upon this theme: "I always have this dream where I'm a little girl and my mother holds me and feeds me and takes care of me." And her ordinary conversation regularly returns to it, "Well if I could have anything I wanted I would want to be a little girl in a family which loved me and would take care of me so I wouldn't have to worry about anything because they would always do everything for me and which I could always depend on them."

Martha's life is consumed by her efforts to be seen as a normal person, by her denial that she is mentally retarded, and by her need for benefactors upon whom she can depend. She is a lonely, frightened figure.

THE OUTLOOK

Six months later Martha was again visited. Her practical circumstances had changed little: she was as isolated as ever, she had not found a job, she was still living in the motel, and the motel manager was still watching over her interests. There was but one change and that was entirely consistent with Martha's past. Martha had discovered a new benefactor.

Martha now leaves the motel only on Tuesdays, the day when she visits her new protector—a social worker with whom the motel manager had put Martha in touch. For Martha, this woman is all good and all wise—a completely dependable goddess who will very shortly "make everything all right." Martha carries a picture of this woman clipped from a newspaper. She identifies it to anyone who will listen as the person who is protecting her against all the inequities of the world. Martha spoke of her new benefactress with pride, confidence, and a tone bordering on ecstasy:

"Mostly I got nothing but bad breaks out of life. The best thing I ever got out of life was meeting somebody like (the social worker). She's been so kind and patient with me; she showed me so much interest. Other people just took me as an inji—inji—I can't say that word—(illegitimate child) that was with a mental ailment, that had a mental disease, and that wasn't fair. (The social worker) told me how that wasn't true and how I was really as good as anyone. I couldn't tell my problems to anybody until I went to her. I feel free to talk to her and tell her my troubles which I could never tell to anybody without crying. You see, the big blow is how people don't treat me like I was a normal person, and that's not right because I was the manager of a thirty-unit motel, and I was a worker in a store, and at the hospital I took care of the clothes of a hundred patients, and gave medicines and knew the names of over a hundred patients. But nobody will give me a job because they say I'm not experienced. Well, if they were just patient and would take their time to show me I could learn. (The social worker) says I could learn. But people just turn me away like I didn't know anything and that's what hurts me. They look at me like I was crazy or I was a criminal because I was put away.

"Oh, but everything is going to be OK now. (The social worker) understands people like me. She's more than a friend to me and I can't thank her enough for all she's done for me. She's so good and she's wanting me to get out of the habit of going to pieces. When I've done that she's gonna get me a job—the right kind of job for me. I don't have any friends that understand me except for (the social worker). Well, I see people here and there, but they would never understand my problems. Because a lot of people think that the hospital is a place for crazy people. In fact, I wouldn't like the lady that I met the other day; she said she's going 'to work where the crazy people are.' And she dreaded it but she had to work, because she needed some money, and I said what did she mean? and she said, 'The hospital here in Pomona.' And I says, 'That isn't for crazy people, the crazy people are doing the work for employees,' I said, 'that's why the employees have the trouble with patients because they go there with the impression that the patients are crazy.' Well, nobody would like to be locked behind bars and the employee going there with the impression of you being crazy and then trying to pick a fight with you, you won't stand there and let them pick at you and push you around just 'cause they got the impression that you're crazy. And I said, 'They shouldn't hire employees that go with the impression that the patient is crazy.' There's people that's just put away there because they have no home, and the State think it's too expensive to take care of them, so they throw them in there.

"Well, (the social worker) understands and she's gonna take care of everything. She just means everything to me, so it would sure break my heart if I should lose her. She's better than a mother to me."

So Martha continues in her search for understanding and respect in a world that seems to her unwilling to grant her the right to live "like any normal person would want to." Her suffering in the face of such inexplicable rejection is great; but her confidence that someone (perhaps her new benefactress) "will make everything all right" somehow seems to endure.

Postscript—1992

In 1963, Martha lost the last job she was ever to hold because, as had happened so often in the past, she could not get along with the other employees. Since then, she has lived on welfare payments; yet, as the years have passed, her reliance on benefactors has diminished. Martha still has emotional ties to one benefactor, a former recreational therapist who knew her in the hospital, but in recent years this woman was rarely called upon for any kind of support. Instead, Martha's independence has grown quite steadily, so much so in fact that at least since 1972 she has refused to accept any aid unless she can reciprocate fully. Indeed, when her oldest and closest benefactor became terminally ill, Martha took on the difficult role of caring for her until she died.

Martha's desire to help others is a central theme in her life and for over fifteen years she has found satisfaction by volunteering in a Senior Meals program developed by her church. Four days a week, Martha arrives before any of the other workers to organize the meal preparation and delivery activities that involve seven or eight other older women from the church. Because of her excellent memory for numbers, which allows her to recall how many ingredients will be necessary for the preparation of the day's meals, she has taken on a leadership role in the group. However, her frequent irritability and domineering ways often alienate other workers, and she has made no real friends in the group. Indeed, she is almost totally isolated from other people except for a few casual acquaintances she knows from the church. In 1992, at the age of seventy, she has still had no relationship of any kind with a man, nor, apparently has she ever wanted one. Each night before dark, she locks herself in her apartment where she watches television or reads magazines until it is time to go to bed. She is a painfully lonely woman who must devote herself to finding things to do with her time until she is tired enough to sleep. It is odd that although she loves animals and often visits a nearby pet shop to see and play with the dogs, cats, and birds, she has never had a pet. In fact, when asked why she hasn't had one, it is apparent that she has never seriously thought of doing so. Even today, Martha lives with the pain of her hospitalization and the humiliation of having no family. She continues to lead a sad and lonely life, almost pathetically reaching out to people for friendship but invariably driving them away if they return her interest.

Martha is not an easy person to be with. She is anxious, demanding, childlike, domineering, angry, and fearful, all at the same time. Of all the former patients, she has the least appropriate interpersonal skills. But what she lacks in this domain of life, she makes up for by her sheer determination and her intelligence. She is the hardest working and perhaps the most competent of the Senior Meals volunteers. She has made herself entirely self-sufficient, doing all her shopping, food preparation, and household tasks quite well without any need for assistance. She knows her way around her neighborhood and can take the bus wherever she needs to travel. She maintains lively interests in the world, and although her tastes tend to run to tabloid sensationalism, she is very much aware of what is taking place in the world around her. Except for an occasional bout of painful facial neuralgia, her health is excellent. Martha's IQ has been tested between 67 and 72, but scores of this magnitude appear to greatly underestimate her cognitive abilities. Her memory is remarkable, her numerical skills are adequate for any everyday task including banking and dealing with bureaucracies. Despite her limited education, she reads and writes adequately and her problem-solving ability, too, suggests that her IQ scores inadequately represent her intellectual ability. Indeed, she is unique among the former patients in that she possesses better cognitive than social skills. Perhaps she is in reality a casualty of her orphaned childhood and hospitalized young adult years. Surely the trauma of those times and events is still with her.

Martha will probably always be lonely and fearful, but at the age of seventy she is self-reliant and seems to feel better about herself than she ever did before. She is healthy, vigorous, and in control of her environment. In earlier years, she often expressed the hope that someone would come along to "make everything right." No one did, but although Martha herself may not fully realize it, she herself made her life worth living and considering her past and her burden of pain, that is a tribute to her will and her strength.

Case D. Mary: A Woman Married to a Normal Man

LIFE BEFORE THE HOSPITAL

Mary's father was a hard-drinking man named Joe, who worked, when he worked, as a common laborer for the railroad. Mary's mother came from a large, desperately poor farming family. When Joe expressed a matrimonial interest in Mary's mother, her family was quick to agree to the match if only because the marriage would mean one less mouth to feed among their eight, perpetually hungry, children. So, Mary's mother was taken out of school in the seventh grade at the age of thirteen, and she was married to Joe. She frequently ran away from her husband, but each time her parents or other relatives would find her and return her to him. Soon she was pregnant, and at the age of fifteen she gave birth to Mary.

Mary was born in a small town in Missouri in 1928. The birth was normal and uncomplicated. Mary was a pretty, healthy baby who began to walk at eleven months and to talk at one year. Shortly after Mary's birth, her parents moved to a small town in Arkansas where they endured three years of mutual mistrust and hostility before Mary's mother finally left for good, leaving Mary behind with her father. Mary's father could not or would not care for her and had her placed in a State-operated children's home when she was just four years old.

Mary spent the next four years of her life in a rural home for children. No records of this period survive but Mary recalls these years as very lonely and sad. She remembers that she was "so happy" when her father's parents came to take her home with them. Mary lived with her paternal grandparents in another small, rural Arkansas town. She had begun to receive some schooling in the children's home but this was highly informal and sporadic. Now she attended school regularly, and by the time she had reached the third grade it was reported that she did not learn as quickly as her classmates. Despite Mary's obvious slowness in learning, she remained in school and advanced through the primary grades on schedule, although everyone, except perhaps Mary, knew that the promotions were unearned. Mary recalls the school experiences with displeasure, but she did enjoy living with her grandparents and still remembers this period with happiness.

When Mary was thirteen, her mother came to claim her. Mary's mother had been living in Oklahoma and had recently married for the second time. Mary's father, Joe, who had also remarried (for the fourth time), rarely visited his daughter, and made no objection when Mary's mother wanted to take custody of her.

Mary, her mother, and her new stepfather soon traveled to California, where the stepfather found employment in Los Angeles as a skilled auto mechanic. Mary now lived where there was an adequate income, but despite having a room of her own, new clothes, and some spending money—all for the first time—Mary was not happy. Her stepfather, in her words, "never liked me. He never wanted me around and sometimes he was real mean to me." Going to school was not enjoyable either, as her classmates were far ahead of her and the teachers were not indulgent of her slowness. She was urged to learn more quickly, and when she could not, she was ignored by the teacher and treated as the class dunce by the pupils. Mary was now fourteen years old and very attractive, with a full figure and a pretty face. The only persons in her new world who took an interest in her were boys. Mary responded to this attention, perhaps too warmly.

At this point her mother became deeply worried about Mary's welfare. She had been pregnant at fifteen herself and had always felt that this early pregnancy had "blighted" her life. More than anything she feared that Mary too would become pregnant. She felt that Mary knew no restraint with boys and could not defend herself against their sexual aggressiveness. She worried constantly about Mary and devoted much of her time to supervising her; she believed that Mary would easily be seduced by any boy with whom she might be left alone. Mary did occasionally slip away to talk to a boy, and once she was kissing a boy in her parents' garage when her mother discovered them, in what was to her a flagrant sexual embrace. There is no evidence that Mary ever did any more than kiss a boy, but her mother decided that she must be someplace where she could receive constant supervision and protection, as well as training. In 1944, at the age of fifteen, Mary entered Pacific.

LIFE IN PACIFIC

Mary entered Pacific with strong feelings of bitterness toward her mother and stepfather, both of whom she accused of wanting to "get rid of me, even though there was nothing wrong with me. They knew it, too." Mary went to school at Pacific for about a year and was able to improve her reading and writing considerably. Moreover, her IQ score increased in this period from 44 to 56. She was given jobs in the hospital and learned to care for children and to perform simple housekeeping tasks. She was never a troublemaker and got along quite well with the employees. She also lived fairly happily with the other patients and in her "cottage," where she made many friends among girls of her age.

Despite such generally pleasant experiences Mary was usually very unhappy in the hospital and was always anxious to leave it. Mary never accepted any suggestion that she might be mentally deficient. She was firmly convinced that her "mind was as good as anybody else's," therefore it was obvious to her that she did not belong in Pacific and was only being kept there through the "meanness" of her mother and stepfather. She resented her loss of freedom, privacy, and individuality; she disliked some of the girls in the institution, especially the homosexuals; she felt that the food was not fit to eat; she was disappointed to discover that there was no swimming pool or riding stable as she had been led to believe; she wanted to leave Pacific as soon as possible. She was normal, she insisted, and did not belong there.

Only a little over a year after entering Pacific Mary went home for a visit. This reunion proved to be short-lived when Mary could not conceal her disaffection for her parents and they, in turn, found her hostile, intractable, and difficult to supervise. She quickly returned to the institution, where she stayed four more years.

Her good behavior in the institution, principally working for physician's wives, doing housework and baby-sitting, earned her an opportunity to prove her ability in the work-leave program. Mary had three jobs in the community, provided for her by Pacific—all of them in private sanitariums—and in each one she had serious difficulties with her employers. The details cannot be verified but it appears that both the employers and Mary were at fault. The employers made unreasonable demands and displayed little confidence in Mary while failing to show her any consideration or kindness. On her part, Mary was nervous and quick to show anger when she felt she had been wronged. Mary tried hard but made mistakes—some, of the most elementary and irritating nature—and must be rated as an exasperatingly poor worker during this period. "I admit it. I was hard to get along with, but I just can't stand snotty, stuck-up people. You go out of your way for people, then they are snotty to you."

On her fourth work placement, after these three prior failures, Mary found a sanctuary. She was placed in the home of Mrs. Gould (the owner of still another private sanitarium), where she was required to work as a "mother's helper," cleaning the house and caring for the children. Unlike her previous work assignments in which she was expected to perform her work well, day after day, without supervision and without any personal satisfactions in the form of praise or friendship, in this job, Mary worked *with* her employer at all times. In this relationship, Mary always knew what was expected of her, decisions were made for her, and her work was always gently guided in the desired directions. Mrs. Gould was an extraordinarily kind and sensitive person, who was consistently able to provide Mary with the warm affection, security, praise, and freedom that she so greatly needed. Mary's self-esteem was further raised by the respect and affection she received from the children in the family.

In a short while, Mary had become completely dependent upon her employer. She rarely left the house and then only to take the children for a walk or to run some errand. While both Mary and Mrs. Gould were completely content with the situation, Mary's dependency became so great that her social worker from the hospital felt obliged to take action. It was only after more than a year of urging and cajoling that the social worker was able to convince Mary that she must leave her sheltered life and demonstrate some ability for independent living before the institution would consider granting her a complete discharge. By this time Mary had saved some money, and her relationship with her parents had improved, so that when her mother joined the social worker in coaxing Mary to get a job on her own, Mary finally agreed.

She moved to downtown Los Angeles, where she took a room in a rooming house on the fringe of the skid-row area. This rooming house was occupied by several other former patients from the hospital, by a few retired men, and by an occasional prostitute. The building was shabby but the rooms were large, clean, and adequately furnished.

Mary's reluctant experiment in independence was not a success. She was completely unable to find any suitable job on her own. She made only a few dollars per week as a domestic servant, and within a few months her savings were exhausted. At this point, her social worker stepped in once again to find her a job in another sanitarium. She also found Mary a place to live. This time Mary moved into a small apartment in a large apartment building which was managed by the husband of yet another former patient from Pacific.

After several weeks of reasonably successful work in this new situation, Mary's mother decided that Mary was now capable of self-support and deserved to receive her discharge from Pacific. Mary's social worker agreed, and consequently Mary was discharged in the summer of 1957. Shortly after discharge she was married.

LIFE AFTER DISCHARGE

When Mary was located in the summer of 1960, she was still a rather attractive woman. She is of average height, perhaps ten pounds overweight. She has a flawless complexion that needs and receives little makeup, and she successfully maintains a deep suntan that contrasts strikingly with her light blue eyes. Her dress is usually appropriate and neat, although at times it can be garish and even sloppy. She is proud of her figure, and she has reason to be, although her bustline is sagging and she must sometimes wear a girdle. Her hair is black with prominent touches of gray. In all, she is an attractive woman who looks somewhat older than her thirty-three years.

Nothing about Mary's appearance would betray her limited intellectual capacity; her grace, grooming, and dress are all quite acceptable for a woman in her status. But when she speaks, the impression of "normal" mentality is shaken if not completely destroyed. When nervous or excited Mary stutters and becomes highly inarticulate. Even when she is not under stress and is speaking normally she is breezy, superficial, perseverative, and sometimes disoriented. Her speech is liberally punctuated with illiteracies that follow one another in rapid succession, as, for example, these during a short discussion of motion pictures: "spectracular", "Cecil D. (for B.) DeMille," "Charleston (for Charlton) Heston," and "Primm (for Pimm's) Cup." She also pronounces the word-ending "-ing" as "-ink"; thus, "darlink." She says in this regard, "I learned to talk Jewish real good from Mrs. Gould but I can't remember it anymore." The overall first impression is that of a not very well educated, "scatter-brained" housewife, but not necessarily a mentally retarded one.

NEIGHBORHOOD, HOME, POSSESSIONS

Mary and her husband Bill live in a small, one-bedroom house behind a larger house which the owner occupies. The neighborhood is quite pleasant, with wide, tree-shaded streets. The lots are large and the modest houses are well cared for. In general, the yards are carefully maintained and the street has an air of quiet respectability. Just one block away is a commercial street with heavy traffic, stores, and markets, but the area is so arranged that having stores so near by is a convenience rather than a nuisance.

Approaching Mary's home from the street, one first sees the owner's house, a moderate-sized stucco house that is exceptionally well cared for. The front yard is immaculate. At the back of the lot is a small stucco house surrounded by a large back yard that is only fairly well maintained. The house has four small rooms: living room, bedroom, bathroom, and kitchen. It is rented unfurnished except for a refrigerator, and the monthly rent is sixty dollars. The floor is linoleum throughout, unpolished, with a few small throw rugs. The living room contains two old-fashioned but serviceable sofas, a large shabby chair, two old but unscratched end tables, and an old coffee table. Next to the false fireplace is a large television set that dominates the room. The set is five or six years old but it still operates and is turned on almost constantly. There is also a large floor lamp and a small table lamp; a bulb was burned out in the floor lamp, and the lamp shade was quite dusty. All this furniture was a wedding present to Mary and Bill from Mary's mother.

The house derives its character from other features. Throughout the living room, on every available shelf, there are curious souvenirs and knickknacks that Mary has picked up here and there. A small cabinet contains some china given to Mary by her mother. These things have significance for Mary; she thinks that they are decorative, but each also recalls to her some important event in her life. They are kept as souvenirs rather than as display items. Much of the wall space is crowded with photographs which mark events or persons in Mary's life. Near the door hangs the only "religious" article in the house, a picture of a young Indian woman holding a cross above her head with one hand. Her voluptuous body is transparently clothed, creating an effect more erotic than spiritual. Bill won this picture at a fair. There are no books in the house and no newspapers. The only magazines are Mary's movie magazines scattered throughout the living room; some are old and some are current, but all are badly worn.

The kitchen is clean and neat and appropriately equipped. It is small but adequate for two persons. Mary has all the necessary dishes, glasses, cooking and eating utensils. Much of the kitchen equipment also came to Mary from her mother, but Mary and Bill have added a few things since their marriage. The bathroom is small, clean, and adequate. Mary looks at movie magazines in the bathroom and sometimes leaves them about, but usually the room is neat.

The bedroom contains a double bed with a neat pink bedspread, a dresser, a chair, and a closet. There are clean pink curtains on the windows. Mary keeps a large, rather soiled teddy bear on the bed. This room, too, is neatly kept but has a barren appearance. Mary and Bill bought the furniture for this room themselves and are still paying for it. They have occasionally fallen behind in the payments but have not yet lost the furniture. This furniture is Mary's "pride and joy." Some of Mary's jewelry is on the dresser. It is cheap costume jewelry but some of it is tasteful and fashionable. Both Mary and Bill seem to have only cheap, poor-quality clothing. Mary's most prized article of clothing is a red cloth coat that cost twenty-five dollars. She mentions the price with awe and calls the coat her "pride and joy."

When Mary and Bill were first married, Bill drove an ancient, dilapidated automobile that finally "completely fell apart." Bill then purchased a 1958 Chevrolet convertible (at that time only two years old), and this car is their most valuable possession. Making the payments has been extremely difficult, however, and has caused them many problems. Because of quarrels with the telephone company over non-payment of bills, there is no telephone in the house.

MAKING A LIVING

Mary's working days ended when she married Bill. He insisted that no wife of his was going to work. He still feels this strongly, asserting that no proper man would permit his wife to work. Mary has worked very hard at being a housewife during her marriage. She keeps her house clean and reasonably neat and takes some pride in doing so. She irons passably well and is, according to Bill, "a pretty good cook."

Bill works at a nearby steel company, where he hauls steel around on a forklift. He has had many jobs in the last few years, from unskilled manual labor, to driving trucks, to his present job. He makes between $350 and $400 per month now and he and Mary are enjoying their greatest affluence. Their past has often been very difficult, with Bill out of work and unpaid bills accumulating.

Mary and Bill do some of their shopping for clothes and household items at a fairly expensive department store. They also buy at discount stores but deny ever shopping at the Salvation Army, Goodwill Industries, or other similar stores that deal in low-price, used, and refinished merchandise. Bill and Mary usually do the grocery shopping together, with Bill making the decisions and handling all the money. Once in a while, Mary will walk a block to the market to pick up some small item, but the major shopping is done by Bill "with Mary along." She says, "Bill does most of the shopping—you know, with money and all that." Bill also buys many items of food at a nearby liquor-delicatessen store, where he is granted credit. Bill's purchases of liquor at this store account for his good relations with the management; at the very least, he spends fifty dollars a month on such beverages. Often he spends a great deal more.

RELATIONS WITH OTHERS

Next to that with her husband Bill, Mary's most important personal relationship is with her mother. After the early years of separation and the later years of hostility, Mary and her mother are now in fairly amicable, frequent contact. The quality of the relationship is obvious. Mary is the "not-too-bright," semi-competent "child" over whom her mother feels obliged to exercise supervision and maternalistic care. Although Mary still resents her mother's past actions and fears her continuing authority, she nevertheless does not rebel openly. Indeed, she gives every indication of needing and wanting her mother's affection and direction. Although Mary receives far more direction than affection, she continually returns, seeking both.

Mary's mother writes to her daughter about once a week with questions and instructions (she always encloses a stamped, self-addressed envelope). Mary and Bill receive these letters rather resentfully and apprehensively, for they resent her interference in their activities, although they appreciate her past favors and gifts (furniture and money) and do not want to alienate her as a benefactress. Her letters are answered with careful dissimulation by Bill, aided by Mary's anxious suggestions. Mary visits her mother perhaps once a month. Bill sometimes accompanies her, but usually she goes alone and spends several hours with her mother.

Mary's mother is a handsome, well-groomed woman who reigns over (rather than resides in) a sensationally well-appointed and decorated home. The house itself is modest but the interior is done in expensive yet decorous fashion. During her visits, Mary usually avoids her stepfather altogether and tries to talk only with her mother. Her mother's role is that of an omnipotent and condescending deity, prepared to extend kindness and to overlook Mary's incompetence but also ready to punish when Mary's actions become unacceptable. Mary is repeatedly told (indirectly and directly) that she is not adequate mentally. For instance, upon hearing that Mary was planning to learn to drive a car, Mary's mother told her, "You should not do that. You aren't ready to learn to drive. You'll just hurt yourself or somebody else." Mary's reaction is highly selective. She gives some indication of perceiving and resenting her mother's slights, yet she plays a completely dependent, submissive role. She neither rebels outwardly nor attempts to assert her independence. Mary says she sometimes feels these meetings to be unpleasant but cannot explain why: "She makes me so uncomfortable. I just don't feel right with my mother sometimes. I don't know why, I guess it's just because she's mother."

Mary has no contact with Bill's relatives, all of whom live in the East, but she does maintain an intense affection for her former employer, Mrs. Gould. Since leaving Mrs. Gould's employ, Mary has had occasional contact with this woman but had actually lost touch with her at the time of this study. Still, Mary retained great affection for her and recounted tale after tale of their close, sympathetic relationship. When taken to visit Mrs. Gould by one of the researchers, Mary bounded into the house with childlike enthusiasm. She was warmly greeted by the younger child, but the older child was very aloof, and Mrs. Gould herself was interested but very distant. Mary was quite insensitive to these rebuffs and enjoyed herself thoroughly.

Another important relationship for Mary is one with a woman who is a former patient of Pacific, and her husband. This woman, whom we shall call Ellen, married a "normal" man and together they manage an apartment house. It was in this apartment that Mary lived when she met her husband. She is terribly ambivalent toward these people. On one hand Mary regards them as surrogate parents (they are some fifteen years older than she) and calls them "Ma" and "Pa." Face to face, she is very affectionate toward them and they toward her. Yet, out of their presence, Mary defames them with awful vehemence: Ellen is a "liar" and a "thief"; her husband is equally reprehensible. Mary seems to resent their past authority over her and their somewhat greater intellectual ability. Still, Ellen is important to Mary as a person with whom she can share experiences and talk over old times. Ellen is especially valuable as a source of information about other ex-patients whom she and Mary knew at the hospital. Mary is greatly interested in the lives of these people but does not have the means to maintain contact with them, except through Ellen. Ellen retains such contacts and passes her gossip along to Mary.

Mary's only other friends were actually made through her husband, yet Mary regards them as her own friends. In fact, she and Bill interact with two couples so often that they have actually become Mary's friends. The first of these couples is John and Kitty. John works with Bill and they have known each other for years; they first met in Detroit, then came to California together. John is a ruddy-faced man of about forty, taciturn and unimaginative; he likes to drink, and becomes much more outgoing under the influence of alcohol. His girlfriend is Kitty. They met in a bar and have lived together for several months. Kitty is the stereotype of the B-girl;

gawdy, sexy, vulgar, and tattooed, a blond woman of twenty-five to thirty, who has graduated from an earlier life of sexual delinquency in a Negro section of town. John and Kitty have vague plans for marriage but neither seems very dedicated to this purpose.

The other couple is Frank and June, who also met in a bar. Frank is a Mexican-American of twenty-five. June is a rather mousy girl of twenty-five whose major attraction for Frank is her figure. Mary and Bill often join with John and Kitty, and less often with Frank and June, for a "good time." They drink together and otherwise enjoy each other's company. Mary is able to interact on a basis of partial equality with these people. They are slightly indulgent toward her, but Bill shields her from most situations that could become difficult.

In all her interaction with relatives and friends, Mary shows an odd lack of perception. For example, she often makes appropriate remarks or actions without knowing why they are appropriate; that is, she usually knows what people expect of her but not always why they expect it. In some situations she is wildly gauche, in others she is hopelessly wrong. In neither instance does she have the skill to save the situation by covering her blunders. For example, during a casual conversation she reminisced about buying a bathing suit from a woman she had known some years ago. As Mary tells it, the woman had paid nine dollars for the bathing suit and had sold it to Mary for ten dollars. Mary presented this statement with pride as though she had received a bargain. Bill reminded her that ten dollars was more than nine dollars and Mary seemed uneasy about the contradiction but never fully understood or resolved the absurdity.

However, Mary usually does know when she is being kidded and is able to respond in kind. Bill often jokes with Mary, using some "funny" word that Mary either finds amusing or does not understand. Mary retorts by saying "I'll—you," or "Go eat some—," repeating the word being used. One of her favorite expressions, "Go and eat them apples," serves in a multitude of situations. In well-structured situations, where Mary is comfortable and where no pressures are put upon her, she is able to hold her own.

Mary's reaction to criticism or contradiction by others is typically submissive, at least initially. For instance, she commonly puts forth her own views on matters, such as the impropriety and untrustworthiness of Negroes and Mexicans. When others contradict her, she swiftly retracts her opinion and absurdly, even fulsomely, voices a completely opposite view. But her later reaction to the same people—apparently when the frustrations have become great—is often a violent display of temper.

Her contacts outside this small number of people are extremely limited. An occasional grocery clerk and her landlady are the only additional persons she encounters alone. She expresses an uneasiness about meeting and interacting with such persons but interactions of this kind are rare and very few were observed during the three-month period of contact.

SEX, MARRIAGE, AND CHILDREN

Soon after admission to Pacific, Mary developed considerable aloofness toward boys, an attitude that pleased her mother. Six months after admission, Mary was sterilized. This greatly relieved the fears of Mary's mother and reduced her insistence upon avoidance of boys, but it was several years before Mary herself was able to establish any friendship with a boy. When she finally did find a boyfriend at the hospital with whom she felt comfortable, she soon left him and the hospital to go on work leave. While working outside the hospital, Mary continued to avoid contact with men. She "slipped" on only one occasion. One night while on her second vocational leave, Mary and another girl had gone to a drive-in restaurant and were walking home. A car stopped and the man driving it offered them a ride. They both got in, but a moment later, when the man stopped the car, Mary became frightened and said (no doubt to his vast puzzlement), "Don't touch me, I'm from Pacific Colony." Although the man promptly released her, it was fully a year before Mary was willing to have anything to do with another man.

Once Mary permitted herself to date men, she found many male friends. Before meeting her husband, Mary had had five "serious" boyfriends, all but one of whom were former patients at Pacific. The first of these affairs was transient and ended when Mary met a more attractive man. The second involved much more emotion. This young man wanted to marry her but she put him off demanding that he save some money and find a good job before marriage. Eventually he drifted away, but only after accusing Mary of physical coldness toward him. At this point, Mary had not yet formed any sexual relationship with a man. The third match failed when the man left Mary to marry another former patient from Pacific. This unhappy affair, in which there was substantial romantic involvement, left Mary in a depressive state for several months. The fourth boyfriend swept Mary off her feet. At this time Mary was making $26 per week and had saved $280. When this man, who was not a former patient, began to show Mary attention and to flatter her outrageously, she accepted his invitation to move into his apartment. After only a few days, he disappeared, taking with him Mary's radio and all her money. Mary was completely crushed. It was at this point in her life that she began her dependent relationship with Mrs. Gould, who for several years sheltered her against similar unhappiness.

After leaving her sanctuary with Mrs. Gould, Mary moved into the apartment managed by her friend Ellen and her husband. Here she met and began to date another former patient named Don. Don became seriously interested in Mary and was making overtures of marriage when Mary met Bill, who was also living in the same apartment building. Mary then dated both men but clearly favored Bill. She tried to discourage Don entirely, but he lingered hopefully and made renewed efforts to win Mary back. This was a complicated situation with all three persons living in the same apartment building. One day Mary and Bill were talking in his apartment when Don stormed into the room and said to Bill, "You better hang off where Mary is concerned." He further announced that he had two rings (engagement and marriage) and wanted Mary to put them on. Bill said that they should talk things over together and offered Don a beer. Bill recalls that "four beers later" he stated his refusal to leave Mary, and Don was too drunk to argue. Don fell asleep on Bill's bed and Bill and Mary "went out for a good time," which did not end until early morning, when they returned and found Don still slumbering on Bill's bed. Don awoke, was offended, and asked Mary if she loved Bill. She answered that she did, and he left, very upset. The next day, Don sneaked up behind Mary while she was working and tried to slip his rings on her finger. She rejected him coldly, saying that she did not like him and that he didn't even have a decent job (he did odd jobs). "I told him that Bill had a good steady job."

From this point on, Mary and Bill conducted their courtship without the interference of another man. They went to movies and drank beer and drove around in Bill's old car. A few weeks later, Bill and Mary were in a bar and Bill proposed, suggesting that Mary move into his apartment with him. Mary accused him of kidding, but Bill said that if she didn't believe him, he "would come and drag her into my apartment." She "believed him then" and agreed to marry him. She also moved into his apartment immediately. A week later she went to a jewelry store and picked out an engagement ring and two wedding rings. She told her parents then and they were pleased, offering to pay for a honeymoon in Las Vegas. Mary had tearfully confessed to Bill about her stay in Pacific and he had said that "it didn't matter." Bill had responded by telling Mary about his first wife; it seems that this woman had been "cheating" on him. They had had a daughter and Bill had permitted the little girl to remain in the custody of his ex-wife. Bill has never seen his daughter since the divorce.

On the day of the wedding, Bill picked Mary up in his old car and together they headed for the minister's house where Mary's parents were awaiting them. Both were formally dressed, Mary in a long white gown and Bill in white tie and tails. (She had been given the dress and he had rented the tails.) Unfortunately, the car broke down en route and they were two hours late. Mary was humiliated but Bill laughed it off. The minister was tolerant and the wedding took place. They were married in 1957. Mary was thirty years old.

Bill says that he is very happy with Mary as a wife and this is almost certainly true. She has always been completely submissive, allowing him any action, any extravagance. She cares for the house all day and can be relied upon to have things in order when he returns from work. She cooks for him, irons his clothes, and drenches him with affection. He does not have to worry about her flirting with other men. He rules completely but with a light touch. Bill (who possesses normal intelligence) realizes that Mary is less intelligent than most women, but she provides him with what he wants—a faithful, dependent woman who will keep house for him, gratify his sexual wants, and permit him any behavior he wishes.

Mary, in turn, is very happy with Bill. He gives her stability and confidence: she can depend on him. He is kind to her, buys her things now and then, and takes her to interesting places. What is most important, he makes her respectable—she is married to an "outside guy," not a "guy from the Colony." Bill is affectionate and never belittles her. For example, he often says, "We never use the word *stupid* in our house." She thinks that it is unfortunate that he drinks so much and spends so much money on his friends, but if this is what he wants, then it is all right. She is proud of Bill and praises him to all who will listen; she believes that he is a wonderful person and she is willing to do anything to make him happy.

Their sexual relationship may not be completely fulfilling, although both say that they are satisfied. She feels that sex is just fine with Bill, but he seems to be somewhat dissatisfied with Mary and apparently has an occasional furtive relationship with another woman.

It is Bill's drinking that worries Mary most. He does drink heavily almost every night and spends considerable sums of money on beer and whiskey. Recently, Bill and his friend John spent the night drinking at a nearby bar and returned to Bill's house in an advanced state of inebriation. They demanded entrance from Mary, then fell fast asleep upon the couches in the living room. About three in the morning, Mary awoke and found the house filled with smoke. She was unable to wake either man, so she ran screaming to a phone booth a block away to call the police. When she returned, she found that the men had awakened, had extinguished the fire, and were now sitting outside on the lawn drinking beer while they waited for the smoke to clear. It was a small fire started by a cigarette and it was easily put out. They highly resented Mary's calling the police, as it was embarrassing to greet the police, the firemen, and the landlady in their condition, so they chided Mary for acting precipitously. Mary regrets such incidents but is completely unwilling to criticize Bill in any fashion beyond lighthearted joking.

Mary is disturbed over being sterilized at Pacific. She feels deprived of her right to be a woman and wonders why this was done to her without her "permission" or without "warning." She would like to have children and is envious of her friends who do have them. In a sense, she regards the operation of sterilization as a stigma of her days in Pacific, which she would prefer to forget. However, Bill does not want children and is secretly delighted that Mary is sterilized. He says that it saves him the trouble of employing contraceptive devices. He feels that "children would tie us down." He had earlier given up his daughter and appears to have no regrets over his action. To some degree, Mary has come to accept Bill's feeling that children would be a burden.

In general, Mary and Bill have a happy, if not always stable marriage. She is utterly devoted to him and he is genuinely fond of her. Each needs the other and is willing to admit this need.

SPARE TIME

Every weekday Mary gets up early in the morning and prepares breakfast for Bill before he goes to work. Bill leaves at seven-thirty and Mary turns to her housework. She cleans the kitchen and straightens the house. Then she irons, sews, or otherwise busies herself around the house. Often she turns on television very early in the day and watches old movies. After a light lunch, Mary frequently takes a nap so that she will be able to stay up and watch the late movie on TV. In the late afternoon, she gets out of bed and prepares dinner for Bill. Often she has time on her hands and watches TV or looks at a movie magazine until Bill comes home. When Bill returns, he opens a can of beer and relaxes, talking to Mary before having dinner.

After dinner, Bill usually proposes a trip to a bar or to a friend's house for a few drinks "and a little mischief." Sometimes Mary goes along, but often she stays home. Mary does not drink beer very often because she feels that it is fattening and she is trying to reduce. She seldom drinks any alcohol, because, as she says, "it makes me heave." When she accompanies Bill on his escapades she usually does not drink. Only on occasional evenings do Bill and Mary stay home together and then they go to bed early.

Weekends are inevitably devoted to full-time recreation. Bill and Mary very often leave the house early on Saturday and do not return until very late on Sunday. They enjoy overnight trips to the beach, the mountains, or Las Vegas. These trips involve swimming, dancing, gambling, and drinking. Mary loves movies but Bill does not, so they very seldom go to one. Another typical weekend involves a prolonged party for Bill's friends. These parties begin early on Saturday evening and seldom conclude before daylight on Sunday. Mary used to love the excitement of preparing for these parties and of being a hostess to Bill's friends. But recently these parties have become increasingly disorderly, leading to cigarette burns on the furniture, drunken fights, vomiting on the floor, and broken glassware. No one ever stayed to help Mary clean up. She now dislikes such parties and tries to dissuade Bill from inviting his friends.

Mary develops intense personal attachments to motion picture and recording stars. She follows their careers closely and refers to them as though they were personal friends. Bill does not share these interests and sometimes derides Mary slightly for devoting so much time to these things. Similarly, Mary does not understand Bill's interest in sports. However, they live an exceptionally active life and spend much of their spare time together. They love "going places" and "getting into mischief." They are together a great deal, and for the most part they enjoy each other's company. In comparison with other former patients, Mary and Bill have an extremely varied and full leisure life.

SELF-PERCEPTION

There is no evidence that Mary has ever accepted any suggestion that she is mentally deficient. She is perfectly aware that she has been thought deficient by others but she has rejected this definition of self. She has worked out a long and complicated story of her life that carefully explains the events of her past and shows her to be the victim of cruel circumstances. It concludes triumphantly by indicating that her present successful life proves that she always "had what it takes" if only she were given the chance.

Ever since her release from Pacific on work leave, she has attempted to associate with non-patients and either to avoid or to dominate former patients. For example, while on work leave Mary used to attend a friendship club, a recreational club for former patients of several hospitals that is supervised by California State Department of Mental Hygiene personnel. During her visits to this club, Mary was most officious in her efforts to dominate and control the other patients. She ordered them about and otherwise made it clear that she considered herself far superior to them. Eventually, these other former patients became so annoyed that Mary was made unwelcome at the club. Her efforts to find friends among non-patients were singularly unsuccessful with the exception of her one unfortunate experience with the man who stole her money. Still, she insisted that she wanted to associate with non-patients. Despite her failures, Mary was making efforts to "pass" and be accepted as a perfectly normal, nonretarded person.

Mary was never markedly successful in her "passing" until she met Bill. Her marriage to him was the turning point for her perception of self; it not only convinced her of her relative normality, but it greatly facilitated her "passing." Mary saw Bill as an attractive and desirable man. He was handsome, had a regular job with an adequate income, an automobile, and, in her mind, vast knowledge and savoir faire. That such a man should marry her was tremendously self-assuring. But beyond this, Bill has provided her with increased confidence in her ability to control her social and material environment. Although he has chosen to play a profoundly protective role toward Mary, he has not done so in a manner that lowers her self-esteem. She says, "Before I married Bill, I told him about my trouble figuring out money and reading and writing and all that, but he said, 'That's OK, you're just the kind of wife I want.' I've never told anybody else about being in that place." He has never undermined her own confidence, and he has buttressed her against the complexities of modern urban society. For example, Bill has tried to teach Mary to drive a car. He patiently explained the manual gearshift to Mary and then took her out for a lesson in his car. She promptly ran headlong into a parked car. Bill quickly changed places with Mary and insisted to the police that he was driving. His insurance covered the damage and he has never reproached Mary for the accident. He still insists that she should learn to drive, but she says she is "too nervous." Bill also admits that he is too nervous to try to teach her again.

Despite all that Bill can do for her, Mary is confused and uncertain in some situations. Mary's inability to quantify is almost complete—where numbers are concerned, she is *always* confused. For example, in response to a question about her husband's salary she said, "I don't know. I think it's two hundred seventy dollars a week or something." When asked the same question later she replied, "It must be three hundred seventy dollars either a week or a month. I'm never real sure about that." She still cannot read or write with any facility and when forced to do so publicly she is greatly frightened and generally retreats from the situation. When, during the course of normal interaction outside her home, someone makes a disparaging remark, Mary is humiliated and angered. Her reaction is a hopelessly ineffective retort or excessive anger; neither is appropriate and neither saves Mary's self-esteem from damage. Also, she is grossly incompetent in many public situations. For example, a researcher joined Mary, Kitty, and June in a trip to Mary's mother's house. Kitty was driving and Mary was giving directions. Mary became hopelessly lost. She had no means whatever for finding the house or for explaining her own confusion. The researcher finally determined the address of the house from a phone book and located the street. They first drove in the wrong direction, as numbers were difficult to see. Mary pointed out a large restaurant as they passed it. The researcher finally noted that they were traveling in the wrong direction, and the car was turned around. Mary quickly pointed out that they must be going in the wrong direction "because there is that restaurant again and we were going wrong when we saw it before." That she was passing the restaurant while traveling in two different directions never occurred to her and she could not be made to understand this fact. Many other embarrassing circumstances are brought about by Mary's inability to remember names, addresses, or phone numbers, or to do such things as dial a telephone correctly.

A good part of Mary's time is devoted to fantasies in which she visits awful punishment upon all those persons who have wronged her. For example, she relives (verbally if she has an audience) an experience in which a "snotty" salesgirl was "stuck-up" with her. In recreating the scene where she "told her off," Mary describes ripostes, which she relates as having utterly devastated the erring salesgirl. Friends who have wronged her are similarly bested in Mary's fantasies. She tells of the clever things she said and how her opponents were crushed by these retorts, or of the ingenious means she used to punish the person. For incidents where she was accused of making a mistake, she always concludes by "proving" to her listener that "I was right after all."

Mary maintains a lively interest in the careers of her former acquaintances at Pacific. Even though she does not want to associate with them, she is eager for news of them. She is particularly anxious to learn of their problems and their failures after leaving Pacific. Rather than feeling threatened by the failures of her colleagues, she seems to be emboldened by the knowledge that she is "doing better" than many of these persons. It appears to convince her that she is truly more capable than they.

Mary and Bill live primarily in the present, but Mary, far more than Bill, is sometimes concerned with plans for the future. She sees herself as able to achieve worthwhile things in the years to come. Right now she is "a little heavy but I'll take that off and get some really nice clothes." She has distinct aspirations for better clothes, a better car, a more expensive house, more money, and ultimately, her own servants. She treats these aspirations not as dreams but as attainable goals that she and Bill can someday reach. For the moment, she wants a washing machine of her own and a slightly bigger house, but she feels that she is someday capable of acquiring a "nice" home in a "nice" neighborhood, and all the "good things" that go with this. She is by no means obsessed with these hopes but she does now and then think and speak about them. To date, neither she nor Bill have made any efforts to save money or defer present gratification for any future rewards.

In summary, it seems that Mary suspects that she is mentally less capable than others and is mortified by this self-accusation. Yet, she will never admit to others that she is at all deficient and she struggles to deny this to herself. She does realize that she would be lost without her husband; he means everything to her self-esteem and to her ability to cope with everyday life.

THE OUTLOOK

At the time the study was terminated, serious changes had taken place in Mary and Bill's life together. Mary tells the story that one night Bill and his friend John had been a little short of money and had decided to drink some "cut-rate" vodka. They both became violently ill and were unable to go to work for ten days. When Bill returned to work, his boss accused him of drunkenness and threatened to fire him. Bill became angry, demanded his back pay, and quit.

Bill's reaction to the loss of his job was to go on a two-week vacation spree with Mary, John, and Kitty. Bill told Mary that there was nothing to worry about, that he had been planning to get a better job anyway, and now he could get the job he really wanted. Mary believed him. Bill said that he intended to apply for a job driving a truck for the motion picture studios (he claims to know some people who do such work). This work pays very well, and sometimes when the studio goes on location he would be paid to go along and he could take Mary with him, all expenses paid. He and Mary talked about going to Africa together with the studio paying the way and Mary said that she thought it would be "fun with lions and tigers and all that." Bill then told Mary that he would have to wait a week or so before hearing from the studios, and that since they had not had a good vacation for a long time, they should "live it up" for a week, or perhaps even two.

This they proceeded to do. Every day for the next two weeks was spent in a dizzy round of driving, drinking, gambling, dancing, and once in a while, sleeping. Bill and Mary, sometimes accompanied by John and Kitty, went to almost every vacation area within three hundred miles during those two weeks. They would drive a few miles, stop in a bar for a few drinks, and then continue on their way. They spent four days in Las Vegas, where Bill drank and watched the shows while Mary gambled in the slot machines. They had a "marvelous" time and Mary believes that she discovered a way to win, playing the slot machines. "You can't pull the handle real quick and jerky or you'll lose. If you pull it down nice and easy you win."

They went to the beach, to night clubs, to desert resorts, to amusement parks, and to Disneyland. After two weeks of this merriment, or as they call it, "mischief," Bill and Mary had spent every cent they could muster—all their cash on hand and all his severance pay, some eight hundred dollars. Bill now confided that he didn't think that the studios were going to offer him a job "after all" and he began to look for other work. He said, very nonchalantly, "I'll take anything that comes along," and he meant it. He waited in a State employment office for days, and once in a while found a job for a single day, but never longer than that. Both Bill and Mary applied for aid from "unemployment," but before any emergent aid could be received they were reduced to eating potato soup and nothing else. Further, their landlady gave them notice to vacate their house. The ostensible reason was to permit occupancy by the landlady's mother, but Mary believed that it was their "wild parties" and present reduced financial condition.

The most shattering blow for Mary was the sudden desertion of their friends. John and Kitty, Frank and June—all quickly disappeared. Bill and Mary had only recently spent their few remaining cents on cigarettes for Kitty. Now that Bill and Mary needed help and could not provide money, entertainment or liquor, their friends were unavailable. Or at least so Bill and Mary saw it. They are both extremely generous people, who give anything they have to anyone they consider a friend. Further, they do not require anything in return. So, when their friends ignored them during their impoverishment, they were angry and bewildered.

Bill had no income, and the modest aid being received from unemployment benefits was in danger of being cut off. Their friends had forsaken them and they were being forced to vacate their house and look for new lodging. Neither Bill nor Mary was willing to ask her mother for assistance. They hid their problems from her and were determined to solve them alone. Still, their final word was "We'll try to get on our feet alone, but if things go wrong we can always get help from Mother." They wanted to be independent but they knew that they had a benefactress to fall back upon, though they would be somewhat embarrassed to do so. Their past actions and their plans for the future both seem to be based upon the realization that this sourse of aid is available if needed.

Mary was sincerely distressed by their misfortune but she steadfastly argued, "It will be OK. Bill will work things out. He knows lots of ways to do things. You'll see, everything will work out OK."

Postscript—1992

Mary was right. With help from his mother, Bill was able to rent an apartment and found a job driving a truck. Mary and Bill made new friends and, as far as one can tell from telephone conversations, for the next ten years they lived very much as they had before. In 1972, they moved to Toledo, Ohio, to be near Bill's mother who was critically ill. Bill found a job as a forklift operator in a factory and continued to provide for all of Mary's needs, including doing all the grocery shopping. Mary enjoyed cooking (especially chili, macaroni and cheese, and buttered veal cutlets), watching television, and chatting with neighbors and Bill's many relatives. After fourteen years of marriage, Mary still could not read, write, or understand money, but she was pampered by Bill, accepted by his family, and according to her, happier than she had ever been before.

In 1978, Bill retired with a pension and a disability allowance for emphysema, which he apparently contracted on the job. Soon after, Bill and Mary moved to Arkansas. Mary was as happy as ever. Bill enjoyed his retirement by fishing and "lounging around" as he put it, but his health deteriorated and he died half a dozen years ago. Mary missed him greatly, saying that "he was a good man," but like many other formerly dependent wives, she rapidly learned to cope with life on her own and to enjoy new experiences. She made the decision to move to Oklahoma to be near her much-loved stepmother who encouraged her to convert to Catholicism. A friend from her church volunteers to take Mary shopping and helps her to manage her money which, thanks to Social Security and Bill's pensions, is adequate for her needs.

Mary has a VCR that she uses to tape movies. She particularly likes John Wayne and Humphrey Bogart movies, perhaps because they were Bill's favorites, but she also likes *Home Alone* and *The Sound of Music*. Now sixty-four years old, her health is excellent and so are her spirits. She enjoys her new friends in Oklahoma and loves shopping at Walmart and K-Mart, saying that she is "always into mischief." Of her many moves, she says without regret, "You do what you have to do." She is definitely enjoying life: "I'm on my own now, and I like it that way. I do what I want to do!"

CHAPTER THREE

Some Central Concerns of "Life on the Outs"

The preceding chapter provided a detailed introduction to the lives of a small number of the former patients. This chapter will build upon that background by turning attention to all of the former patients and by discussing some of the central concerns of their lives outside the institution, or as the former patients put it, "life on the outs."

Since it would be impossible to discuss every relevant aspect of the ex-patients' lives in the outside world, this account will be confined to a limited number of concerns that are central in their lives. Both the important commonality and the variability in their lives can be understood by concentrating upon those dimensions of life that the expatients themselves saw as being either critical to their ability to exist "on the outs" or as foci upon which their interests and energies centered. By these criteria, there were three central concerns: (1) how to make a living, (2) the proper management of sex, marriage, and reproduction, and (3) the ways in which leisure can best be utilized.

Before we turn to a discussion of these central concerns, we should know something about where, and under what conditions, the former patients were living at the time of research contact. Unfortunately, we have no firsthand knowledge of the living and housing conditions of the members of the cohort after discharge but before the period of the actual research. However, all available evidence, obtained by interviewing the patients as well as those normal persons who knew them, indicates that there have been few dramatic changes in the level and style of living of the ex-patients during their post-discharge lives. Though they change residence often, they typically change to a similar type of housing in a neighborhood of similar socio-economic status. We may conclude, then, that the conditions seen during the twelve-month period of research are representative of a fairly stable pattern.

At the time of the research, ten of the forty-eight patients for whom there were complete data were located in a downtown commercial area or slum. Another eight were in downtown boarding-house areas. Sixteen were living in lower socio-economic residential areas and two were in upper-middle socio-economic status areas. Three former patients were transient—one was a girl who traveled from man to man, and two were Mexican-American men who received hospitality from a far-flung system of relatives and friends. The types of housing they occupied were varied. Twenty-one lived in houses, thirteen in apartments, eight had rooms in their places of employment, two lived in hotel rooms, two lived in trailers, and two lived in their parents' homes.

Wherever the location and whatever the type of housing, it was typically the case that the furnishings were few, old, worn, and inexpensive. The condition of the dwelling was often lamentable, even when it was located in an otherwise proper neighborhood. Over half of the dwellings were conspicuously ramshackle or run-down even in comparison to other dwellings in the neighborhood. For example, in eleven instances, the dwelling occupied by an ex-patient was the most dilapidated one in an area of several blocks. On the other hand, the neatness and cleanliness of the living quarters was usually much less substandard than the condition of the dwelling itself. No more than fifteen of the ex-patients were living in markedly substandard conditions of cleanliness and hygiene—nine of these were only moderately below the presumed norm of "middle-class" housekeeping, but six were living in appalling filth. Eight cases were clearly above the norm, even for compulsive "middle-class" housekeepers, and the other twenty-five cases were judged to be about average. Here, too, there is substantial variation.

Finally, none of the former patients was the owner of his dwelling place, although several of the women, as we shall see later in this chapter, married normal men who owned homes. These, then, are the outlines of the ex-patients' living places and conditions. On the whole, the subjects were realistic about their housing circumstances, and indeed, about their whole life-style, pretending neither that they were used to something better nor that their chances for significant improvement were good. One ex-patient brushed aside his living conditions this way:

> Look, it ain't like I don't give a damn how I live. It ain't like I don't want to live no better. I could live better than what I do, I know that, but I could live a damn sight worse too. The problem is I ain't no millionaire, see, and money is the stuff what really counts. You got money, you got no problems; I got no money, so I got problems. You don't get no money without you get off your butt and work. Everybody wants a good job but good jobs ain't easy to find. Work's work and that's no joke. We used to bitch about the food in that hospital, but out here, if you don't work you don't eat nothing at all. You gotta work. That's the whole thing.

Making a Living

For the ex-patients, the ability to work is fundamental in more than one sense. Had they not demonstrated an ability to perform well on a job, they would never have left Pacific on work leave, and had they not continued to perform well on a job in the community, they would never have been discharged. The importance of employment is not reduced following discharge. For the ex-patients, holding a job after discharge has an importance even beyond the importance that employment has for normal persons. Every ex-patient held a job at the time he was discharged, but there was no guaranteed tenure to this job. To hold it, the newly released retardate had to perform well. The ex-patients, one and all, fear that unemployment means a return to Pacific. In fact, this fear is greatly exaggerated, for it would require more than unemployment to bring the released retardate back to the attention of the authorities, but the fear exists nonetheless. Unemployment also menaces the self-esteem of the ex-patients, for whom employment is necessary as a demonstration of worth in the normal world.

As might be expected, several years after discharge the employment status of the forty-eight ex-patients was varied. Several were steadily and happily employed, with some security and hope for the future. Others were unemployed and despondent. We begin with the unemployed.

THE UNEMPLOYED

Six of the released retardates were unemployed. Two of these were men, four were women (this excludes housewives who will be discussed separately). At the time of discharge, of course, all these persons had jobs. We must ask, then, how they came to lose them and why they did not find others. Surprisingly, for so intrinsically complex a matter, the answers seem to be simple. Three of the women who are without jobs lost their original jobs because of their massive anxiety. The fourth woman was led astray by her half brother, who convinced her to leave her job of seven years, to withdraw all her savings, and to take a trip with him. In a short while he left her, without a cent. One of the unemployed men lost his job because he was sent to prison, the other lost a series of jobs through a combination of his anxiety, his incompetence, and his grandiose aspirations.

Three of the women have endured unemployment thanks to support by the Bureau of Public Assistance, and the fourth woman (who was bilked of her savings) is now a ward of the State in a foster-care home. The two men are supported by relatives. All six of these individuals express—with convincing sincerity—their desire to be employed again as soon as conditions, or their health, permit.

The following account, by one of the three women who lost her job as a result of "nerves," is typical:

I used to Work for Mrs. —— there at —— (a restaurant). I washed dishes and cleaned up and put things away and sometimes I made salads—you know, chopped lettuce and things. I did good. I worked good and tried real hard and all, but everyone was always picking at me, like I was never no good any time. I got so nervous with them always crabbing at me. Why couldn't they leave me alone? I just couldn't take it. I was nervous, crying all the time. Mrs. —— picked at me one day and I just walked on out of there. Never went back. Never even got paid. (How long ago was that?) Must have been a year ago. I been getting the welfare since. I can't work with my nerves all shot. When my nerves get better I'll get a job OK. I can work OK but it's my nerves that's the trouble. It's not that I can't get a job, it's my nerves that's bad.

This man's account is instructive because of its clear expression of concerns that trouble many of the ex-patients:

Well, since I been out, I've had lots of jobs. Some were real good ones that I found myself. I was a busboy at —— (an expensive restaurant), but I had to quit there. Then I was a clothes sorter at the Goodwill. I was there about a year. It wasn't my nerves that was wrong, I just didn't like doing nothing all the time. And I was, uh—what do you call it?—handbill man, a handbill man. I went along and put them bills in mail boxes and other places. I liked that job. I was my own boss. But it got too hot in the summer so I quit that job too. I been a busboy at a lot of places—one place I worked a long time, but my nerves got bad from all the noise so I quit that too (actually, he was fired after he dropped a tray of dishes on a customer). Then, I got a terrific job. I was with the union and I got three twenty an hour building bridges (the salary is correct). I was a construction man for a great big company (his stepfather got him the job as a laborer through his contacts in the union). I handled all kinds of equipment and I was doing real fine. The foreman liked me so I thought maybe I'd catch on regular and go with them on their next big job in Hawaii or Seattle or someplace like that. But something went wrong and the foreman started to yell at me and I got nervous again so I quit that job too. I could do real good if people would just let me do things my own way (in fact, he caused the loss of several hundred dollars worth of tools and was fired despite his stepfather's attempts to protect him). I'm thinking I'd like to start my own car-washing company so's I could be my own boss. Why won't people let me do things my own way?

The unemployed are not properly a class with common characteristics. They are anxious, to be sure, but so are many of the ex-patients who remain employed. And they are fearful, but that is not unique either. The most remarkable thing about the unemployed is that there are so few of them.

THE HOUSEWIVES

For the women among the former patients, marriage offers the opportunity for a legitimate exit from the labor force. Twenty-one of the women in the cohort were married, and eighteen of these women had removed themselves from regular employment by becoming housewives. Fourteen of these housewives were completely unemployed; four others worked only a few hours each week.

All of these women had worked successfully before they were married. The obvious question is why they should have stopped. Part of the answer lies in the fact that fifteen of these eighteen women married normal men. With three exceptions, these men have not permitted their wives to work. The following comments are typical of these twelve marriages:

(A normal husband) I didn't marry Corliss so she could support me. I'm the man of the house and I'm the one that'll do the working. I want her here at home. She don't have to do much of anything here, just a little housework and cooking, but I want her here all the same. Even if she could make more money working than I could, I wouldn't let her work. I'm the man and I work. She's the woman and she stays home.

(The retarded wife of a normal man) I had a pretty good job before I got married (she worked on an assembly line in a factory), but when I married Harry, he said to me, "Ain't no wife of mine gonna work. I want you here in the kitchen and in bed and I don't want you off gallivantin' around lessen I'm with you." So I just stay right home and I'm real happy.

The strength of this value—that a proper man should not "send his wife off to work"—is clear and pervasive. Several men admit that they could use the income their retarded wives could earn doing part-time domestic labor or "taking in" washing or ironing, but these men nevertheless do not want their wives to work. In only one case is the husband's income sufficiently large that additional income from the wife would not be useful. And, with rare exceptions, none of these women has children whom she must remain at home to care for.

Of the four women who work a few hours a week, three are married to normal men. One of these women helps her husband manage an apartment building, but her duties are never trying and they do not take her away from the home. Another wife sometimes helps her housepainter husband on jobs, but more often she stays home. The third housewife seldom sees her unemployed husband and is consequently compelled to work twelve to fifteen hours a week doing washing and ironing in order to support herself.

To be a wife, at least to be the wife of a normal man, tends to mean relief from the need, and the possibility, of employment.

"SAN WORK"

A category of employment that the ex-patients recognize and discuss is "san work"—work in a sanitarium. There are many sanitariums in the Los Angeles area that provide long-term residential care for infirm patients, particularly for elderly, bedridden patients. Most of these sanitariums require large numbers of semi-skilled, low-salaried employees to work in kitchens, on wards, and on the grounds. Many of these private institutions are licensed by the State and are utilized by the various state hospitals as work placements for patients on vocational leave. Pacific State Hospital has utilized the sanitariums in this fashion for a number of years. In fact, thirty-one of the forty-eight persons in the research cohort had spent some time working in sanitariums before or after their discharge.

At the time of the research contact, eight of the ex-patients were working in sanitariums. These sanitarium jobs regularly offer long hours, hard work, and low wages. However, they provide room and board in addition to salary. For example, the average wage of the eight ex-patients was $94 per month, but all eight of these employees also received full room and board. By virtue of the fact that these sanitariums have the character of institutions encapsulated against the outside world, they are places in which all the needs of the ex-patients are met, protection is offered, and the challenges of the outside world are held at bay.

Life in a sanitarium is discussed by this ex-patient (a thirty-four-year-old man):

> I worked in three, no, I guess it's been four, sans now. They're OK. The work's hard, you know, lots of dishwashing and cleaning up, and sometimes I don't like being around all those old, sick people, but it ain't so bad. I got my room and my food and I got some dough. I can go where I want to, and do what I want. The work's OK but the hours is too long. I gotta have more rest than what I get around here. Mrs. (the manager) is OK though. She runs me ragged lots of time but she looks out for me too. I get in trouble or I'm broke and she'll help me out. Some of the ones from the hospital, they don't like it here. They want to be more out on their own like, but I got no complaint.

The owner and manager of a large state-licensed sanitarium reflects upon her experience with retarded patients and ex-patients as employees:

> Over the last thirteen years I've had a lot of the retardeds in here. Some were good and some were bad. They're all limited mentally, of course, but more than that, most of them don't like hard work and can't stand being told what to do. A great many of them stay a short while and then they quit or

I have to let them go. But a few ofttimes work out all right. I've got two here now and both of them are good kids. The real thing about working here is that we're all one big family. We live here on the grounds and we eat here and we have some of our own recreation here. My employees don't want for anything while they're here. The food's good and I pay well and I see that they're taken care of and happy. My employees, especially the retarded ones, couldn't ask for anything more than what they find right here.

The "san" job always remains as a possibility for the ex-patients; such jobs are usually available if the ex-patient is out of work. But "san work" is a kind of backwater where the ex-patient knows that in return for a sheltered and safe existence he will be less than fully independent. Not only is the ex-patient's past "known about" when he works in a sanitarium, but he is also continually brought into contact with that past in the form of a stream of patients from Pacific who work at the sanitarium while they are still on probationary status. The sanitarium remains in the ex-patients' view as a half-way house between the full control of the hospital and the freedom of an "outside" job that has no connection with an institutional past. The ex-patients refer to a job in a sanitarium as a "State" job (one found by and connected with the State); most of the ex-patients prefer to find an "outside job."

"KITCHEN WORK"

A common type of "outside job" for the ex-patients is "kitchen work" in restaurants. "Kitchen work" is the ex-patients' term for restaurant jobs that combine dishwashing, general kitchen cleanup, and some food preparation or handling. Many of the former patients received training in such procedures while at Pacific by working in the hospital cafeteria. Since discharge, nineteen of the ex-patients have done "kitchen work" at one time or another. At the time of the research, seven of the cohort members were employed in restaurants.

One forty-one-year-old man did general kitchen cleanup and dishwashing at a small cafe for $33.20 per week plus meals. A second man, aged thirty, has worked in the same Italian restaurant for seven years. He began as a dishwasher for $10 a week but he has advanced to a position ("cook's helper") that requires simple food preparation and cooking and he now earns $67 a week. A third ex-patient, a thirty-one-year-old woman, also worked in an Italian restaurant. She has worked in this same kitchen for eight years preparing food, making sauces, and doing most of the dishwashing and cleaning. She is paid $1.25 an hour, plus meals, and she is a reliable and competent worker.

Two married couples also do kitchen work, again in Italian restaurants. The first husband-and-wife pair works together in the same kitchen but he receives a dollar an hour and she receives only seventy-five cents. The second couple also works together—often for twelve to fifteen hours a day—and both earn a dollar an hour. Husband and wife prepare sauces, do some cooking, and all the cleanup work. This restaurant is small but quite expensive, and its business is thriving.

In addition to the curious finding that six or seven kitchen workers are employed in Italian restaurants, it is noteworthy that while most of these employees work long hours, their wages are not markedly substandard when it is considered that they also receive free meals plus many gratuities and favors. In every case, however, the ex-patients remain secluded from public view. Despite frequent requests from the ex-patients to "wait tables," no former patient has been permitted this responsibility. Indeed, it is extremely rare for a former patient to be permitted even busboy duties. One employer who has had several ex-patients in her restaurant gave this typical explanation: "I wouldn't let Lester or Bertha go out in the dining room because it wouldn't look right. Customers expect certain things, and Lester and Bertha don't dress right and don't talk just right, and if somebody asked them for something they might botch it up. I don't think it would be good for business. Besides, they might drop a bunch of dirty dishes or spill a glass of water or something like that. They can be all right in the kitchen but I wouldn't want them out front."

OTHER "OUTSIDE JOBS"

Others among the ex-patients have located non-traditional "outside" jobs, often after much seeking and many prior job changes. Two of the cohort members work only irregularly. For example, one man, who says that he is an "odd-job man," has never had, nor wanted, steady work. He has taken a number of temporary odd jobs, usually indoor janitorial work or general cleanup work at ranches. He has never earned more than a dollar an hour. During the period of the research, he held and quit three jobs: cleanup work at a ranch, sweeper at a county fairground, and dishwasher at an all-night cafe. "I work so I get some money. Then I quit and spend it. Then I work some more. That's how I like it."

Much of the same is true of a woman in the cohort. This attractive young woman began her post-discharge life as a live-in domestic for three years at $25 to $40 per week. For eight months following this she worked in an automated car wash. She then married a normal man who had a well-paying professional position. During her marriage she was supported by her husband. Following separation from her husband, she found a series of jobs at an amusement park, first as the girl the magician throws knives at, next as the face that baseballs are thrown at, and finally as a general magician's assistant at fifty cents an hour. At the time of the research she worked only now-and-then and preferred to be supported by a lover. She said of herself, "I don't work unless I have to, and when I got a guy I don't have to work."

A few ex-patients have improved their employment only by dint of diligent effort. One man, for example, has found eight jobs and left seven of those in the three years since his discharge from Pacific. Chronologically ordered, these jobs included: painter (two weeks at $25 per week); janitor at a pet hospital (seven months, $25 per week); handyman, miniature golf course (one month, $55 per week); handyman, amusement park (twelve months, $25–$40 per week); dishwasher at a cafe (two days); door-to-door salesman (nine days); hand sander for a furniture manufacturer (ten months, $1.65 per hour); and, presently, grounds maintenance for a large chemical company at $1.75 per hour. When the research terminated, this last job had endured for seven months.

A few others have held one job for a considerable period, principally because the job was one that no one else would take. One such former patient had worked as a janitor, a gardener at a motel, a general hand at a chicken ranch, and a dishwasher at a sanitarium. However, for the past five years he has worked for a metal-processing firm, feeding metal into a furnace. The work is exhausting and the heat is extreme. The job demands long hours (sometimes twelve or more) and pays only $1.25 per hour, and provides, rent free, utterly wretched living quarters. The employer admits that he was never before able to get anyone else to do the same work, even at higher wages. For his part, the former patient is proud that he can do work that no one else is able, or willing, to do.

Of the remaining ex-patients who have found their own "outside jobs" few have found any degree of job security, either through the excellence of their performance, through the personal guarantees of their employers, or through union membership. One of the two most secure ex-patients is a man (age 39, IQ 56) who, since his discharge six years ago, has held the same (union) job at a trucking company. He loads and unloads trucks for $2.45 an hour. He is a reliable, competent worker with six years of job tenure. A second man (age 40, IQ 68) worked as a handyman shortly after his discharge in 1949, then enlisted in the Army, where he served as a cook under combat conditions in Korea for three years. During the past eight years he has worked as a tile presser in a tile company; he earns $240 per month and fully supports a wife.

Although it is true that relatively few of the ex-patients are unemployed, it is also true that most of these forty-eight retarded persons are highly marginal economic performers. Indeed, the realities of their economic conditions are worse than this brief review has been able to indicate. Most of these persons are in debt, few have any appreciable job security, and fewer still have marketable job skills.

The feelings of these former patients concerning making a living are exemplified by the following comments of a man who is married to a cohort member: "I think it's easier for a girl to come outside and make an adjustment than it is a man. Because a girl can come outside and maybe she can meet some nice guy that's working and she can take care of the house and stuff. Where a man when he comes outside, you know he can't get an outside woman. You know she ain't going to take care of no institution guy. So I do believe that a girl, if she comes outside and she has just a little bit of mentality. then she can make it because she can find some outside guy." His wife: "Honey, that's easier said than done." He: "No it ain't. A man has to come out and he has to go to work, and a girl comes out and meets some guy where maybe she don't have to work. A man's got to worry about working every day and stuff. Ain't nobody going to feed him on the outside." Economically, the ex-patients remain unskilled and insecure.

Sex, Marriage, and Reproduction

Sexual behavior is of special importance in the everyday lives of these former patients because it has so often caused them trouble in their pre-hospital lives. For all of these former patients, sexual matters were an ever-threatening source of trouble in the community, and for many of these persons, real or fancied sexual misconduct was the ostensible reason for their original institutionalization. Moreover, sex remains potentially a highly troublesome matter for these people after discharge. For example, improperly managed sexual desire can lead to prostitution, promiscuity, child molestation, rape, or venereal infection, and it can easily produce all manner of interpersonal conflict. Obviously, then, skill in the management of sexual conduct must be developed if the ex-patient is to avoid serious difficulty in life outside the hospital.

The former patients' desire for marriage and for children in marriage are also vital concerns, for both marriage and parenthood are cherished goals in the ex-patients' search for self-esteem. As patients in the hospital, they were denied the right to marry, and because surgical sterilization was routinely performed as a precondition to discharge (Sabagh and Edgerton, 1962), they were also permanently denied the ability to bear children. The critical importance of marriage and children to the ex-patients' maintenance of self-esteem will be discussed in subsequent chapters. Here, the emphasis will be upon an outline of the practical circumstances of their sexual and married lives. It is hoped that, in addition to the material necessary for an appraisal of this aspect of the ex-patients' lives, a perspective can also be provided from which it will be possible to evaluate the competing stereotypes that have grown up concerning the sexual conduct of mental retardates.

Comparatively little has been recorded about the sexual behavior of the retarded, either as such behavior occurs in institutions or in the community. Although facts may be lacking, stereotypes are plentiful. One such has it that the retarded are "oversexed" and hence are often desirable as sexual partners to "perverted" normals. A corollary insists that this same excess of sexuality makes the retarded dangerous to unprotected normals. However, an opposing stereotype holds that the retarded are sexless and infertile.

Table 5 *Marital Status of the 48 Former Patients*

Marital status	Men	Women	Total	Mean IQ
Single	9	5	14	64
Divorced or separated	2	2	4	56
Married to retardate (non-cohort)	2	0	2	64
Married to cohort member	5	5	10	67
Married to normal person	2	16	18	68
Total	20	28	48	

If anything about the sexual lives of these ex-patients is certain, it is this: none of the stereotypic views is accurate. The experiences of these retarded persons with sex and marriage are varied, but for the most part, they are quite conventional.

The marital status of these retarded individuals offers us an important, and surprising, insight. Table 5 indicates the marital status of each of the 48 cohort members at the time of the research.

The most striking aspect of this table is the number of ex-patients who are married. Thirty of the forty-eight are married, and eighteen of these are married to a normal person. Further, only four are divorced or separated. Because marital status is so important to the ex-patients—and to an understanding of them—the common experiences of persons in various marital statuses are illuminating. Each status will be discussed in turn.

SINGLE MEN

Although there are some commonalities, the nine single men cannot easily be characterized. For example, one man (age 41, IQ 83) has had continual difficulties in confining his sexual interests to appropriate persons. Sexual problems were prominent in this man's pre-hospital life, and one incident of "indecent exposure" led to his arrest and subsequent institutionalization. Since discharge, difficulties have continued. In fact, he was arrested for child molestation three years ago and is currently on probation. He still has an active interest in pre-adolescent girls, whom he ogles but tries not to follow; however, he also has a girlfriend with whom he has sexual relations. He says that he wants to marry her but that she refuses. She says that he is simply "one of my boyfriends." He recognizes his problems in controlling his sexual impulses and regularly seeks religious support "for my problem."

Another man (age 34, IQ 85) is a homosexual. This Mexican-American had no record of pre-hospital sexual problem. Since discharge, however, he has lived as the homosexual partner of several men. One such relationship has been very stable and has given him a haven in the community, but his earlier casual homosexuality led to several conflicts with the police (one led to arrest on vagrancy charges), one known venereal infection, and rejection by Mexican-American friends and relatives from whom he might otherwise have received assistance. He continues to live as a homosexual.

A third man (age 29, IQ 77) is overtly psychotic, and the nature of his psychosis has precluded all possibility of sexual relationships. His delusions contain grandiose sexual masochism with countesses, movie stars, and famous women. In his delusions, he is usually seduced by the wives of famous men. In reality, he is almost completely a recluse, and his sexual delusions have not led to any social difficulties.

Two men are notably inept in their relations with women. One of these men (age 33, IQ 64) is obsessed by his sexual desires and fantasies, yet in all his actual approaches to women he has failed. He tells elaborate tales of his sexual conquests with one particular woman who is an ex-patient. This woman openly laughs at his claims and insists that she only dated him twice and on both dates he was "so silly that I went home with another guy." This man also maintains the fiction that a normal married woman in his neighborhood is in love with him. He insists that she is soon to divorce her husband, leave her children, and marry him. For her, however, he is but a retarded man who sometimes does odd jobs for her. He is obsessed with desires for sexual relations and marriage with a normal woman and spends much of his time worrying about what he must do to accomplish his dream.

The second romantically inept man (age 20, IQ 61) is obese and is tormented by his lack of physical attractiveness. Although he has never had a girlfriend, he persists in seeking dates with attractive, normal girls, and he is deeply hurt when they reject him. He has recently become a voyeur, but he has not yet been in trouble with the police. He is a pathetically unhappy young man, for whom the desire for sexual experience is becoming very difficult to control.

Four of the nine single men might be considered "gay bachelors" who enjoy being single and, as one of them put it, "free like a bird." One of these men is Fred who is described in chapter 2, case B. The other three are Mexican-American men. The first of these men (age 31, IQ 51) has never married, but he has never suffered a shortage of girlfriends. He insists that, despite his prison record, what he wants most is to marry "a good girl." Then he laughs and says, "Of course, I ain't never met one of those." He enjoys his transient life and has no regrets concerning his sterilization. Sex is no problem for him. Since discharge, the second Mexican-American man (age 34, IQ 48) has been continually "on the go." He has enjoyed many "parties" and many girlfriends, and he has not the least desire to marry. Neither does he worry about being sterilized. Indeed, he regards his infertile condition as a favorable one: "They sterilized my balls, but I don't mind; now I don't got to worry about no troubles." The third man (age 45, IQ 64) was the father of an illegitimate child before being hospitalized at Pacific. Since discharge, he has known a multitude of girls—principally those he picks up at a bar where he drinks beer, as well as some ex-patients he met at the hospital—but he never thinks of marriage. His sexual behavior has not led to any trouble since discharge, and he says that he enjoys life as it is. His principal girlfriend says, "Oh, he is all right. He's harmless and he buys me beer. He don't bother me none." He thinks she is "lots of fun. We go for walks and we talk and all kinds of things. I'm what you could call real happy."

SINGLE WOMEN

The five single women are more easily characterized than were their male counterparts. One is an innocent wanton, the other four are fearful maidens who have fled from any thought of male companionship.

"The innocent wanton" is a caricature of sexual impulsiveness. This woman (age 56, IQ 47) has repeatedly demonstrated her lack of sexual control by engaging in public acts of sexual intercourse with any available male. She is now closely protected and supervised at her place of employment (a sanitarium), but even at the age of fifty-six she will occasionally slip away, only to be found in sexual congress in a work shed, the laundry basement, or in the garden. Her partners range from teenage boys to elderly patients at the sanitarium who were previously thought to be senile. She has been sterilized since 1929 and has never expressed an interest in marriage.

The other four women are similar in their dedication to an avoidance of men; however, their reasons for seclusion differ. One of these women is Martha, whose complete disavowal of sexual interest was described in chapter 2, case C. A second woman attributes her avoidance of men to "nerves" arising from her conviction that men, especially normal men, are lustful "beasts." Accusation of promiscuity (probably unfounded) led to her original institutionalization. Although she is a fairly attractive girl, since discharge she has probably never had a "date" with a man, surely no formal or romantic date. She expresses fear and distrust of men and says that she is waiting "for the right man." She does want to marry and is distressed that she has not yet done so, yet her fear of sex far overrides her girlish dreams of romance.

A third woman (age 35, IQ 64) has apparently had no sexual experience in her entire life. She has never dated, fears men and sex, and doubts that she will ever marry. Rape and sterilization figure prominently in her thoughts, however; she fears rape, and is glad that she is sterilized so that she could not become pregnant if she were raped. She says, though, that if she were not sterilized she would be able to marry. "I'd like a fellow that goes to church and has nice habits, but it's kind of hard to find one like that." She is now completely secluded from men in a foster-home placement.

The fourth woman (age 31, IQ 83) has come to her total avoidance of men through differing experiences. This young Mexican-American woman comes from a large, delinquent family. Three of her siblings are in prison and another was shot at a party and remains paralyzed. Her own sexual delinquency as a teenager led to her hospitalization. Since discharge, however, she has been the soul of propriety. She has dated only the most proper men and has behaved very conservatively. Her inability to bear children (she was sterilized at the Pacific) has tormented her, however. She almost married four years ago but could not bring herself to do so because both her prospective husband and his parents wanted children very badly. She feels that as a Catholic it is her duty to bear children and that since she cannot, she has no right to marry or to enjoy sexual relations.

She now says, "I got no right to marry anybody. I can't be no real woman." For three years, she has lived in seclusion with an older woman, and has had no contact of any sort with men.

DIVORCED OR SEPARATED

Although the circumstances surrounding their marital problems are unclear, at the time of the research, three of the four separated or divorced retardates were conducting themselves in what might be regarded as a promiscuous manner. For example, one of the separated ex-patients is a very attractive young woman (age 25, IQ 66). Her pre-hospital experiences were filled with episodes of sexual delinquency, and one spectacular act led to her hospitalization at Pacific. Sexual misconduct continued in the hospital, yet she was discharged in 1954. After discharge, she married a rather well-to-do man (an engineer in an aircraft plant) and they had three children. Two years ago he was admitted to a mental hospital, diagnosed as a schizophrenic. It is said that her suspected infidelity contributed to his problem. Since his hospitalization, she has been drifting from man to man, staying only as long as the man will support her. One of her children is dead, another lives with her mother-in-law, and the third accompanies her as she drifts about. She is regarded by her relatives, and even by her temporary lovers, as a promiscuous woman.

A second attractive woman (age 30, IQ 50) has had a somewhat similar career. Her pre-hospital life was marked by repeated sexual misbehavior, some of which led to police action. After discharge from Pacific, she married a normal man one month after she had met him on a bus. They were married but briefly, principally because her husband insisted upon inviting friends to spend the night with them, then suggesting that they all get in bed and change partners. After this unhappy marriage, she returned to a life of episodic drinking and sexual affairs. She is now quite promiscuous, is often exploited sexually, and is thoroughly unhappy: "I guess I'm never gonna get married again. I never meet a man I can trust. They take what they want from me, then they run off. I don't know what's wrong."

A divorced man (age 30, IQ 53) has been equally promiscuous. His pre-hospital life was characterized by sexual irresponsibility. He fathered one illegitimate child, was suspected of rape, and had several venereal infections. After discharge he married an eighteen-year-old, normal girl, but their marriage was annulled a few days later by her parents. He now dates several girls and enjoys his "freedom." He has no plans for marriage and is happy with his regime of casual contacts with women he meets in bars.

The final divorced ex-patient (age 39, IQ 56) presents a different picture. As an adolescent, his sexual escapades led him directly to Pacific State Hospital. After discharge, however, he married an ex-patient and was able to support her. Later, his wife "fell in love" with a dentist and "ran away." Since this divorce, he has had several girlfriends but has dated his current girl exclusively for almost a year. They enjoy each other's company, especially on long overnight trips that they take on their bicycles (they belong to a bicycle club). They expect to marry, "Some day—when we can afford it." They appear to be a happy and devoted couple.

MARRIED TO A FORMER PATIENT

Twelve of the cohort members are married to former patients. Two of these are married to ex-patients from Pacific who are not members of the research cohort; ten members of the cohort are married to each other. Although all of these couples face similar problems, there are only a few apparent similarities among them concerning their sexual or reproductive lives. For example, several of these persons were arrested for sexual misconduct prior to their hospitalization; none has encountered similar trouble since discharge. And, in only one instance are sexual matters prominent in the marriage. In this marriage, the husband is a small, passive man who has little interest in sexual relations. His wife is an enormous, extremely aggressive woman who believes that marriage gives her the right to demand vigorous sexual relations at any hour. Despite this conflict, their marriage is relatively happy.

The only common problem in each of these marriages involves infertility. Without exception, the wives complain about their surgically produced sterility. Further, each of these women employs her childlessness as an excuse for whatever difficulties she may be experiencing in her marriage. Even though the husbands tend to accept these excuses, not all the men have any desire for children. One spoke with unusual candor: "We got enough problems getting along as it is. We got no business having no baby, even if we could, which we can't. We got no business adopting one either. Right now, we got to take care of our ownselves."

Some of these marriages between former patients are happy, while others are obviously less so. But this is hardly surprising. The most important fact about these marriages is that they have endured, and at the time of the research, all gave signs that they would continue to do so.

MEN MARRIED TO NORMAL WOMEN

As might be expected, it is no easy matter for an ex-patient to marry and support a normal woman. Yet at the time of the research, two men were married to normal women and were supporting them. One of these men (age 29, IQ 66) was introduced to his normal wife by his mother, who insisted that he ask her for a date. The normal woman was a divorcée who had two small children and little alimony. After a few dates, the marriage took place. The ex-patient's mother was active in the promotion of the marriage and was delighted that "Now he'll be taken care of and happy at the same time." The marriage has lasted three years and it has worked out surprisingly well. The ex-patient's wife dominates him completely and often orders him about like a child, but he works regularly and (with some assistance from his mother) provides adequate support. Both he and his wife say that they are happy, and there is evidence to suggest that both are sincere.

The second man (age 40, IQ 68) who married a normal woman met his wife at a church social gathering. They were married in 1955. Although she is an attractive young woman, she is noticeably unintelligent. The ex-patient has supported her without outside assistance. Although their marriage appears to be stable, there are some problems, and two of the most serious of these involves sex and infertility. He complains that his wife is sexually unresponsive and he is very troubled by this "coldness": "I don't know, she seems like she doesn't care at all. I try everything but she just lays there. I don't know what to do about it." His other major problem arose from their failure to have a child. His wife worried about not having a child but he worries more, knowing that he had been sterilized at Pacific but being unwilling to confess to this part of his secret past. It was finally discovered that his wife was sterile, so his secret was kept.

The probability that an ex-patient will marry a normal woman is low at best. The two instances in which such a marriage did take place were not necessarily exceptions to this rule. In one case, the marriage was virtually arranged and supported by the ex-patient's mother. In the other, the "normal" woman was normal only in that she had never been institutionalized; she apparently possessed borderline intelligence at best. However, if male former patients have difficulty locating normal wives, the obverse is not true. Female ex-patients do marry normal men, and often.

WOMEN MARRIED TO NORMAL MEN

Sixteen of the women in the research cohort were married to normal men at the time of the research. The marital circumstances of these women cannot easily be summarized, for the variations in their circumstances are as impressive as are the similarities. Still, there are a few general patterns that tell us a good deal about the sexual and marital lives of these retarded women who are married to normal men.

For example, five of these women led notably troubled and dissolute sexual lives before entering Pacific; however, following discharge, each married an older man and "settled down" to a stable, trouble-free life as a housewife. One of these five women was Ellen (age 49, IQ 84). Prior to hospitalization, sexual restraint was a problem for Ellen. She was twice arrested as a prostitute and she had an illegitimate daughter. After discharge at the age of forty-two she had few male admirers, but one night she was, in her words, "picked up" in a downtown movie theater by an older man. They were shortly thereafter married. This man was a widower who had been married to his first wife for thirty-two years, and had worked in several mental hospitals before moving to Los Angeles. Ellen and this man have been married for seven years and seem to be quite content. Her sterilization has not been a problem in the marriage; neither has any sexual problem. As her husband says, "I know she was kinda wild when she was young but she's settled down now."

A second woman was a sexually delinquent member of a juvenile gang before she was arrested and sent to Pacific. A third was accused of spectacular sexual wrongdoings (including public exhibitions of bestiality) prior to her admission to the hospital. A fourth was regarded as such a sexual menace to the teenage boys of her neighborhood that the mothers of these defenseless young men besieged her parents with demands that she be "put away."

After discharge, each one of these women has found a tranquil and happy marriage with her older husband. In turn, each of the husbands involved regards his retarded wife with satisfaction and affection.

In the fifth and final instance, the retarded woman has followed the same pattern but her normal husband has not. Before hospitalization, this woman's life was an epic of misdirected sexuality. She produced at least five children by an unknown number of casual lovers. She was also in frequent trouble with the police for soliciting and child neglect. Following discharge, she began another round of casual sexual contacts, but this time somewhat more discreetly. Five years ago, she was picked up in a downtown movie theater, and two weeks later the man married her. Her sterilization is thought to be a "blessing" by her husband, but she would like more children ("so he'd treat me a little better"). The marriage has become distressed by the apathy and sometimes brutal mistreatment of her husband, whose current romantic interests rest upon his stepdaughter. Still, the marriage continues and she remains hopeful: "Yeah, he does wrong sometimes, but he's my husband and I want to do good for him." She has been faithful and does try to be a good wife.

Three additional women have led entirely sexless lives. These women were secluded against all sexual experience before and during their hospitalization. All three married elderly men and their marriages have remained devoid of sex. In two cases, the marriages have never been consummated; in the third, there has been no sexual relationship for the past eight years. The third woman said, "No, we don't do that anymore. I don't know why, really; I guess my husband is just pretty old."

Two women have approximated a life of middle-class grace by marrying normal professional men. Neither of these women was accused of being sexually delinquent either before or during hospitalization. Both women have established a stable marriage with men of ample economic resources, and both have become the mothers of adopted children through the resources of their husbands' churches. In both cases, many of the responsibilities of child care and socialization are taken over by the husbands' mothers. Although (or perhaps because) the husbands of these two women isolate their wives against the community almost completely, these marriages appear to be exceptionally happy and stable.

Two unsterilized women who married normal men became natural mothers. In both cases these women have been markedly successful in raising their children. One of these is a Negro (age 29, IQ 73) who has two children and was again pregnant at the time of the research. Her husband was hospitalized for tuberculosis, yet she maintained her children well and gave every indication of being a responsible and affectionate wife and mother. Her principal concern is that her children "get an education like I didn't get." The second of these women (age 27, IQ 77) was so attractive as a younger woman that she was often thought guilty of sexual misconduct, or at least provocation. To illustrate, on two occasions she lost jobs as a live-in housekeeper when distraught wives accused her of tempting their husbands beyond their powers to resist. However, there is no evidence that she has ever been guilty of anything but looking pretty. She married a normal, but unskilled and unstable, man shortly after discharge. They now have four boys, all of whom are attractive, intelligent children. Their earlier married years were troubled by her husband's use of narcotics, and his subsequent loss of earnings. Even so, the marriage seemed to be happy. Even during her husband's imprisonment for possession of narcotics there was no evidence of sexual misbehavior on her part. Indeed, her husband and her neighbors regard her as an excellent wife and mother.

In contrast, two other women who married normal men are quite unhappy. One of these women was never in any sort of sexual difficulty either before or during her stay at Pacific. However, following her first release from the hospital she made a friendship with an "army wife" and began to accompany her to bars and parties. Her aunt finally accused her of "promiscuity" and had her returned to the hospital. After a second discharge, she married a normal man. The marriage was happy for four or five years, but her husband has recently begun to drink and stay out all night. She is very unhappy and says that the whole problem is that she is not attractive anymore: "I guess I just don't look good to him anymore. All he's got eyes for is those girls at the taco stand where he eats at. I don't know what I'm gonna do."

The second woman was reported to be only slightly delinquent before marriage. After discharge she married a man who was addicted to heroin. She insists that "he was only interested in my sex, and besides he was a hophead." After one year, she divorced this man. Her present husband, who is seldom in the home, is obese and probably retarded; she calls him a "drunk" and says that "he is nothing but a big hunk of blubber." She laughingly describes how she denies him sexual relations in order to control him and how she enjoys witnessing his frustration. Her marriage is foundering but she is still faithful to her husband. She can still show some compassion for him too: "You know my husband come home one night and found his first wife in bed with another man. They both laughed at him, too. He was real hurt by that. I could never do him the same way."

Obviously, these patterns are subject to overlap, and to change. Indeed, in Mary, whose life was described in greater detail (chapter 2, case D), we can find many of the features of the lives of these other retarded women who have married normal men. Only one of the sixteen women who have married normal men has developed what appears to be a unique life-style. For this last woman, sex is *everything*. She was accused of sexual misconduct before hospitalization, and these accusations may have had a factual basis, because she was twice treated for syphilis. After discharge she dated several men and had affairs with at least three ex-patients. She finally married a non-patient and they have made sexual relations their principal interest in life. They read and reread sexual manuals, worry greatly about technique, and attempt to have relations as frequently and in as many postures as possible. She says, "If you get the right, uh, movement, it can be real good." They regard sex as their major "hobby." Both would like to have children and both resent her sterilization, but they have no plans to attempt adoption.

No review of these marriages could conclude without noting the remarkable fact that sixteen of a group of twenty-eight retarded women were able to marry normal men. This percentage would appear to be substantially higher than there was any reason to expect. Who, then, were these normal men? Too little is known about these men, especially about their previous lives, to permit any detailed or definitive answer. Nonetheless, two patterns in these current marriages are obvious. First, ten of the retarded women married much older men, all of whom were divorced or widowed. On the average, these ten men were seventeen years older than their retarded wives. In each of these ten marriages, the normal husband admitted—usually quite freely—that he sought, in his marriage to a former patient, the dependent, submissive, appreciative wife he had not had in his earlier marriage or marriages.

The remaining six normal husbands were approximately the same age as their ex-patient wives, and only two of these men had been married before. However, these men were all marginal wage earners at best, and they were troubled people. All six had a history of one or more of the following: narcotics addiction, alcoholism, criminal conduct, or mental illness. In these marriages, the women were called upon to support the normal husbands emotionally, if not financially. The characteristics and the goals of these sixteen men do not fully explain why these particular men married these particular women, but they do make less noteworthy the fact that these former patients were able to marry "normal" men.

In summary, the current marital circumstances of these ex-patients present a remarkable diversity. Theirs is no single or simple pattern. Among them we find everything from extremely promiscuous men and women, through devoted and happy marriages, to fearful maidens dedicated to the avoidance of men. Indeed, their conduct does not seem notably different from that of the other low socioeconomic status persons described in American cities (Rainwater *et al.*, 1959).

It is also apparent that despite fairly active sexual troublemaking before hospitalization, these ex-patients now appear to present many fewer such problems. Indeed, while at least twenty of these former patients had serious sexual problems before entering the hospital, only five or six ex-patients (mostly unmarried) could now be counted as having similarly severe troubles. One explanation is that after discharge they are less directly under the supervision of fearful relatives who feel constrained to protect them against themselves (particularly against pregnancy), or to protect themselves against the complaints of neighbors by instituting some legal action. But it may also be true that behavior that is extremely troublesome when displayed by teenagers goes "unnoticed" when it is displayed by adults.

Sterilization is frequently a perplexing problem but it is seldom an overpowering practical concern. Only a few ex-patients were dramatically impaired in their adaptive ability by virtue of their sterilization. However, the importance of sterilization to their self-esteem and presentation of self is great. This problem will also be considered in detail in a later chapter.

In conclusion, it would seem that the sexual and marital lives of these retarded persons are more "normal" and better regulated than we could possibly have predicted from a knowledge of their pre-hospital experiences and their manifest intellectual deficits. And even this cursory view of their lives makes it clear that no simple stereotype can be applied to them.

The Use of Leisure Time

Another central concern for the former patients is the use of leisure time. The ex-patients pursue "recreation," or just plain "fun," with a single-mindedness that is impressive. The former patients themselves trace their relentless pursuit of happiness to their long history of being deprived of the right to seek leisure-time pleasures when and how they wished. They speak of lives—before hospitalization—of restricted recreation, and they shudder at the memory of their hospital years, during which they always felt controlled, scheduled, and restricted: "We was always cooped in and pushed around. We couldn't do what we wanted in that place. It was like a jail with all them rules and locks on the doors." The freedom of life in the community intensifies the search for "fun," for the full and free use of leisure time. To fill spare time with "fun" is a central focus for the discharged ex-patient. As one man phrased it: "I feel like I got a right to fun now that I'm out, to make up for all the years I was in that place."

A consideration of the uses of leisure time is critically instructive because, better than anything else available to us, the use of leisure serves to indicate the richness or impoverishment of the lives of these retarded persons. What do "morons" do with their spare time? The question is neither rhetorical nor cruelly sarcastic; it must be asked if we are to understand the lives of such persons.

Because the use of leisure time is so important to an understanding of the nature of the lives of these persons, each of the former patients will be described in a brief sketch and identified by number in order that comparisons can be made with similar sketches to be presented in chapter 5. The sketches will be organized under rubrics which, despite their overlap and imprecision, help to provide a sense of the range of leisure-time activities in the lives of these former patients.

CONVERSATION

The basic leisure-time pattern for the ex-patients is a combination of conversation and television. Those former patients who prefer conversation to television will be discussed first.

8. Maggie   Age: 46   IQ: 70   Discharge: 1956   Married

Maggie's time is spent at home with her husband. They talk ("I like to listen to him, mostly, I guess"), and watch TV, or listen to music on the radio. Once in a great while they take a short trip in a car together "and see the sights," and occasionally they go grocery shopping together. But these are rare excursions. Usually, they stay home together, where her time is spent talking: "We love to talk—it's mostly what we do."

9. Ellie   Age: 27   IQ: 77   Discharge: 1956   Married

Ellie is largely confined to her home by her four children. She plays with them, cares for them, and on the infrequent occasions that she has time, she watches TV. She says that she enjoys movies but she seldom goes to one. She loves to take the boys to the beach or take them visiting. She says with obvious conviction, "You don't have much time for yourself when you have four boys. I guess what I do mostly is talk. Just gab to anyone when I get the chance. I guess women like to gab."

12. Ellen   Age: 49   IQ: 84   Discharge: 1953   Married

Ellen's time is devoted to conversation with anyone she can corner: "I just love to talk. Why, I'll just talk about anything." She rarely sees movies but always enjoys them "when we can afford to go." She and her husband also like to watch TV and "go out to dinner every once in a while." But they haven't actually gone to a restaurant for five years. Her delight is conversation, and her best listener is her husband. "I guess you could say I've got a real gift of gab."

14. Maria (Mexican-American)   Age: 31   IQ: 83
Discharge: 1952   Single

Maria's leisure is spent almost entirely in the company of the older woman with whom she lives. They talk and look at magazines. Maria also likes to ride the bus and "just see the sights" but seldom does either. She attends church every Sunday and likes to talk about religion "sometimes." In her own words, however: "I try to keep busy all the time, because I don't like having no time on my hands."

19. Rosie   Age: 39   IQ: 65   Discharge: 1953   Married

Her leisure is unusually impoverished. Her only pleasures are talking with her casual friends or her daughter, in drinking to drunkenness, and in sexual relations. However, in the past she has enjoyed sewing and her pets, which at one time included three dogs, two cats, and a parakeet. "Nowadays I just talk. Talking's the only fun I get."

20. Ruth   Age: 29   IQ: 85   Discharge: 1952   Married

Her leisure is spent at home with her children and, sometimes, with her husband. Ruth talks and watches TV. Once in a while Ruth and her husband shop together, but they rarely go to a movie, although Ruth says that she "loves" movies. Ruth's great passion is dancing but she says that, now that she has two children, she goes dancing "only about once a year." In fact, she hasn't gone dancing for over two years because "my husband doesn't approve, so all we ever do is sit home and watch TV. . . . What I really like to do is just talk. I love to talk to just about anybody."

21a. Arnold   Age: 32   IQ: 61   Discharge: 195
Married to cohort member

21b. Bessie   Age: 26   IQ: 61   Discharge: 1957

The leisure of this couple consists almost exclusively of "sitting home with a can of beer." They talk and argue and watch TV, and once in a while their friends, or Arnold's mother and brother, will join them, and talk becomes more animated. For them, TV is secondary to conversation. As Bessie says, "We just love talking. Seems like we can talk all day and all night and never get tired. We love to hear all the news and the gossip."

23. Noreen (Negro)   Age: 34   IQ: 57   Discharge: 1949
"Married"

This woman enjoys little of her leisure time. She talks with her "husband" (common law) and they drink together. She listens to an old radio, watches TV (when it works), and sometimes walks around the slum neighborhood. She seldom talks to anyone but her husband. Neither she nor he has any hobby or interest that they could think of. "Sometimes we talk, that's all."

33. June   Age: 35   IQ: 74   Discharge: 1956   Married

When June is home alone, she spends her time watching TV and listening to music on the radio. When her husband is home they talk. On weekends they sometimes go for a ride, but they seldom leave the house for any other reason. She says, "All I'm really interested in is my husband. What he likes to do I like to do too. I love to listen to him talk. I talk to him too."

35. Alma   Age: 39   IQ: 65   Discharge: 1951   Married

Her time is spent at home with her invalid husband. She listens to music incessantly, and sometimes watches their ancient TV set, purchased for $19. She also makes doilies, knits, and rolls her own cigarettes. She likes to talk over the back fence to her neighbors and to visit them for multiple cups of coffee. Mainly, however, she talks to her husband whom she inevitably (and usually affectionately) addresses as "you ole fart." "I guess what I really like to do best is talking. I'll gabble to just about anybody."

38. Myrtle   Age: 31   IQ: 56   Discharge: 1958   Married

Her leisure is spent entirely with her husband. They stay home together, talk, and watch TV. They used to attend social meetings of "a handicapped persons club" (he is paraplegic) but they no longer do so. Except on Sundays when they attend church, they rarely leave the house other than to shop: "We just stay home and talk and enjoy things."

39. Corliss   Age: 28   IQ: 65   Discharge: 1955   Married

Corliss spends most of her time with her husband in the familiar pattern of watching TV, but she also enjoys looking at the pictures in all manner of magazines, and listening to radio music. Occasionally, she and her husband take short trips "just for fun," and during the summer they spend considerable time at a riding stable in the mountains. In fact, however, almost all their time is spent at home where Corliss attempts to "talk my husband's leg off. I love to talk to him but sometimes he falls asleep. He's old, you know."

41. Helen (Negro)   Age: 29   IQ: 73   Discharge: 1952   Married

Life with her two children leaves Helen little leisure time. Her husband has tuberculosis and is confined to a hospital. Her time is devoted to housework and her children. She watches TV with the children and sometimes reads to them. Once in a great while she will take the children to a movie: "Can't do much else with the kids and all. I love talking to folks best of all, but I can't seem to find nobody to talk to these days."

TELEVISION

1. Lulu   Age: 30   IQ: 48   Discharge: 1956   Single

Her spare time is usually spent in her room watching TV or looking at magazines, mostly pictorial ones. Perhaps once every six weeks she goes to a nearby movie, and on Sundays she likes to get on a bus, ride to the end of the line, and come back again. She enjoys talking to anyone who will listen, but television is her great passion. She watches a variety of programs avoiding only "the heavy or sad ones." She says fervently, "I just don't know what I'd do without TV. It's my only friend."

3.   Roberto (Mexican-American)   Age: 34   IQ: 85
**   Discharge: 1952   Single**

This homosexual man enjoys television "more than anything." He likes all kinds of TV, except westerns. He also loves to drink beer, alone or in bars. He goes to the beach once a week, where he says he likes to swim, although there is some evidence to suggest that he actually visits the beach to look for homosexual partners. He also loves the rides and games at the amusement park. For the most part, however, he stays at his friend's apartment and watches TV. He never reads, saying, "I don't like to read. It hurts my eyes. I'd rather watch TV."

22a. Lester   Age: 39   IQ: 84   Discharge: 1952
**   Married to cohort member**

22b. Bertha   Age: 28   IQ: 57   Discharge: 1953

Although Lester works very long hours and has little spare time, he enjoys his leisure immensely. He watches TV with his wife—they especially like westerns and sports and they also go to movies whenever they can afford it. Their favorite film is *Psycho*. They also enjoy drinking and "visiting" with their ex-patient friends who sometimes stop by in the evening. But almost all their spare time is devoted to TV: "We love all those western shows. 'Wagon Train' and those kind are so good."

24. Henry   Age: 30   IQ: 80   Discharge: 1957   Married

Henry's time is spent at home with his wife watching TV. "We really like that TV; movies are no good and they cost money too. TV's much better." When they leave their apartment they take short walks or trips with one or another of her relatives, who sometimes take them shopping or on pleasure trips. However, they seldom leave their apartment and its TV set. "My wife loves those quiz programs but I like the old movies. I watch one or sometimes two every night."

25. Lois   Age: 31   IQ: 57   Discharge: 1954   Married

Most of her time is spent at home with her husband, talking and watching TV, and they often stay up late to watch "monster" movies. She also loves to sew and does so most of the time while she sits at home with her husband. They occasionally go to company picnics and dances but seldom "go out" for anything else except an infrequent movie. She takes great pleasure in the company of her pets—a small dog and four parakeets. "Mostly, my husband and me, we love to sit home and watch TV. I love the scary movies best."

27. Betty   Age: 35   IQ: 64   Discharge: 1953   Single

Her leisure is spent in her room in her foster-care home. For the most part, she watches TV alone. Only rarely does she join in the family conversation. She occasionally rides a bus to the end of the line and then returns, and she regularly attends church on Sunday. However, she says emphatically, "Mostly what I like is that TV set. I can watch anything I want."

28. Martha   Age: 39   IQ: 72   Discharge: 1956   Single

She spends most of her time alone in her room, watching TV. Once in a while she will take a round trip on a bus to "see things," and she loves to sit outside the motel in which she works and lives and watch people and cars go by. Her evenings are spent alone with her television set (for details see chapter 2, case C).

30. Agnes   Age: 56   IQ: 47   Discharge: 1953   Single

Her leisure is totally dominated by the television set, which she greatly loves. "Why, since I got this TV I wouldn't read nothing if you made me." She favors Lawrence Welk and murder mysteries but will watch "anything that comes on." She rarely goes out, as her benefactress watches over her very closely. She has a parakeet that she talks to while she is watching TV.

31. Dorothy   Age: 51   IQ: 66   Discharge: 1957   Married

She too spends all of her spare time at home watching TV. Her husband is usually with her, but he also spends considerable time in church, where he goes to pray alone. She loves to talk, and does so at every opportunity, but when she is alone she watches TV and tries to teach her parakeet, Bobby, to talk. She seldom goes out except for essential shopping, and this is almost always in the company of her husband. "That old TV is my best friend, I guess you could say."

34. Grenville   Age: 29   IQ: 66   Discharge: 1954   Married

Grenville spends his leisure at home with his wife and two children by her earlier marriage. He likes to do "chores" around the house and play with the children. After the children go to sleep, he and his wife usually watch TV. Once in a while they go for a drive, or visit his mother, but they rarely go out for any other reason. He says, "I guess you could say I don't do much recreation. Sometimes I go bowling but mostly I just watch TV now and then."

36a. George   Age: 35   IQ: 52   Discharge: 1954
   Married to cohort member

36b. Ramona (Mexican-American)   Age: 37   IQ: 64
   Discharge: 1953

This man and his wife spend almost all of their free time together watching TV or listening to the radio. They converse very little. They do enjoy sports and follow baseball to some degree. Once in a great while they will go to a movie, take a trip to the beach, go for a walk, or simply take a long round-trip on the bus. He usually reads the Sunday paper (at least the comics), but aside from that neither of them reads anything. She says, "We watch TV lots; it's full of real high-class things which we like." He adds, "Yeah, there's classy things on TV, and interesting things, too."

37. Harry   Age: 40   IQ: 68   Discharge: 1949   Married

He complains that he and his wife "never go anywhere," that they do nothing but "sit home and watch TV." He used to bowl and play miniature golf (his wife went along but seldom participated). He would like to bowl on a league team but isn't "quite good enough." He also used to collect stamps and would like to take up photogra-

phy but finds it too expensive. So he and his wife spend their evenings and weekends watching TV. He explains, "Sometimes I can't
stand that TV but what else is there to do?"

40. Prudence Age: 32 IQ: 60 Discharge: 1953 Married

This lonely woman spends almost all her time alone. Her husband
rarely visits her and she stays home with her radio and TV. She loves
all westerns on TV but doesn't particularly enjoy the other shows.
She also loves to talk but seldom finds anyone who will listen. She
says that "TV's the only one thing that I like, seems like."

"CAROUSING"

Five of the former patients have devoted their spare
time to alcohol and the opposite sex.

2a. Hal Age: 39 IQ: 82 Discharge: 1954
     Married to cohort member

2b. Midge Age: 38 IQ: 67 Discharge: 1958

He sometimes watches TV (sports and westerns) and once in a
while goes to a baseball game when his employer gives him tickets.
He also enjoys "walking"—translated, this means visiting bars on
skid row, drinking beer, and "meeting" girls. But this is only on
weekends because, as he says, "Usually I'm too tired at night to do
anything." In addition to his wife, he has a "steady girlfriend" but he
also "looks for new 'gals' every weekend."

10. Nora Age: 25 IQ: 66 Discharge: 1954 Separated

Nora's leisure time seems to be devoted almost entirely to drinking and sexual relations. This attractive young woman says that she is
not interested in "anything like TV or movies," and her current life
would seem to bear this out. When she is not working she is lying in
bed—asleep or with a bottle or with a man.

13. Roy Age: 30 IQ: 53 Discharge: 1953 Divorced

This man's leisure is spent wholly in the pursuit of alcohol and
women. When he is not working or sleeping he is in a nearby bar,
drinking beer and attempting to meet women. He has no other interests. He confided, "I gotta admit I like that beer. I meet a lot of
friends that way too."

18a. Hank   Age: 33   IQ: 70   Discharge: 1958
     Married to cohort member

18b. May   Age: 35   IQ: 70   Discharge: 1958

He devotes his spare time to drinking beer and searching for willing female companions. He spends considerable time in the apartment of one such companion. He is also a prodigious walker,
sometimes traveling thirty miles in a day. His energies are usually
spent in the pursuit of girls, however (for details see chapter 2, case
A).

26. Josephina (Mexican-American)   Age: 30   IQ: 50
     Discharge: 1957   Divorced

Her leisure time is confined to drinking and "running around"
with her boyfriends, some of whom are highly raffish persons who
live either on the margins of the law or completely outside it. Her
only other activity is an occasional visit to her mother. She never
watches TV, or reads. "But I do like to visit with people. I try to stay
away from men. They're nothing but trouble. Seems like they're poison to me."

SPORTS

Only two of the ex-patients devoted most of their leisure time to an interest in sports.

2b. Midge   Age: 38   IQ: 67   Discharge: 1958
     Married to cohort member

2a. Hal   Age: 39   IQ: 82   Discharge: 1954

Midge loves baseball and regularly listens to the games on the
radio; she also enjoys movies, TV, and loves to go roller-skating. She
says that she used to love the beach, where she and her husband
would swim and sunbathe, but they "haven't gone for two years at
least." Her major interest and pastime is baseball—she follows the
standings, learns averages, and idolizes the Dodger players. She goes
to games whenever she can, but because her husband is "too tired
after work," she must usually go alone. Actually, her interest is usually confined to listening to games on the radio.

11. Luis (Mexican-American)   Age: 31   IQ: 51
    Discharge: 1954   Single

Luis is a serious sports fan, attending all sports when he is able. Most of his spare time is spent watching sports on TV (especially boxing and baseball), but he also likes to drink and talk to his friends and relatives. He sometimes plays on a Mexican-American softball team. He seems to have no recreational interests beyond these: "I like to follow sports. I been a fan since I was little."

VARIED LEISURE LIVES

The following five persons had exceptionally varied leisure-time interests.

4. Tony   Age: 41   IQ: 83   Discharge: 1953   Single

Tony enjoys an occasional movie, loves to listen to music on the radio, reads the newspaper (comics and sports section) every morning. He says he loves to travel "most of all" but seldom has the opportunity. He has a driver's license but no car. Three times in the past, he has purchased cars but all were repossessed. He does go fishing (either from a pier at the ocean, or at a nearby trout "farm" in the mountains) perhaps once a month. He also greatly enjoys religious meetings; he attends evangelist services with his benefactress every Sunday. In all, he has a relatively rich leisure life.

5. Fred   Age: 32   IQ: 52   Discharge: 1957   Single

Fred also has a highly varied leisure life. His true love is eating, and he delights in eating everything, everywhere. He also loves to talk about food. He sometimes enjoys TV (westerns), movies ("sex movies, mostly"), and radio music. He buys records and has a collection of Artie Shaw and Bennie Goodman that he plays on his own record player. He also travels on the bus to the beach, to amusement parks, and to visit his girlfriends. He has a collection of "girlie" magazines which he regularly adds to, but most of his time is spent walking around the downtown and skid-row area, eating, looking in windows and visiting acquaintances (for details see chapter 2, case B).

6. Mary   Age: 32   IQ: 56   Discharge: 1957   Married

She loves TV, "all kinds of movies," and movie magazines. She also enjoys "visiting"—talking at length to anyone about everything.

Mary and her normal husband usually spend each weekend in a round of dancing, drinking, gambling, and traveling (for details see chapter 2, case D).

15. Ricardo (Mexican-American)   Age: 45   IQ: 64
Discharge: 1957   Single

This man greatly enjoys his spare time, spending most of it in bars, watching sports on TV, drinking moderate amounts of beer, and talking volubly. He also likes to bowl, to swim in the ocean, and to fish off the pier, but he does these things very seldom. He spends some time with his girlfriends and enjoys walking or riding in a girlfriend's car. He also likes to listen to music, which he accompanies with his own, very spirited, vocal renditions. "I'm happy. I'm always happy. I have all kinds of fun."

29. Leonard   Age: 33   IQ: 64   Discharge: 1957   Single

Leonard enjoys the usual combination of TV and movie fare, but he also goes out frequently with his girlfriend. They drive all over Los Angeles in his ten-year-old wreck of a car for which he has no license. In addition, he often goes to the beach looking for "excitement." His search for excitement caused him to join the Army National Guard, from which he was discharged when his background was discovered. He is now trying to enlist in the Marine Reserve because "everybody knows how great it is to be a Marine." He also attempts to sing and has plans to become a "recording star." He has recorded several songs himself which he has attempted to sell to "the big record companies in Hollywood." He thinks too that he might become an actor, if he only had "the right break." He explains, "I'm always shooting for a star." Indeed, by following movie companies on location he did succeed in being filmed in a mob scene. He now considers himself an actor.

IDIOSYNCRATIC INTERESTS

16. Richard   Age: 39   IQ: 56   Discharge: 1954   Divorced

Richard occasionally enjoys radio music or a TV program, but virtually all of his spare time is spent in *travel on his bicycle*. He is a member of a bike club that travels all over southern California. He rides almost every evening after work and relishes the freedom that he feels he gains by his mobility. He also looks forward to weekend trips that he takes with his girlfriend and other members of the bike club. "My bike cost me over a hundred dollars and it's worth it. I can go anywhere whenever I want. That's what I like, getting away and going places."

42. Ronald   Age: 28   IQ: 47   Discharge: 1955   Married

Ronald spends his time at home with his wife, watching TV and seldom talking. About once a month he and his wife walk to a near-by movie. When he can accumulate any sum of money he takes a bus to the *race track*, where he regularly loses all his money and comes home drunk. "But, you know, some day I'm gonna make me a real lot of money on them horses."

7. Jose (Mexican-American)   Age: 34   IQ: 4
        Discharge: 1957   Single

He loves to talk to friends, "tease" girls, and simply enjoy his freedom. "I just walk wherever I want to go, like a free bird." His only regular pastimes are drinking beer and an occasional visit to a thirty-five-cent movie on skid row. Of course, most of his time is leisure time, and one of his favorite time-consumers is *sleep*: "I love to sleep. I sleep almost all the time, it seems like."

43. Walter   Age: 20   IQ: 61   Discharge: 1958   Single

He sometimes watches TV at home with his parents, but he finds life at home so unpleasant that "I got to get out with the boys." He devotes himself to a *masquerade as a delinquent teenager* by following normal teenagers about and hoping for acceptance. He tries to talk to to them of cars, music, girls, drinking, and fighting, but they consistently ignore or insult him. Nevertheless, his activities continue to center upon efforts to be accepted as a normal teenager. When he has some money, he can buy a moment's contact with this teenage world, but never becomes a participant in it.

17. John   Age: 29   IQ: 77   Discharge: 1953   Single

This psychotic man's leisure life is extremely *bizarre*. Most of his time is spent reading *Popular Mechanics* and aviation magazines; he examines them closely for evidence that evil parties have indeed stolen another of his many inventions and made huge profits thereby. He insists that many recent electronic and aeronautical advances are actually of his invention (inspired by the "flashing blades" of his ice skates) and that unscrupulous "manufacturers" and "master spies" have stolen them for great financial gain. He only rarely leaves his quarters, but when he does so it is usually with a flourish. For example, he may go ice-skating dressed in an ancient fur coat, fur hat, and leather gloves (attire which he also favors as he performs his work duties in the heat of summer). And he often announces to one and all that he is the Grand Duke Ivan, the richest and most powerful man on earth.

32. Billie Mae   Age: 30   IQ: 74   Discharge: 1954   Married

Billie Mae used to love to dance to "country music" but doesn't have an opportunity anymore, as her husband objects. They listen to music and baseball games on the radio and are mildly interested in sports, but she doesn't like TV because "my eyes are lousy." Billie Mae seldom goes out for any reason. Her principal interest is *sex*. She loves to stay home and read marriage manuals: "We like to see if we're doing everything right. That's important, you know. My husband and me, we really like that sex better'n anything."

18b. May   Age: 35   IQ: 70   Discharge: 1958
Married to cohort member

18a. Hank   Age: 33   IQ: 70   Discharge: 1958

May seems to spend her spare time either lying in bed or complaining about one or another misery. She insists she has no pleasures, hobbies, or interests, and her activities bear out this claim (for details see chapter 2, case A).

It is extremely difficult to attempt any comparative conclusions about the uses of leisure time among these former patients, because the practices of the normal residents of the Los Angeles area at various socio-economic strata are not reported. However, based upon studies from other parts of the country, it would seem that the retarded persons described here are *not* as impoverished in their leisure lives as we might well have expected them to be.[1]

It is certainly true that their utilization of leisure is limited by a shortage of money, transportation, and in some cases, by time itself, but they do have interests and they do enjoy their leisure. Their preeminent joy is television; but that their leisure time should be dominated by television is by no means unusual. And they are not interested only in TV. They also enjoy conversation, on a surprising

---

1. For comparative material on leisure, see Denney and Meyersohn (1957), Kaplan (1960), Jordan (1963), and Parker (1964).

variety of topics, and a few enjoy music or sight-seeing or sports. They do not read, but it would also seem that their normal counterparts of low socio-economic status also read very little. They also have few hobbies, almost never "eat out," and seldom entertain. Their most unusual practice is riding buses to the end of the line and back for sight-seeing purposes.

It would appear that, at least in the manifest form of their recreational pleasures and use of leisure time, they do not differ greatly from the "normal" persons who live near them in lower socio-economic status neighborhoods. That this should be so is truly surprising, for if there is great impoverishment of life among these retarded people, it should have become apparent here. Of course, any such comparative conclusion must be offered with caution, for without fully comparable data on the leisure practices of so-called normals, we cannot properly judge the leisure lives of these mental retardates.

Conclusion

The foregoing overview of the character of the lives of these former patients was a partial one, confined as it was to three central concerns. The direction of this report is toward the critical problems that these retarded people face in the management of their incompetence, and the descriptive material in this chapter is offered as a preparation for an examination of those problems.

One other aspect of their lives—what might be called their social pathology—is essential in the present context. These former patients have not become pillars of society, but neither have they been conspicuous in their opposition to social norms or to law. For example, they use alcohol sparingly; only a handful drink to what might be considered excess. For the most part, they drink little, and that little usually consists of beer that is consumed in a neighborhood bar or before a television set at home. Furthermore, only three members of the cohort have used narcotics—and two of these three have been arrested for that use. But, in an interesting counterpoint, only a handful of the former patients attend church or profess any religious inclination. What is more, none of them has voted in any local, state, or national election.

At one time or another since discharge, 32 percent of the ex-patients have received social welfare aid. But relatively few have been found guilty of law violation: three have been imprisoned (two for narcotics possession, one for child molesting) and another six have had minor brushes with the police for vagrancy, traffic citations, drunkenness, and theft. Whether this rate would be high or low compared to normal controls, I cannot guess.

In conclusion, it seems obvious that these former patients have achieved a measure of success in their return to the outside world from which they were once expelled. Few characterizations of the form of their lives in this outside world are wholly satisfactory, because, as we have seen, their lives are so markedly varied. Consequently, few stereotypes can be matched to the realities of the lives of these forty-eight persons—especially if these stereotypes call for an exceptionally simplified mode of life. It is fair to conclude that whatever else these lives are, they are complex rather than simple. Here again, we encounter difficulty because this analysis was not equipped with a normal comparison population. Yet, we might legitimately ask how different would be the lives of persons of normal intelligence who had undergone the same life experiences of deprivation, rejection, and institutional confinement. Unfortunately, no completely comparable population of normal persons can be said to exist. And, certainly, none was available for this study.

Perhaps it is appropriate that the impossibility of comparison with normals should signal the end of this chapter, for the intention of this study is not to relate the actions of these retarded persons to the chimera of a supposed normal control population. For this analysis, and probably for any analysis, normal counterparts are something that ought to exist in the real world, but do not. Instead of pursuing this will-o'-the-wisp, the present chapter serves as an overview of the life circumstances of these ex-patients and as an introduction to a more intensive discussion of their modes of dealing with their incompetence.

Although the problems outlined in this chapter are real and pressing, they are less critical than other problems. The most critical of these problems relate to the stigma of mental retardation and thus to passing and denial. The next chapter will begin a consideration of these fundamental factors.

CHAPTER FOUR

Passing and Denial: The Problem of Seeming To Be Normal

What has gone before has been a description of the general nature of the lives of "morons" in a large city. We have seen that throughout the lives of these mentally retarded persons there are many difficulties, many problems, many crises. But one problem dominates their lives and becomes the quintessential problem, both to them, as the living persons who must deal with it, and to the social analyst who attempts to understand and narrate their life experiences. This fundamental problem is the necessity for "passing" and "denial."

We, in our everyday affairs, regularly and easily accuse others and ourselves of stupidity. We joke about real or fancied incompetence, we estimate the IQs of our friends and foes, we make invidious comparisons of all kinds about the intelligence of many persons with whom we come into contact. Usually we mean little by these remarks and usually neither we nor the victims of our speculations or accusations suffer very much as a result.

For the ex-patient of an institution for the mentally retarded, however, matters are very different. The ex-patient *must* take his intelligence very seriously, for he has been accused and found guilty of being so stupid that he was considered incompetent to manage his own life. As a consequence, he has been confined in an institution for the mentally incompetent. This research has shown, and our common sense would agree, that such an accusation of stupidity has a shattering impact. The stigma of having been adjudged a mental retardate is one which the ex-patients in this study reject as totally unacceptable. Hence, their lives are directed toward the fundamental purpose of denying that they are in fact mentally incompetent. These former patients must at all times attend to the practical problems of seeming to others to be competent and of convincing themselves that this is so. The label of mental retardation not only serves as a humiliating, frustrating, and discrediting stigma in the conduct of one's life in the community, but it also serves to lower one's self-esteem to such a nadir of worthlessness that the life of a person so labeled is scarcely worth living. Thus the "moron" who is released from Pacific State Hospital must "deny," must "pass" with himself. He cannot, and he does not, accept the official "fact" that he is, or ever was, mentally retarded.

To understand the processes of passing and denial in the period following the ex-patients' release from the institution, we must first review prior events in the life experiences of these persons. In an earlier study, the pre-hospital and hospital careers of the same patients who formed the cohort for this research were examined (Edgerton and Sabagh, 1962). It was rarely possible to reconstruct the pre-hospital biographies of these patients in adequate detail, yet it was possible to determine that their pre-hospital experiences were typically highly mortifying. These experiences commonly involved both direct and indirect communication by normal persons to the retarded person to the effect that his or her intelligence was deficient. Parents, peers, teachers, neighbors, and even strangers presented a consistent refrain of rejection and humiliation. Notwithstanding this concerted onslaught, the retardate resisted the accusation that he was mentally retarded, and he usually found allies in the form of parents or peers who would aid him in denying that his intellect was subnormal.

However, entry into Pacific State Hospital presents the retarded person with a new dilemma. Although he is by now thoroughly familiar with mortification and has probably developed means of self-defense against suggestions of mental deficit, he is surely not prepared for the experiences that the hospital will inflict upon him. The cumulative impact of the initial period of hospitalization (at the time of the research) was greatly mortifying, leaving the patient without privacy, without clear identity, without autonomy of action, without relatives, friends, or family, in a regimented and impersonal institution where everything combines to inform him that he is, in fact, mentally inadequate. A typical patient reaction is seen in the follow-

ing words of a teenage boy who was newly admitted to the institution: "Why do I got to be here with these people? I'd rather be dead
than in here."[1]

At this point, when the hospital's impact has taken full effect, the
patient's self-esteem has probably reached its low point. However, at
this critical point, circumstances arise to provide the patient with an
opportunity to aggrandize himself and reconstruct his damaged self-
esteem. This opportunity results from (1) the presence in the hospital of large numbers of manifestly severely retarded persons with
whom comparisons of intellectual ability may profitably be made—
the newly admitted mildly retarded person is clearly superior to most
of the more severely retarded patients in the hospital, thus it is not
surprising that he concludes that he does not really belong in a hospital that contains such patients; (2) friendly, accepting peer-group
relationships that, in comparison with pre-hospital relationships, sustain a positive conception of self—these relationships often provide
the patient with the first instances of acceptance by peers that he has
ever experienced; (3) contacts with well-meaning employees who encourage favorable self-esteem—many of these employees not only
provide acceptance and affection but also do much to provide au-
thoritative assurance that the patient truly is not retarded (Edgerton
and Sabagh, 1962).

The patients in the research cohort, then, had an opportunity to
rebuild and even to aggrandize their self-esteem while in the hospital. Nonetheless, they felt acutely uncomfortable about being in the
hospital and hoped for release. There is no necessary contradiction
implied. The patients were able to aggrandize their self-esteem by
being in the hospital, but a vital feature of their own aggrandizement
was their contention that they did not belong there in the first place.
In addition, the patients seldom appreciated either hospital confinement or its regulations. As a result, freedom from institutional confinement was a primary goal for every patient in the cohort.[2]

Release, when it came, was always received as an expression of
justice, long overdue. Again and again, the words "I never belonged
there in the first place" were recorded. As one ex-patient put it: "I
was never mental like the others that couldn't remember nothing or

1. See Edgerton and Sabagh (1962), p. 267.
2. A few patients were not eager to be discharged from hospital supervision after
they were living in a community on "work leave" status, but all patients in the cohort
wanted to leave the confines of the hospital itself.

do nothing." Members of the cohort commonly saw their release as confirmation of the error of the original diagnosis of mental retardation that had sent them there, and as affirmation of their right as "normal" persons to live their own lives, "without anybody telling me what to do." Release from the hospital was indeed the beginning of their right to live "like anybody else," but it was emphatically not the end of their problems, nor of their need for passing and denial. They now had to face the multiple challenges of living independently in the "outside" world. Each former patient knew that failure to meet these challenges would not only be ruinous to self-esteem—it might also lead to a forcible return to the hospital. Consequently, the outside world was entered cautiously and fearfully.

One of the first needs of the ex-patients was concealment of their institutional history, a "past" which, if revealed, could be gravely discrediting. This concealment was regularly attempted through a stereotyped "tale" which explained and excused their confinement in the hospital by revealing the "real" reason they were there.[3] Such excuses were collected from all of the forty-eight ex-patients. The excuses fell into nine categories. The excuses, with the number of persons who gave them, are as follows: "nerves" (2), mental illness (2), alcoholism (3), epilepsy (4), sex delinquency (5), criminal offenses (5), physical illness—usually a need for surgery—(7), need for education (8), and the enmity of, or abandonment by, parent or relative (12). The first four categories of excuses admit of some degree of mental or physical abnormality; the last five excuses admit nothing more than errors of conduct, and sometimes admit nothing at all. Examples of a typical excuse within each category:

"Nerves": "I don't miss that institution. I should have been put out of there years ago; they shouldn't have kept me in there like they did. That's what I think. They kept me too long. I only went there 'cause I was nervous, but they kept me so long I got worse. They ruined my life. Those people in that institution was much worse than me. I'm just as good as anyone in there or anybody I've seen on the outside."

Mental illness: "That place was horrible. Everybody there was crazy. You know, there was one girl that actually ate a table—took bites right out of a table. Another girl stood on her head and drank milk.

3. For an introduction to the concept of the "sad tale" see Goffman (1961).

I was a little crazy myself, that's why I went there, I guess. But I got over it OK."

Alcoholism: "I used to be a pretty heavy drinker. Now I kind of control myself a little bit. That's why I went to that institution. The drinking mostly brought it on. When I stopped drinking I got out OK."

Epilepsy: "Well, the hospital was good in some ways—I made friends with the girls, but I really didn't belong with those other patients. (Why?) Well, they're mental, you know. Low mental."

Sex delinquency: "When I was younger I used to make mistakes with boys. I was put in that hospital so's I could learn to behave myself with boys. I done OK. You learn when you get older. But I sure didn't belong in there with all those dopey people."

Criminal behavior: "Yeah, I was in there because of the robberies I was doing when I was a kid. Cops caught me, so I was sent up to that place. I was never supposed to be there with those mental patients. I was there because of those robberies, you know."

Physical illness: "That hospital was OK. If it wasn't for that place I wouldn't be alive today. I went in when I was only fifteen and I had three surgical operations. I was only there on the surgery ward because of my kidneys. I didn't have nothing to do with them handicapped patients."

Need for education: "Well, that place didn't do me no good. I was sent there to go to school because I missed lots of school when I was little. But I didn't get much schooling in there. Might just as well not of been there. I never belonged in a place with all those low-grade patients. I was just there for my schooling."

Enmity of, or abandonment by, a parent or relative: "I got plenty of kick coming. I spent five years in that hole just because my stepfather always hated me. As soon as my mother died he got together with some doctor and framed me into that place. I never should of been in no place like that full of those mentally handicapped patients. Those people need to be there because they can't take care of themselves. Hell, look at me. I can take care of myself OK. It was a real frame-up to put me in that place."

Entering the world outside the hospital, or as the ex-patients put it, "life on the outs," means facing an often bewildering array of demands for competence. The reaction to this initial contact with the

outside world is typically a kind of "release shock."[4] All patients experienced this shock. Some reacted by exaggerated attempts to remain inconspicuous: "I didn't say nothing to nobody. I would just
listen and stay out of the way. After work I'd come straight home
and stay in my room. Sometimes I'd be shakin' all over by the time
I got home." Others sought a personal guide to direct their actions
in the earliest days: "I was all confused, sort of puzzled up. I don't
know what I'd done if Mrs. —— hadn't of shown me the ropes. I
just didn't know how to do nothing. Mrs. —— had to show me
how to shop and go places and everything. Oh boy, I was real scared
in those days." All remarked that this period of release shock was
extremely difficult for them. A man who married another cohort
member remembers it this way: "I did twelve years in that hospital,
so I know what rough times is like, but it was even tougher outside.
A man's got to worry about working every day and stuff. Ain't nobody going to feed you on the outside. It wasn't no cherries for us,
I'll tell you."

For some, the initial period of release shock was overcome in a
few weeks; for others it lasted for many months. But despite the
shock of finding oneself alone in the outside world, each ex-patient
immediately had to come to grips with his or her need for passing
and denial—for dealing with the practical problems of seeming-to-
be-normal. As mentioned earlier, the ex-patient faces the two related
problems of denying to oneself that one is mentally retarded, and of
"passing" with others, so that they neither suspect nor accuse one of
exceptional stupidity.

Passing

The second of these problems—the "passing" problem
—will be dealt with first. The practical problems of everyday life
have to be solved, not simply in order to get along, to live successfully, but also because, as every patient saw it, failure would lead to
a forcible return to the hospital. But the demands of everyday life
also had to be coped with in order to "pass," simply because no
ex-patient was willing to seem to others to be mentally retarded.

4. Cf. Goffman (1961).

What follows is a discussion of the practical problems these retarded persons encountered in meeting the challenges of everyday life in the outside world. Only those problems that seriously challenged most of the ex-patients will be examined. For convenience of exposition these challenges will be grouped together under four general rubrics: making a living, finding a mate, managing material possessions, and interpersonal problems.

MAKING A LIVING

Finding a job when one has no demonstrable skills is difficult enough, but when the job-seeker also has a past that would tend to discredit him in the employer's eyes, the difficulties are increased many times over. Obviously, very few employers are looking for employees who, in addition to being unskilled, are also mentally retarded. The ex-patient approaches a job interview burdened with his discrediting past and with extreme anxiety. The following quotations are typical:

(A woman) "When I try to get a job they always ask me where I'm from. I don't tell nobody I'm from there (Pacific State Hospital)—I say I'm just an 'outsider' like anybody, but I've been working in the East. They want to know how long I've been away and I say that it's been pretty long. I don't tell anybody where I'm from, or I'd never get a job."

(A man) "I get jobs by walking the streets and answering ads. I know I'm not qualified but I lie to them. I figure that once I get the job I can learn it. Sometimes they find out about my past and fire me and sometimes they don't. A man's got to eat."

(A woman) "I've got to find a job but I just can't. I go down somewhere and fill out the application, but then when I have an interview I just tense all up because I know they'll find out that I've lied on the application about never being in the hospital. I just break down and cry. I can't ever hide it—they always find out about me. How can I get a job?"

(A man) "I can't get a job because the application always asks where you worked for the last ten years. What can I do? I can't leave it blank, and if I lie they always find out and then they don't want me. I'm good at a lot of work if they let me do it my way."

Finding a job means more than making a living to many patients. Those who continually fail to find employment suffer a serious loss of self-esteem. A man put it this way: "When you been out of work so long and can't seem to get no job you really worry: Is there something wrong with me or something? A man's got a right to work. Besides, you're better off when you're doing something. It puts your mind at ease, makes you feel like you're as good as everybody else."

A woman's view is much the same: "I have to get a job so I can be like other people. I'm all right, it's just that people don't understand that I'm not as healthy and strong as some. I've just got to find a job, else how can I be like other people?"

All but a very few of the patients complain about the job they currently have, arguing that it compromises their claim to normal mentality by suggesting somehow that they are less than normal. Some representative complaints follow:

(A woman) "When I worked for that last family (as a maid) I had to live in a tent in the back yard. They wouldn't let me use the toilet inside. I had to use a can and bury it in the yard. I wasn't gonna stay there and be treated like some kind of animal."

(A man) "On my last job the boss kept saying I was slow—couldn't do right the way he wanted. Kept yelling that I had to do better or faster or something. I didn't stay around that place very long."

(A woman) "On that last job I was supposed to be a stock clerk, you know, putting things on the shelf and all that, but my supervisor made me do the sweeping and clean the toilets all the time. She treated me like I was an idiot. I wasn't getting paid to clean toilets. I just quit that place."

(A man) "I do real good on a job as long as they leave me alone, but they always start telling me what to do just like I was a little child. That makes me so nervous I got to quit. I can't stand everybody treating me like a child—I got to be my own boss."

Despite the acute difficulties of finding a job, and then in finding self-respect on the job, by far the most formidable problems relating to work lie elsewhere. They have to do with the proper attitudes for work: punctuality, regularity, zeal, industriousness, and sober responsibility. When asked to recall the worst problem faced in adjusting to the outside, all but two members of the cohort mentioned these attitudinal problems as being among the most difficult to deal with:

(A man) "God, I could never please that man. He wanted me to get to work at eight o'clock every day."

(A woman) "My first job or two was real bad until I learned to act like I was enjoying the work. They said they didn't want no sourpuss around always griping, so they fired me. Finally I learned to keep my mouth shut and act like I didn't mind working."

A man summarizes the problem this way: "I made good on the outside for just one reason. I learned to work hard, do what I'm told, get to work on time and go to work every day. Most of the people from the institution never had to work like that, so they have a real hard time getting adjusted. Lot of them never make it." Unfortunately, this verdict is correct. Many of the ex-patients who have sufficient skills to hold a job have never developed the requisite work attitudes.

FINDING A MATE

For many reasons, it is imperative that the ex-patient find a mate—if possible, a marriage partner. Ideally this mate should be a normal person. A woman discussed the matter this way: "Every girl wants to marry an outside guy. I know I did. I tried everything to find one. I bought nice clothes and tried to talk right, and I went to nice places. And I didn't go around with no hospital guys either. When I finally married an outside guy I knew my troubles were over." A man sees it as follows: "A guy usually wants to get married, but mostly he can't meet no outside girls. He can only get hospital girls or whores or something. I'm still single because I ain't found no outside girl yet." Another woman states the matter as succinctly as is possible; when asked if she knew another ex-patient in the cohort she said: "Oh yeah, she's doing real good. She's really made good. She married an outside guy."

Many of the ex-patients are satisfied to be married to anyone, even another ex-patient. A man said, "Before I was married I never used to have the same kind of life as other people. I was left out of so many things. Now that I got my wife (an ex-patient) I feel like I'm OK. I feel like I'm just as good as anybody." Another woman made her feelings plain when she answered the question "Are you happy?" by saying incredulously, "Well, I'm married, ain't I?"

Marriage for the ex-retardate is a highly meaningful status to achieve. Not only does it partake of most of the meanings it possesses for normal persons, it also serves dramatically to emphasize their newly won status as free and full members of the outside world.

As patients in the hospital they had been denied the right to marry, or to bear children. By the time of the research, all but fourteen of the forty-eight cohort members had married. But bearing children continued to be a problem.

Forty-four of the forty-eight ex-patients had undergone "eugenic" sterilization before their release from the hospital. Indeed, during the period of their institutionalization, sterilization was generally viewed by the administration as a prerequisite to release (Sabagh and Edgerton, 1962). The form letter sent to parents or guardians to request permission for the operation stated, *inter alia*, that sterilization would "permit parole, leave of absence, and visits with less fear of undesirable complications." Consequently, unless there was a profoundly negative reaction on the part of a relative or guardian, surgical sterilization of both males and females was routinely performed.[5]

A few ex-patients, almost without exception the single men, approved of sterilization on the grounds that it gave them greater freedom to enjoy sexual relations without fear of pregnancy. As one male put it, "It ain't so bad. This way I can play around with the girls and I don't have to worry about getting into no trouble." However, most of the ex-patients held strongly negative feelings about sterilization. They objected to it because it suggested to them their mortifying, degrading, and punishing past; sterilization for them had become an ineradicable mark of their institutional past. As such, it served as a permanent source of self-doubt about their mental status. One woman gave expression to this doubt in the following typical fashion: "I still don't know why they did that surgery to me. The sterilization wasn't for punishment, was it? Was it because there was something wrong with my mind?"[6] Another woman gave these words to her torment: "I love kids. Sometimes now when I baby-sit, I hold the baby up to myself and I cry and I think to myself, 'Why was I ever sterilized?' "

But more important to the present discussion is the extent to which sterilization impedes the course of "passing." As the following characteristic remarks should indicate, it sometimes does so to a marked degree:

5. Not only is eugenic sterilization no longer performed at Pacific State Hospital as a routine prerequisite to release, but currently employed medical and psychological criteria for performing such surgery are so demanding that very few patients are now being sterilized.

6. Sabagh and Edgerton (1962), p. 220.

(A woman) "Naturally, when a girl comes out of the hospital and meets a guy and gets married—well, if she is sterilized, then the guy wonders why she can't have no children. She's either got to tell the guy the truth or lie to him and say, 'Well, I had an accident,' or something."[7]

(A woman) "Two or three times I could've got married but I didn't dare tell the man I was sterilized. How could I tell a man a thing like that?"

(Another woman) "I was all engaged to marry a man that I really loved. He loved me too, but one day we were sitting and talking with his mother and father and they were saying how happy they would be when we were married and had children. I couldn't do it, because his parents wanted us to have children. When I heard this, I said, 'No, I don't never want to get married.' I almost told her (the mother) why but I just couldn't bear to tell her."

Another sterilized woman lies to all her friends, telling them that she has a seventeen-year-old daughter. She says, "I feel like being in that hospital wrecked my life. They made it so I can't have kids."

Women regularly explain the prominent abdominal sterilization scar to their husbands or lovers as the result of an appendectomy. "When I first had, you know, sex with a guy after getting out (of the hospital), I could just feel him looking at my scar and wondering what it was. I was gonna cover it up, but then I thought that would look bad, so I told him it was my appendix scar. He believed me OK." This is a nice irony, since sterilization surgery at the hospital was usually described to the patient as an appendectomy[8] rather than what it actually was.

Men, too, can suffer this same dilemma. One man was inordinately proud that he had courted and married a normal girl. He had revealed nothing of his past to her, least of all his sterilization. But after several childless years of marriage, he was feeling immense guilt and anxiety about his infertility. "It almost worried me to death. I was scared she would find out about me and divorce me." Then, without his knowledge, his wife went to a doctor and discovered that *she* could not have children. He was tremendously relieved and has still not told his wife anything about his own sterility.

It is evident, then, that sterilization can complicate the problems

7. *Ibid.*, p. 219.
8. *Ibid.*, p. 221.

of passing by standing as a permanent and visible mark of a secret and humiliating institutional past.

MANAGING MATERIAL POSSESSIONS

Whether married or single, ex-patients face some unusual difficulties in the management of material possessions. They enter the outside world without any of the large or small possessions which normal persons accumulate. Many normal folk may come to regard these possessions as impedimenta, but the released retardate sees them as the essential symbols of being normal in the outside world.

For one thing, the ex-patient lacks the ordinary souvenirs of a normal past. When he leaves the hospital he ordinarily has few, if any, souvenirs that could be displayed in the outside world. The ex-patients recognize this lack and make efforts to remedy it. It is quite common for souvenirs, photos, and oddments of all kinds to be picked up in junk shops or trash cans. Others are borrowed from friends. And more or less legitimate memorabilia of trips or experiences are collected with a passion, as though to make up for lost time. For example, one married woman had a photograph album filled with photos of assorted relatives, friends, and family—and not a single photograph in the album was legitimate. She had accumulated the photos from several old albums at a church rummage sale and was now happily representing the album to be a record of her allegedly normal, almost illustrious, past. Another woman had over forty china cups, saucers, and dishes, for each one of which there was a history involving travels, good friends, fine memories, and the happy exchange of gifts. All these tales were false also—she had picked up the lot of china for a few dollars in a junk shop. A man had over a dozen trophies of supposed skills in golf, bowling, tennis, and even archery, presumably dating back to a happy, athletic boyhood; these too were acquired in junk shops. To a great extent, the presentation of these fraudulent souvenirs is typical. Not all former patients collect and display bogus souvenirs with as much dedication as the patients mentioned above, although all but a few do so to some degree.

The ex-patients also acquire actual souvenirs at a great rate. When they visit a fair, amusement park, or any tourist attraction, they buy inexpensive items, bring them home, and display them proudly. When they acquire a photograph of themselves or some relative or friend, they often have it framed and then display it in a conspicuous manner.

Still the search for memorabilia continues and most of the ex-patients feel the lack acutely. For example, one woman who is married to an ex-patient keeps the following lists in a small, grimy notebook. She keeps the lists up to date and proudly shows them to visitors. The lists are given below just as she wrote them:

Things I Have Made
12 dish towels
 8 pillow cases
 6 scarbes
 3 bed spread
 2 pot holders
 1 clothes pin bag
 1 rug bag
 2 pillows
 1 quilt
 7 curtanes

Things I Found
cloths pins
dish pans
knife
silver ware
ash trays
pillows
skirts
underware

Things I Bought For Home
soap
bleach
starch
2 salt and pepper
   shackers sets
silver ware set for six
"rolla way bed"
egg beater
table cloth
coffee pot
2 potato pealers
dish drainer
ice cream scoop
silver serator
blankets (sheet)
books on sex

Things We Are Interested In
sex
sports—baseball
sewing
gardening
music Western
match covers
ash trays
picture taking
collecting odd ends

Things Given To Us
lamp
dresser
dish
2 trays

Reading is something which few of the ex-patients do adequately and only one practices as a recreation. In general, beyond the occasional picture magazine or newspaper, reading is simply not done. However, many of the ex-patients recognize that books and magazines are read and displayed by some of the normal people they meet in the outside world. These ex-patients pick up used magazines here and there, look at the pictures, and then keep them around as display items. Others acquire and display books in the same way. Large, pretentious book displays were maintained by five of the married couples (ex-patients married to each other); these books were *never* read. One man explained his book collection this way:

"Well, you know old —— (another ex-patient). He's always putting on. He went and got these books at the junk shop for ten cents apiece, and now he's got 'em all over his place like he was some kind of millionaire. Well, I went and got me some books too, real classy ones. I paid a dollar for some of 'em. Got all kinds. I think they look real nice."

His books included obscure, old texts on economics, electrical engineering, and mathematics, some old and undistinguished novels, many *Reader's Digest* novels, and a copy of *War and Peace*. The owner admitted that he had not read any of the books but felt that he "might" do so when he had more time.

The receipt and display of mail is something else which concerns these former patients. Very few send or receive mail, and when they do send it, they usually need help. All, however, love to receive mail, because receiving mail is "what outside people do all the time." The living quarters of the former patients often seem virtually littered with mail that was apparently addressed to the occupants. This curious fact does not accurately represent the volume of mail received; most of the ex-patients very seldom receive mail. It is this lack of mail that causes the ex-patients to surround himself with real or fraudulent letters: "I like it to look like I get a lot of letters. You know, like people you see in the movies. So I keep lots of mail around—most of it ain't mine, but some of it is." One woman regularly looks for discarded letters in the trash cans around the apartment where she lives. When she finds a letter or an envelope, she brings it in, folds it neatly, and adds it to a stack of letters she keeps on a small desk near the door. A man has but one letter—a legitimate one—and he keeps it prominently propped up against a lamp in his living room. He admits that he recently had to recopy and replace the original envelope because it was beginning to yellow and grow dirty. He says the newly addressed envelope "looks a lot better." Even bills from utility companies are often retained and displayed as though they represented the invoices of a busy commercial enterprise.

One final problem concerning material items must be mentioned—the problem of the automobile. The automobile represents perhaps the most enticing yet unattainable of commodities for the ex-patient. Nothing else so represents the cultural focus of the outside world, yet nothing else is so difficult to acquire, legally operate, or properly maintain. For the ex-patient the automobile is the ultimate symbol of success, but for all except a very few it is a symbol quite as elusive as the Holy Grail.

In the first place a serviceable car is expensive, and no member of the cohort was able to purchase a car that ran with any regularity. At the time of the research three ex-patients had cars, but all these vehicles must be described as wrecks that ran seldom, if at all. Of course, some women who married normal men had a car in their family, but none of these women herself owned an automobile. One man paid four hundred dollars for a ten-year-old car only to see it almost immediately burn oil, lose all compression, then cease to function at all. He never was able to find the money for major engine repairs that were necessary, so the automobile sat on blocks in front of his apartment for over two years before he finally sold it for scrap metal for twenty-five dollars. And, of course, a major problem for the person who attempts to purchase even a very inexpensive car is upkeep—the cost to operate and maintain such a vehicle is prohibitive. No member of the cohort has successfully kept an automobile in operating condition for more than a month or so at a time.

However, even an inoperative car can be a worthwhile symbol. One man kept a completely nonfunctioning automobile parked on the street in front of his living quarters and unfailingly stopped to examine it and to refer to it as his property whenever he was in the company of someone he wished to impress. He never had the money necessary to put it in running condition, and he privately admitted that he probably never would, but rather than sell it for junk (he had been offered thirty-five dollars) he preferred to retain it as a symbol of his affluence and competence. He loved to remark to friends, "I'd take you for a ride in my car but I've got to get that generator tuned up. It's dangerous to run it the way it is."

Even more forbidding than the expense of buying and maintaining an automobile are the requirements for a driver's license. So formidable is the licensing process of written exams and driving tests that only one member of the cohort has ever obtained a license (and he has never owned a car). Only three others have even attempted to pass the tests, and they have all refused to attempt the tests more than once. The lure of driving is sufficiently great, however, that five men and three women drive automobiles occasionally without benefit of an operator's license. Of course, none has the personal liability insurance (or the ability to post bond) that is mandatory in California. When questioned about the risks of driving without a license or insurance, these drivers expressed ignorance of any need for insurance. "I don't think that applies to people like me who ain't got much money." None of these illegal drivers was much worried about lacking a license, either: "I don't drive very much anyhow, so I don't think I really need one"; or, "I only drive this other guy's car, so I don't need a license for that." Only one person would admit frankly that the driver's tests were simply too great an obstacle: "I took the tests they got there—the written ones—and I guess I didn't do so good, so they gave me a book and told me to study it before I come back. I looked at the book but it was just too hard. I don't need a license anyway."

And so the unattainable automobile is surrounded by excuses: "I wouldn't have one of them cars—they cost too much." "It's much easier to get around on the bus—cars are too dangerous." "I'd rather walk, you know—cars are too much trouble." "I'm not interested in cars; those things just cause you trouble." Under more intensive questioning, however, the lure of the automobile is readily admitted. It attracts *all* the ex-patients as surely as a lamp does moths. The following two statements are typical of their unguarded feelings about cars:

(A man) "I'd give anything to have me a car of my own. I could ride around wherever I wanted and do anything and really feel great, if I could only get a car."

(A woman) "Me and my husband (cohort member) are shooting for the moon. We're saving our money so someday we can get a car. Then we can go places and be just like anybody else."

INTERPERSONAL COMPETENCE

Of all the ways in which the ex-patient's competence is challenged, none is more serious than the multiple demands that are posed in interpersonal relations. Here the ex-patient must contend with demands for intellectual skills that he does not possess. In an effort to produce the competencies demanded, the retardate must often dissemble, lie, or fake in most ingenious fashion. Here, in its most classic form, we see "passing." And here also we see the constant danger of failure, disclosure, and shame.

One of the major concerns of the released retardate is the avoidance of any public association with other retardates. This kind of association could be highly discrediting, as the following typical remarks show:

(A woman) "I guess once a girl's been out—the real bright ones that has a lot of sense—they don't like to talk to the girls or boys they knew at the colony. They just don't hardly want to be seen with them. I remember one time I was in San Diego. I guess I went to buy a pack of cigarettes or something. Well, I seen a girl in there I used to know at the colony. I turned around and walked out, then I snuck back in there to be sure she was the one I used to know. She was the one, all right, so I got out of there. I didn't want nobody to see me with her."

(A man) "All that's past history (the hospital). I don't want to have no more to do with that place. I don't want to have nothing to do with people from there, either. I just don't associate with those people that was patients. I like to associate with outside people."

Association with "outsiders" carries an obvious burden: demands for social competence and consequent danger of disclosure as an incompetent. One of the first demands is for appropriate speech. A male ex-patient states the problem: "I just don't associate with very few State hospital people—maybe I want to get out and associate with more of the outside people. Maybe you've noticed the different change in me since I've associated with outside people. I more or less speak a little different than what the State hospital people does. Maybe you've noticed that I've got class now."

"Class" in speech requires that hospital jargon be avoided. Lapses into this jargon can be dangerously discrediting: "I always got to watch myself that I don't slip and use some words which somebody would know I'm from the hospital. One day I called somebody a 'low-grade,' then I almost bit my tongue off, because outsiders don't use that word. I'm usually real careful about that." "Class" also depends upon the use of "all the big words" and a liberal infusion of "sayings"—in both instances, solecisms predominate. For example, one man pretentiously explained to all that his poor health was due to his "need for a lack of vitamins." And a woman explained why it was so hot in Florida by saying, "It's not the heat, you know, it's the low humidity." But most of the ex-patients manage their verbal deficit by saying as little as possible when they are in public. Naïvely paraphrasing the well-known saying, one man put it this way: "The best way to get by when you're with outsiders is just to keep your mouth shut. You know, if you just keep your mouth shut you won't say nothing foolish—if you talk you're just gonna say the wrong thing."

Reading and writing also present enormous problems for the "passing" retardate. Everyone in the cohort was able to read and write, at least in a rudimentary way. But rudimentary skills are often not enough, especially where reading is concerned. Everyday life offers a variety of situations in which the retardate's reading ability may prove insufficient, for example, reading bus destinations, using telephones, shopping in markets, deciphering signs or notices, or reacting to newspaper headlines. The ways in which an ability to read may prove necessary in a modern city are almost infinite. For the ex-patient to fail such a challenge in the company of normals with whom he is trying to pass would be damaging indeed. Fortunately, the ex-patients have developed serviceable excuses for most contingencies. For example, one woman was twice observed to excuse her inability to read labels in a market by saying that she had been drinking and couldn't focus her eyes very well. But one excuse is almost universally valid, and the ex-patients use it often. When the challenge to read cannot be avoided, the retardate simply fumbles about for an instant, then says that he's forgotten his glasses and can't see the words in question. The obliging normal usually can be depended on both to accept the excuse and to read aloud whatever is needed.

Writing can also be a problem but it arises as a problem much less often than the need to read. The ex-patients are seldom called upon to write in public. They can all sign their names so that is no problem. Some have developed a hasty and illegible scrawl that they use if called upon suddenly to write something that is beyond their ability. Others rely upon retreat in the face of difficult requests such as filling out forms or applications; faced with such a request, one simply pleads illness, forgotten glasses, or, occasionally, the need to put pennies in a parking meter, and walks out. If the need for writing is important but can be delayed, the ex-patient can always wait for the assistance of a benefactor. During the course of this study, the researchers were several times asked to perform this service, usually in filling out official forms or writing letters, but even in filling out income tax returns.

By far the most difficult challenge for the ex-patient lies in the use of numbers. Without exception, the members of the cohort had difficulties with numbers; some had more difficulties than others, but all found that numbers—both in the form of counting and in temporal relationships—were serious obstacles to passing.

Numbers obtrude into the ex-patients' lives at frequent and regular intervals, and when they do they are usually important. For example, most of the ex-patients carry little bits of paper on which they have written their address and phone number—few trust their memories for such long numbers. However, one man has responded to this problem by memorizing all the significant dates in his employment history and can easily provide the beginning and ending dates of every job he has ever had. He admits that he "practices" the dates almost every day. A more serious problem is telling time. It has already been pointed out that getting to work on time is a serious problem for the ex-patient. This is in part an attitudinal problem but it is also a problem in telling time. A few ex-patients can tell time without difficulty, but most—justifiably so—must take precautions against getting to work late. The most common precaution is having an alarm clock set by their employer or friend: "My boss sets this old clock for when I should get up, then I just get up and go on over to work." Others have their clocks set by friends. At one time or another, thirty-four of the cohort members have relied upon alarm clocks set by others to get to work on time.

In other circumstances, however, when the ex-patient is unsure of the time of day, he must ask. This raises problems because to ask simply, "What time is it?" would be dangerous. Answers to this question can be exceedingly confusing. For example, "It's twenty of nine," or, "It's eight forty," may refer to the same time, but the effect of such intricate temporal distinctions upon the ex-patient is usually vast confusion. To avoid such potentially confusing answers, many of the cohort members employ a similar technique. The device probably derives from the hospital culture, where it also exists, but regardless of its provenience, it meets the need. Instead of asking "What time is it?" the ex-patient asks, "Is it nine o'clock yet?" The answers to this question—"No, not for a few minutes," "It's way past nine," or "It's only eight"—are much less likely to be confusing. Consequently, the retardate usually asks for the time in this latter form, often holding up his or her own watch, saying, "My watch stopped." Most of the retardates, even those who can't tell time, wear watches. It helps greatly, in asking for the time, to be able to look at one's watch and ruefully remark that it has stopped running. As one man, who wears a long-inoperative watch, put it: "I ask 'em, 'Is it nine yet?' and I say that my old watch stopped, and somebody always tells me how close it is to the time when I got to be someplace. If I don't have that old watch of mine on, people just act like I'm some kind of bum and walk away."

But if telling time is a difficult problem, dealing with money is a greater one still. Again, the degree to which the ex-patients suffer from the problem varies, but all do suffer. It is not simply that, as the apothegm would have it, "a fool and his money are soon parted," but also that earning money, counting it, spending it, banking it, and owing it are all problems of the highest seriousness. For one thing, few of the cohort members are capable of counting money at all well. This makes for multiple problems, such as the case of one man who never knew how much he was earning: "I make a dollar an hour— that's more than four hundred dollars a month." (How many hours do you work?) "Oh, about two or three a day, I guess." (How can you make four hundred dollars then?) "Oh, ain't that right? Maybe it's one hundred dollars. I don't keep such close track." Such confusion is not uncommon.

Purchasing items, as in a market, can also be baffling. Only one of the female cohort members has any confidence in her ability to shop. And when this woman was accompanied on a shopping trip, her alleged competence vanished. She did not know prices, could not calculate change, and had to rely upon the honesty of the employees. She finally admitted: "When I go shopping I just take what I want, then I go up to the check stand and give them the biggest bill I've got. If it's enough, they give me change; if it isn't, I give them another one." Indeed, many of the cohort members spend money as some tourists do in a foreign country—by spreading it out on a counter and letting the shopkeeper take what is owed him. Unfortunately, not everyone is honest, as some of the ex-patients have been made to realize.

Of course, jobs requiring that money be handled are usually beyond their capacity, as witness the previously mentioned woman who served as cashier for a day until she rang up seventy-seven dollars instead of seventy-seven cents and gave twenty-three dollars change for a one-dollar bill to a customer who uncomplainingly accepted the windfall. Another man had similar problems as a gas station attendant; he lost that job when his inability to make change made itself apparent in the discrepancy between receipts and cash on hand.

Banking is not a problem in one sense because no member of the cohort had a checking account and those who had a savings account were always assisted in its use. The confusion of being paid by check is overcome easily enough by presenting the check to a nearby bank and having it cashed. But before some of the ex-patients discovered that banks would cash checks honestly, they lost a good deal of money cashing their checks at various markets and liquor stores.

When numbers become large, the sense of puzzlement and the problems of passing grow apace. The following example of a man's efforts to pass is typical. This man knows that his inability "to figure" has repeatedly ruined job opportunities, and he feels that it has made him appear to be "a dope." He attempts to compensate by carrying a small writing tablet around with him. On the tablet he has figures in five and six rows copied in heavy ink. He sits near someone and begins to compute multiplications in a conspicuous and grandiose fashion, complete with flourishes and grunts of intellectual satisfaction. He then announces—whether he has an audience or not—that he is studying "high math." In fact, he keeps the answers written below each problem in very light pencil so that from a distance only the heavy numbers written in ink are visible. He confesses, and not without pride, that "I've fooled lots of people that way." Another man conceived of the notion of borrowing money to start his own car-washing business—an economic practice common at the hospital and something he felt competent to do.[9] He went so far as to contact a loan company concerning his business plans and asked the agent how much money he would need to start: "The guy told me how much and I wasn't sure just how much that was so I said, 'That's a lot of money; you better write that down.' When he wrote it down it was a six with a whole lot of 0's behind it and I just knew that was too much."

Many of the ex-patients try to conceal their confusion about

9. Cf. Edgerton, Tarjan, and Dingman (1961).

money by using a form of specious precision. They regularly refer to things as costing sums such as "about" $19.24, $7.66, or $100.43. An employer of one of the ex-patients discusses the practice this way: "He just can't be specific about time. He'll say 'two weeks' but you never know what he means by that. With money though he's real specific. He'll never say twenty-two dollars; he'll say twenty-two thirty-one. Of course that's not the real price. He can't remember that. He's just showing off, pretending he really knows."

As one ex-patient put it: "Most of us people that was at the colony just can't figure or take care of money real good. Them things just don't matter when you're in the colony. That ain't so good on the outside, though. Outside you gotta learn to figure or you'll go down the old pot. Seems like most of us goes down the pot."

Denial

It should now be apparent that the ex-patients meet some challenges to self-esteem well and others not so well; they pass in some circumstances and not in others; they "get by" in some instances but by no means in all. As a result they cannot fail to realize that their competence in many aspects of everyday life is clearly less than that of the normals with whom they must associate. Such a realization is potentially devastating to their self-esteem, and if the integrity of the self is to be maintained, imputations of stupidity must be denied. The process of denial is continuous.

For a few ex-patients, denial appears not to succeed. We saw one such instance in the account of May Hatfield (chapter 2, case A). This woman made self-deprecatory remarks, but she was under great stress at that time and her remarks may not have been typical of her. In any case, they were not truly self-accusatory. Indeed, they had a rhetorical ring, and when she was contacted some months later, at a time of greater calm, those self-accusatory comments had ceased. Only one other person—again a woman—frequently made similarly revealing remarks about her possible stupidity. For example, the strongest such remark she made concerned sterilization. When asked how she felt about it she said, "Well, I'm kind of glad. If anybody attacks me, I'd get in the family way otherwise, and I'd have to go

through court and everything, and also I think that the baby probably would not come out normal."[10]

Overwhelmingly, however, they give the appearance of success in
denying to themselves that they are retarded. They succeed by turning their institutional past to good use. They say, and they appear to
believe, that they are relatively less competent than normal people
because they have suffered the depriving experience of having been
confined—wrongly of course—in Pacific State Hospital. This single
excuse is sovereign. It serves in any need and it serves well. Some
typical examples follow:

(A man) "All my problems in making good on the outside is due
to just one thing—I didn't get no schooling at all in that colony.
How can you make good without no schooling?"

(A woman) "I know I can't talk as good as most people. Even my
friends tell me I'm hard to understand. I know I'm hard to understand but that don't mean anything. That's from being in the colony
so long."

(A man) "Sometimes I worry I don't talk as good as other people.
You know, like numbers and reading and all that. But how can I? I
was in that hospital for eight long years and I didn't learn nothing
about how to think or act on the outside."

(A woman) "Of course I'm not good at talking and I get confused
and mixed up. But that's because I was in that place so long. You'd
be mixed up too if you was in there as long as I was."

(A man) "I'm real nervous and I can't always do things as good as
other people, but I'd be all right if they had let me out of that institution. Anybody would get nervous in that place."

And so, again and again, the process of denial continues by employing this excuse. By attributing their relative incompetence to the
depriving experience of institutionalization, and by insisting that the
institutionalization itself was unjustified, the ex-patients have available an excuse that can and does sustain self-esteem in the face of
constant challenge. To what extent they "really," in any psychody-
namic sense, accept their own denial is exceedingly difficult to estimate. They usually give the appearance of being successful in their
efforts to answer their own questions about themselves, but at the
same time they give indication that, fundamentally, they either know
or strongly suspect that they are mentally retarded. Probably the

10. Sabagh and Edgerton (1962), p. 219.

most accurate understanding of the ex-patients in their struggle for denial is to see them as participants in a self-instructive dialogue that is in a constantly changing balance between highly rationalized denial and gnawing self-doubt.

One point remains. One absolutely essential component of the ex-patients' armamentarium for passing and for coping with problems has been mentioned only now and then. This essential component is a "benefactor," the normal person or persons without whom the ex-patients could not maintain themselves in the community. The role of the benefactor will be discussed in the next chapter.

CHAPTER FIVE

The Benevolent Conspiracy:
The Role of the Benefactor

In their efforts to maintain themselves in the community, the ex-patients are not without assistance. With few exceptions, these former patients have located "benefactors"—normal persons who help them with their many problems. These benefactors provide welcome assistance with the practical difficulties of coping with everyday problems, with the multifold problems of passing, and even with the delicate need for denial. This assistance is of immense importance in the lives of the ex-patients.

So vital is this assistance to the former patients that a brief sketch of each of the forty-eight persons will be given in order to show the nature and range of the activities of these benefactors. These sketches will be concerned with the ways in which each former patient relies upon the normal person in order to cope with the demands of everyday life. In these sketches the emphasis will shift from the ex-patients' views of their own circumstances to the views of the benefactors. In this way it is possible to see each retarded person from the perspective of a normal person who knows that individual well.

The forty-eight ex-patients have been rank-ordered by the relative degree to which they depend upon a benefactor or benefactors. The sketches that follow are ordered alphabetically, and each bears an identification number that permits comparison with other sketches given in chapter 3. Each of the sketches also indicates the position of that individual in the relative rank-ordering of dependence upon benefactors. A ranking of no. 1 signifies the least dependence upon benefactors; no. 48 indicates the greatest dependence.

1. Lulu   Age: 30   IQ: 48   Discharge: 1956   Single (no. 11)

Lulu has reasonably good social and verbal competence, but nonetheless she is anxious and often hysterical. In the years following discharge she has been unable to find a job and has become increasingly fearful of any public performance during which she must interact with several people. She admits that she needs some "advice about money matters" and that "when things go wrong I get all confused and mentally upset." In addition to the Bureau of Public Assistance, which pays for "total disability," she depends upon three persons: a doctor, a social worker, and her landlady. The doctor, who is a friend of her sister's family, helps her with her repeated emotional crises and psychosomatic illnesses; his kindnesses are offered free of charge, despite the fact that his phone often rings at night to announce a new crisis. The social worker who has befriended her is not officially assigned by the BPA; she is the original social worker from Pacific State Hospital, who has retained an active interest in Lulu and stands ready to help with advice and assistance on financial and psychological problems. Finally, Lulu's landlady is highly sympathetic and offers dependable help with practical matters such as shopping, housekeeping, and money management.

The ex-patient's sister—a normal and moderately prosperous woman—characterizes her retarded sister's dilemma in this way: "Whenever there's an emergency, she goes to pieces. She has no money; she has no car; she has nothing. She can't do anything. If she didn't have somebody to watch out for her, she'd have to go back to Pacific." This evaluation is essentially accurate. Lulu herself says, "I feel like I need somebody to lean on or I'll just go all to pieces." Yet, this ex-patient is in fact less dependent upon benefactors than are many others in the cohort.

2a. Hal   Age: 39   IQ: 82   Discharge: 1954   (no. 13)
      Married to cohort member

2b. Midge   Age: 38   IQ: 67   Discharge: 1958   (no. 16)

Both this man and his wife, who have no relatives, are closely tied to two benefactors. The first of these is Hal's employer, who not only provides him with a job but also gives him a furnished house (albeit a ramshackle one) and frequently donates large parcels of food. This relationship is strongly paternalistic, with the ex-patient recognizing his strong dependence upon the employer: "Mr. ——— knows I'm a good worker. He wants to take care of me because I'm such a good worker. I'm happy this way; I got no worries." The employer describes the relationship this way: "He does the job I need done. It isn't easy, but he does it, and I have had plenty of others who couldn't do it (the ex-patient works in terrible heat in a foundry). So, I try to keep him happy. He's a good worker, but he doesn't have too much mental ability so I help him out."

The second benefactor is the couple's next-door neighbor. This woman takes Midge to the market every Friday, makes the food selection, and helps with the money. She also watches carefully to protect the couple from salesmen or others who might victimize them. For example, she calls the police whenever she sees a stranger at the door: "I feel I've got to protect them. Midge got took by a vacuum-cleaner salesman a while back—she just don't know what to do with a sharp salesman, so I got to look out for them."

Both husband and wife appreciate the benefactions of these two persons: "Years back, Midge and me could count on Mrs. ——— (a former employer). She was good to us and helped us whenever we had troubles. Now we got other friends. It sure makes life easier when you got friends to count on." This couple is heavily dependent upon these two benefactors.

3. Roberto (Mexican-American)   Age: 34   IQ: 85
   Discharge: 1952   Single   (no. 20)

Although Roberto has no known relatives, he does possess two benefactors. His employer at the sanitarium manages all his financial and official affairs; for example, his money is banked for him and is doled out as an allowance would be, and his official contacts with parole officers are mediated through the employer. She refers to Roberto as "a very irresponsible person. He can never be relied on, but if I take care of all his problems for him, he does a fair job of work most of the time. The truth is, though, that no one can solve all his problems for him." Some of these problems relate to and are solved by his second benefactor, the homosexual man with whom he has lived periodically during the past two and one-half years. This man, who is of normal intellect, provides for the ex-patient's everyday needs. Food, clothing, a place to live, and all the creature comforts are available in his apartment. The former patient describes his situation this way: "I used to have some troubles, with the law and all. But now I'm all taken care of—I got no more problems." His only material possession is a battered transistor radio; but he has the essential possessions in his two benefactors.

4. Tony   Age: 41   IQ: 83   Discharge: 1953   Single   (no. 19)

Tony has an exceptionally close relationship with a benefactress, a woman who was formerly his employer. She has helped him through innumerable past crises. She currently reports with him to his probation officer (offense: child molesting), tells him how to avoid further difficulties, and actively diverts him from temptation. She also supervises his payment of back income taxes with the Internal Revenue Service. Tony lives quite near this woman and her husband, and every Sunday they attend church (a fundamentalist sect) together. When this woman was no longer able to employ the ex-patient, she found him a job in a nearby bakery. His new employers at the bakery described Tony as follows: "God, he is stupid. At first he almost drove us nuts. He couldn't follow simple instructions and we had to tell him everything a hundred times. He couldn't even learn how to grease a pan. He worked hard, though, and was honest, so we kept him. Besides, we don't pay him too much and Mrs. (benefactress) vouches for him." At the time of the study, both this former patient's everyday affairs and his crises were largely managed for him.

5. Fred   Age: 32   IQ: 52   Discharge: 1957   Single   (no. 9)

This man occupies a somewhat equivocal position with respect to benefactors. His emotional dependence upon benefactors (two social workers and a "big friend") is profound and dominates his way of living. Yet he is independent of the influence of such persons for considerable periods. He usually manages the everyday affairs of his life without assistance. It is only in times of crisis that he turns to his benefactors, and they have yet to fail him. However, these crises occur in a regular cycle, and the knowledge that in times of need he can always turn to such persons (particularly his former social worker) seems to be essential buttressing for his capacity to survive in the community (for details see chapter 2, case B).

6. Mary   Age: 32   IQ: 56   Discharge: 1957   Married
       (no. 28, tied)

This woman is almost totally dependent upon her normal husband. She has no life apart from his, and in all but the most trivial aspects of life it is his knowledge and protection that sustains her in the community. Although she sometimes sees her mother and stepfather, she relies upon her husband for her ability to cope with community life, to pass, and to deny that she is retarded (for details see chapter 2, case D).

7. Jose (Mexican-American)   Age: 34   IQ: 48   Discharge: 1957
        Single   (no. 23)

This man's dependence upon normal benefactors is difficult to assess. He is highly transient and seemingly capable of moving easily within a network of friends and relatives in the Mexican-American community. His needs for housing, food, and clothing are thus always met. Jose works only irregularly. One relative, his sister, serves him in a special capacity: She reads for him when necessary, makes phone calls or writes letters to official sources (doctors, BPA, probation department, etc.), represents him when bad debts are incurred, and when necessary, finds him jobs. She describes him as follows: "Sometimes I won't see him for a month or so, then he comes back and lives with me and I have to work out all the problems he brings back with him. Sometimes I get him a job for a while. When he's tired of it, he takes off again. But he always comes back and I try to help him with his problems." His competence and his independence are in the middle range.

8. Maggie   Age: 46   IQ: 70   Discharge: 1956   Married
        (no. 38, tied)

Maggie is married to an elderly normal man who dominates and protects her while he isolates her against the world outside their small apartment. He met her when she was on work leave from Pacific and thought that she was greatly exploited: "I took her away and married her. She's been a good wife. I watch out for her. All she's got to do is cook and clean up a little. I do the rest." They live on BPA aid and whatever he can earn by "trading junk." Her father and brother live nearby but she rarely sees them. Maggie is almost entirely dependent upon her husband's protection.

9. Ellie   Age: 27   IQ: 77   Discharge: 1956   Married   (no. 5)

This young woman, who is married to a normal man, seems to be quite competent and to have as much independence as could be expected for a housewife with four children. Her husband is somewhat unstable and was in prison for narcotics possession at the time of the research. Yet, with BPA help she continued to provide an acceptable home for herself and her children. She receives no assistance from her relatives although she does visit her mother regularly. Before her husband's incarceration she had been both competent and independent, supporting her husband as much as he supported her.

10. Nora   Age: 25   IQ: 66   Discharge: 1954   Separated
    (no. 17, tied)

This young woman, the full sister of case 9 above has always lived in a highly protected status with a normal benefactor. For some time she was married to a normal man with whom she was fully relieved of responsibility for any contacts in the community. Following the onset of his mental illness, she has drifted from lover to lover, exhausting the willingness of one man after another to care for her financial and emotional needs. With her handsome physical appearance, she always seems able to secure another lover. She also periodically receives assistance from the BPA. Her last male friend spoke of her this way: "She is all right. She could keep a job and get along OK if she wanted to, but she'd rather live off some guy and do nothing. She's kind of a leech. If somebody gave her a good kick in the pants it might straighten her out. But nobody will. There's always somebody willing to put up with her."

11. Luis (Mexican-American)   Age: 31   IQ: 51   Discharge: 1954
    Single   (no. 12)

Luis, who was recently released from prison, alternatively lives with his three sisters, his brother, his grandparents, or an aunt or uncle. Currently, he is completely dependent upon them for everything. As one of his sisters put it, "We take turns keeping care of him." However, his current need for benefactors is due largely to his recent imprisonment and surgery for gallstones. With his past record of social competence, it is not likely that Luis will long remain in such a fully dependent situation. Luis says, "I'll be getting a job and moving out of here soon's I get rested up. I like to be on my own."

12. Ellen   Age: 49   IQ: 84   Discharge: 1953   Married   (no. 8)

Ellen's husband is a former ward charge in mental hospitals in the East and South. Together they manage a large apartment building. She is sometimes puzzled by money and receipts, but otherwise she seems both adequately competent and independent. Her husband is quite intelligent but he does not greatly dominate her. She says: "I feel like that I proved I can run this old motel as good as anybody. But then anybody's got to have help, and my husband's real handy." The husband says of his wife, "She does just fine. She's learned how to do things real good. We get along fine. I help her with some things, and she helps me with others."

13. Roy   Age: 30   IQ: 53   Discharge: 1953   Divorced   (no. 35)

Roy is heavily dependent upon his employer, especially upon his employer's wife, who has befriended him. Although he has been a notably unreliable worker, he continues to receive numerous benefactions from this woman. She has provided him with a place to sleep in her garage, has three times posted bond on his behalf following his arrest for "drunkenness and vagrancy," and has continually reduced his responsibilities on the job. She says, "He just doesn't have the ability to do any better." He says, "She's just like a mother to me—but I'd still like to be a bartender." Since it is her bar (at the restaurant she and her husband own) that he wishes to tend, she said, when told of his wish: "A bartender? Is he still on that kick? He's drunk half the time as it is, and even when he's sober he could never learn how to mix drinks or make change. Lord knows, I don't want to knock him, but it takes all the help I can give him for him just to stay alive and out of jail." This appraisal appears to be accurate.

14. Maria (Mexican-American)   Age: 31   IQ: 83   Discharge: 1952
      Single   (no. 26)

Maria is only moderately dependent upon the owner of the restaurant where she works, but she is greatly under the sway of her sixty-year-old landlady. This woman has befriended her and has offered every conceivable assistance and kindness. The two now live as close friends, with the older woman highly maternal toward the former patient, whom she counsels and protects in every area of life. The ex-patient is so close and clinging to this benefactress that she has come to have virtually no life apart from her—despite the fact that this former patient is unusually verbal, has demonstrated good social competence, and has considerable intellectual ability.

15. Ricardo (Mexican-American)   Age: 45   IQ: 64
      Discharge: 1957   Single   (no. 37)

This highly incompetent man is strongly protected and assisted by two benefactors. One is his employer, the other is an elderly man with whom he shares an apartment. Together these two men supervise almost every aspect of this ex-patient's life. Ricardo describes his circumstances this way: "Well, I was at the colony forty or fifty years and that was OK (he was there less than twenty years) and now I'm outside—and this is OK. I'm always OK. Somebody always helps me out." His employer says, "Well, he's always happy but he really isn't capable of managing his own affairs. There are some areas where he is lost. He really doesn't understand money or time and he can't read very well, so I have to help him out with anything like that."

16. Richard   Age: 39   IQ: 56   Discharge: 1954   Divorced
     (no. 2)

Richard is quite independent. He has held the same job for eight years and he receives no unusual assistance from his employer. His former social worker used to intervene in his life—especially a few years ago at the time of his divorce—but there has been no intervention for the past year. Richard is fully self-supporting and is independent of any out-of-the-ordinary assistance from a normal person. His father and mother live within twenty-five miles, but he rarely sees them or any other relative. He is very much on his own, and he is quite competent.

17. John   Age: 29   IQ: 77   Discharge: 1953   Single
     (no. 43, tied)

This psychotic man is totally protected in a sheltered work environment. The owner and staff of the sanitarium where John works take care of his financial needs and protect him against contacts with the community. John works reasonably well and regularly, so his idiosyncracies are overlooked (e.g., he works clad in the heaviest fur coat imaginable, periodically announces that all the land in the area around the sanitarium was granted him by his dear friend Louis XIV, and repetitively states that enemies have "sold my skeleton to the world"). He could not function in the community without complete supervision and protection.

18a. Hank   Age: 33   IQ: 70   Discharge: 1958   (no. 10)
      Married to cohort member

18b. May   Age: 35   IQ: 70   Discharge: 1958   (no. 29, tied)

This man is currently relatively free of the influence of benefactors. He is occasionally helped, dominated, and protected by his landlady, and he used to be assisted by his social worker, and at one point his wife also helped him a great deal, but he has been and still is reasonably independent. His wife, however, has been extremely dependent upon her social worker and, recently, upon her landlady, who is a former mental hospital employee (for details see chapter 2, case A).

19. Rosie   Age: 39   IQ: 65   Discharge: 1953   Married   (no. 14)

Rosie used to be dependent upon her normal husband. For several years he has dominated her life, made her decisions, and in every way controlled her. In recent months he has taken less interest in her, and she has come to rely upon a next-door neighbor for help with shopping, housekeeping, and any necessary contacts with the community. This neighbor woman speaks of the former patient as follows: "Even when she isn't drinking she needs help with so many things. I really don't think she can read and I know she can't manage money. She's a little slow, I'm afraid, but she's sweet and I try to help out whenever I can. People like her need help." Even so, Rosie has shown surprising ability to cope with her life circumstances, and she is less dependent than many of the ex-patients.

20. Ruth   Age: 29   IQ: 85   Discharge: 1952   Married
        (no. 18, tied)

This woman is moderately dependent upon her normal husband and her stepmother. Her husband controls and protects her by making her decisions, doing the shopping, and handling all community contacts. However, he has recently begun to leave her somewhat to her own devices, as he has been drinking heavily and staying away from home for days at a stretch. The ex-patient's stepmother has taken over the role of benefactress in this period. The stepmother describes Ruth as follows: "She's weak, and not very smart, of course, and she's easily led. She used to run around a lot before her marriage, and I've still got to watch her close, but I think she's settled down now and been a good wife and mother. Still she's got to have help with the house and shopping and the kids. She can't do it alone. Without her husband she couldn't manage, and now I'm trying to help out too."

21a. Arnold   Age: 32   IQ: 61   Discharge: 1955   (no. 33)
        Married to cohort member

21b. Bessie   Age: 26   IQ: 61   Discharge: 1957   (no. 24)

This couple is strongly assisted and protected by their employer, the owner of the restaurant where they work. He watches over them with paternal interest, provides food and gifts, and intervenes in any emergency. In addition, Arnold's mother occasionally helps with the rent payments. For the most part, this couple simply stays home together. Their contacts with the world outside their home and their place of employment are few, and these contacts are typically supervised by their employer. The employer puts it this way: "They're real nice kids—both of them. They work hard and don't cause any trouble. But obviously they've got their mental limits and they need some help. He's a pretty dependent guy, to put it mildly. She dominates him pretty good, but she needs help too, to make ends meet. I try to help out. I figure somebody's got to."

22a. Lester   Age: 39   IQ: 84   Discharge: 1952   (no. 15)
     Married to cohort member

22b. Bertha   Age: 28   IQ: 57   Discharge: 1953   (no. 22)

This couple, like the aforementioned one, is assisted by their employer, the owner of the restaurant where all four ex-patients work. In this case, the protection is less intensive because this couple is slightly better able to manage its affairs, but still, they are dependent upon their employer. Bertha puts it this way: "I don't know what we'd 'a' done without him. He's been so good. He's helped in so many ways, we can always count on him." Lester adds this realistic note: "If you're gonna make it on the outside you got to have a little bit upstairs. You can't be a semi. But I know we couldn't 'a' made it without him. He's taken care of us, that's all." The employer sees his role as follows: "Sure, I help them when they need it. Most of the time they get along OK and Lester's a good worker. I help with their problems: money, reading, shopping, getting around town, and things like that. Sometimes I think they depend on me too much, but I don't see how they could make it without somebody helping them, and they've got no family."

23. Noreen (Negro)   Age: 34   IQ: 57   Discharge: 1949
     Married   (no. 6)

This woman has maintained herself remarkably well in the absence of any reliable benefactor. She is able to manage her own practical problems with the occasional assistance of her common-law husband with whom she lives in the back of a dingy, slum-area store where he works. When he is present he deals with many of the problems of money and shopping. But when he is not present she does quite well on her own. The ex-patient receives aid from the BPA, and this seems adequate to sustain her, even without the assistance of a benefactor.

24. Henry   Age: 30   IQ: 80   Discharge: 1957   Married   (no. 1)

Henry is unusually independent. He works ably, regularly, and happily. He budgets his money, attempts to save, and successfully deals with the complexities of community living. His wife (a former Pacific patient) is quite dependent upon him, although she also receives help with grocery shopping from her mother, who takes her shopping every Friday. Except for this, his wife's parents give little assistance, although they live next door and are helpful friends. In all, this man lives quite independently.

25. Lois   Age: 31   IQ: 57   Discharge: 1954   Married   (no. 45)

Lois is completely dependent upon her normal husband. He manages all the family affairs, makes all decisions, and shelters his wife from any unsupervised community contacts. For example, through his church he was able to adopt an infant. Lois was asked how old the child was and answered, "She should be about twenty-two or thirty-four months now or something like that; I've lost tract." She has also lost track of how long she has been married. Her only responsibilities are keeping house and cooking, both of which she seems at least partially competent to do. Her husband admits that he must supervise her actions, but he feels that "She's a good wife. She makes me happy and I don't mind taking care of her."

26. Josephina (Mexican-American)   Age: 30   IQ: 50
      Discharge: 1957   Divorced   (no. 30, tied)

This woman often rejects the aid of a consistent or reliable benefactor and, perhaps as a consequence, her life is very disorganized. She has periods of moderate stability and security when she works regularly at a sanitarium. There she is supervised and protected by her employer, a highly sympathetic woman whom she calls "Mama." More often, Josephina is off on an irresponsible and sometimes illegal spree, which usually terminates when she is blatantly exploited by one or another young man. The security and serenity of her life when she is under the control of her benefactor, "Mama," contrasts sharply with the turbulent and often bizarre periods when she is "away."

27. Betty   Age: 35   IQ: 64   Discharge: 1953   Single   (no. 47)

After a series of failures in community living, this tiny (4'10") woman has been placed in a foster home and is officially supervised by a State social worker. Her final failure occurred when she precipitously left her job and "went away" with her half brother. He induced her to withdraw her savings of seven years ($2,000), which her benefactress had encouraged and supervised, and after a few weeks of traveling, he abandoned her and vanished with her money. Betty may be re-institutionalized, and even now she is totally dependent.

28. Martha   Age: 39   IQ: 72   Discharge: 1956   Single   (no. 40)

Martha's life is a single-minded pursuit of benefactors. She has no relatives or friends, and her attempts to establish personal relationships in the past have resulted in failure and retreat. She now lives only for, and through, her benefactors and, in fact, she could not maintain herself in the community without their considerable and continuing efforts (for details see chapter 2, case C).

29. Leonard   Age: 33   IQ: 64   Discharge: 1957   Single
        (no. 39, tied)

After unsuccessful efforts at independent living, Leonard returned to his mother's home and has since lived there in complete dependence upon his mother and stepfather. They control his activities so completely that he must ask permission to turn a lamp on or off. He is, in effect, conceived of and treated as a small and difficult child. His mother says that "He's more like a child than an adult." His stepfather adds that "If I didn't do everything for him, he really wouldn't know how to get through the day." Leonard complains that "Nobody ever lets me make up my own mind; everybody tells me what to do." Despite his resentment, he makes no further efforts to leave home and to live more independently. He left home several times in the past; each time he returned in failure after a very few days.

30. Agnes   Age: 56   IQ: 47   Discharge: 1953   Single   (no. 48)

This older woman is totally dependent upon her employer and her sister (who owns the sanitarium where she works). Both of these persons order her about and control her quite as though she were a small child. Indeed, she is often confined to the sanitarium where she is employed. Agnes does not seem to object to this treatment and summarizes her condition in this way: "I think I done pretty good to stay out (of Pacific) this long!" Her employer says of her, "She is no better than a child of eight. I have to watch her all the time to keep her out of trouble. She'll jump in bed with anything that wears pants. If we can make her feel she's important, though, she will do some work. It's always a problem because she really can't control herself—she's just like a child. Fortunately her sister and I have been able to take care of her. In fact, her sister has saved almost two thousand dollars for her out of her salary here."

31. Dorothy   Age: 51   IQ: 66   Discharge: 1957   Marrie
     (no. 21)

Dorothy is largely dependent upon her elderly, retired husband. Although he is in his seventies, he is still able to supply the necessary knowledge of community life, and she is able to run errands efficiently. Almost all of her time is spent alone with her husband in a trailer court, and in this limited environment they are able to maintain themselves well. However, she is easily confused by any complex relationship, and despite her superficial appearance of competence, she is dependent upon her husband. As she admits, "I don't think I could make it without the old goat. He takes care of me, and as long as I got him I'll be OK." He says of her, "Dot's a good wife. There's things she don't know and things she can't do, but we get along fine. I help her along when she needs it and we get along just fine."

32. Billie Mae   Age: 30   IQ: 74   Discharge: 1954   Married
     (no. 31, tied)

Billie Mae lives with her husband, her father-in-law, and her brother-in-law. These three men provide her with great assistance in the management of her affairs and they similarly shelter her against difficult community situations. She says, "My husband just does everything for me. He shops, he buys everything; he even buys my Kotex for me. I like it that way. I was going to marry this other guy but he was never sure how to do anything. He was stupid. I think a man's place is to tell a woman what to do. I don't have to worry about anything now." Her husband says, "Sure, she's sort of stupid. When I met her she didn't know nothing about nothing. But I got her trained. She's OK now. I take care of her and she's OK. She cooks real good."

33. June   Age: 35   IQ: 74   Discharge: 1956   Married   (no. 36)

June is totally supervised and protected by her husband. He does all shopping and makes all community contacts. She lives in housewifely seclusion with her husband except for occasional trips that they take together. He enjoys his dominant role: "My first wife was a real bitch, if you'll pardon me. Nothing was good enough for her. June is what I've always wanted. She appreciates everything. Everything is new and enjoyable for her. She stays home and takes care of the house, and that's what I want." June too is happy: "My husband is the most wonderful man. He's so good to me. He takes care of everything around here and we have a lot of fun going places. I don't have to worry about anything."

34. Grenville   Age: 29   IQ: 66   Discharge: 1954   Married
     (no. 34)

This young man has always had a benefactor. In the first years after his discharge, his mother assisted him in every way: she found him an apartment, paid the rent, got him a job, paid for his driving lessons, banked his money, made social contacts for him, and so on. At times he rebelled, insisting that he could not compete with normal persons, but his mother continued to force him to try. With his mother's connivance he found a wife, and since their marriage this normal woman has dominated him greatly. She controls him and the household, making and implementing her own decisions. He seems not to protest, though, saying: "Before I was married I felt different; I wasn't the same as the others. Now I can go bowling or watch TV and be just like anybody else. I mean with a wife and everything." And he can still depend upon his mother whenever her help might prove necessary. She continues to watch over him, from a distance, but closely.

35. Alma   Age: 39   IQ: 65   Discharge: 1951   Married   (no. 32)

With the aid of the BPA and a very beneficent next-door neighbor, Alma is able to maintain herself. Her normal husband, whom she still refers to as her "Daddy," used to protect her, but since his stroke he has been confined to a wheelchair. Her neighbor now helps her with her problems: shopping, dealing with salesmen, and in official contacts with the welfare agency. The ex-patient says that this benefactress has "been like a sweet mama to me and that's the fact truth." This woman, however, is pessimistic on several counts: "She is not very capable so I try to help out, but then she gets very demanding and wants all of my time. You have to be very careful talking to her, too, because you can never tell when you'll be over her head. She's so unpredictable, too. One time she's real sweet to Frank (her husband); the next day she just runs off and leaves him alone all night. She really needs a keeper. I just do what I can."

36a. George   Age: 35   IQ: 52   Discharge: 1954   (no. 25)
    Married to cohort member

36b. Ramona (Mexican-American)   Age: 37   IQ: 64
    Discharge: 1953   (no. 27)

This couple is quite dependent upon his employer and their land-lady. The employer extends help with all money matters, advises with medical problems, and helps with their emergencies. In return for occasional baby-sitting and laundry service, the landlady does all the shopping for them and supervises their housekeeping. They are de-pendent upon this landlady for advice concerning even the simplest matters in their life. She says of them, "They're good kids but they know so little. I try to help them to get on their feet and get along. I feel they need me and they are grateful, so I don't mind. You know, they really can't do anything for themselves."

37. Harry   Age: 40   IQ: 68   Discharge: 1949   Married
    (no. 3)

This man, who is married to a "normal" woman (she has never been hospitalized but appears to be quite unintelligent), is reasonably independent. His only relatives are his five brothers, all of whom are institutionalized for mental retardation. He receives little help or pro-tection from any source. Although his father-in-law lent him some money to buy a car, such assistance from his wife's parents is very unusual, and he is conscientiously attempting to pay back the loan. He has proven himself competent to manage his life and appears able to provide for his not-very-able wife. He saw military service in Korea from 1950 to 1952, and since his discharge he has worked competently at the same job. He has $600 in a savings account.

38. Myrtle   Age: 31   IQ: 56   Discharge: 1958   Married
    (no. 46)

Myrtle is absolutely dominated and protected by her normal hus-band. In the past, she was supported by the BPA and her parents, but when these latter began to exploit her, she was married by her long-time friend, a paraplegic man several years older than she. He does everything for her, including all the talking in any public situation. She has no friends of her own and no contact with the community without her husband being present. But she is very happy: "I got everything now." Myrtle's husband enjoys his dominance: "Of course she is handicapped, but her parents were stealing her blind before I married her. Now she's well taken care of. All I ask is that when I come home from work she has dinner ready and the house cleaned up."

**39. Corliss   Age: 28   IQ: 65   Discharge: 1955   Married
      (no. 44, tied)**

This young woman is greatly controlled and protected by her older, normal husband. He shields her from any public exposure. Her mother-in-law is also very controlling and protective. She still visits her mother and father, but her husband usually insists that he be present, "So they can't take advantage of her like they used to do." She happily admits, "I depend on him for just about everything." Indeed she does, and without much expressed resentment. For example: "We can't afford to adopt a child because my husband is old and he's afraid that if he dies I'll be left alone to take care of the child, and he doesn't think I could do that." He truly does not: "I'll admit she's a problem sometimes. She needs so much supervision, but I don't mind—it all works out all right."

**40. Prudence   Age: 32   IQ: 60   Discharge: 1953   Married
      (no. 4)**

Prudence is relatively competent and independent. Her first husband was a heroin addict who would not work. After she tired of supporting him, she married a younger man. He drinks excessively and seldom works. She says of him: "His Daddy is the biggest drunkard in Atlanta, Georgia, and now he's trying to catch up. If it wasn't for the two kids (his by an earlier marriage) I'd leave him. I can't even give him any money now (from her BPA check) or he'll drink it up." In fact, her husband seldom visits her at all except when he is drunk. She has managed the house and two children on her BPA check without assistance for several years. She recently found a job at a dollar an hour. She now works regularly and leaves the two children with her mother-in-law during the day.

**41. Helen (Negro)   Age: 29   IQ: 73   Discharge: 1952
      Married   (no. 7)**

Helen is relatively competent, although she does receive regular, if modest, assistance from her mother and her siblings. Her husband has given her adequate support until recently, when he was hospitalized with tuberculosis. She has two children and is pregnant with a third. She receives aid from the BPA and rents out a room of her small house for $37.50 a month, and this income with her mother's help is adequate. She maintains a secure and stimulating home for the children and appears to be a completely adequate housewife and mother without much assistance from any benefactor.

42. Ronald   Age: 28   IQ: 47   Discharge: 1955   Married
    (no. 41)

Ronald is fully dependent upon the control and support of his employer. This woman not only provides him with a job, she orders his entire life for him. She forbids further contact with his parents (she insists that they "steal" his money); she confines him to his room if he misbehaves; she banks his salary and gives him an allowance. In short, she manages his life. "Ronnie is so unrealistic that he just makes a mess of everything if you leave him alone. He has all kinds of highfalutin ideas about the great things he's gonna do, and he can't even begin to take care of himself right here. If he gets hold of any money, he loses it all at the races or drinks it up. He's got to be watched over all the time."

43. Walter   Age: 20   IQ: 61   Discharge: 1958   Single
    (no. 42)

This young man is completely dependent upon his mother and stepfather, with whom he now lives. He is treated as a naughty child, and his resentment is monumental. His half brother continually brings teenagers into the house and these young people often humiliate the ex-patient with acts or with omissions. He responds with a frantic effort to establish his competence and independence as a normal teenager, but thus far all his actions have failed and he remains dependent upon relatives, who regard him as little more than an annoyance. Walter states it this way: "They don't respect me at all; they always tease me or act like I wasn't even there." In fact, they do sometimes address him as "fatso" or "stupid" and they generally regard him with annoyed contempt. Still, their care and protection are essential. His mother says, "He really is impossible. He's so unrealistic about his problem that he drives us crazy. We try to take care of him but it isn't easy."

What has preceded is a summary of the involvement of benefactors in the lives of the forty-eight members of the study cohort, prepared as accurately as limited information, abbreviation, and the author's judgment permit. This summary indicates an extensive involvement of benefactors in the efforts of these former patients to manage their practical everyday affairs. Indeed, it suggests such a considerable degree of dependence upon benefactors, that most of the ex-patients were judged to be unable to maintain themselves in the community without the active intervention of one or more benefactors.

Estimating Dependence Upon Benefactors

Many studies have attempted to assess the relative independence and dependence of retardates living in a community.[1] Almost without exception these studies have reported favorably upon the "adjustment" of the retardates, and many have concluded that these ex-patients are notably independent. Adjustment is usually estimated in terms of the degree of self-support shown and by the absence of detected law violation. The current study does not attempt to replicate any of these earlier studies—it cannot, for it has no normal control group, deals with but a small number of subjects, and makes no excursion into the past to attempt pre- and post-hospital comparison. In short, this study is not designed to make broad or definitive statements about the relative adjustment, success, or independence of any large population of retarded persons. Its value lies in the completeness of its information about the lives of a very limited number of former patients. With recognition of these limitations and strengths, the following evaluation is offered.

Table 6 presents a rank-ordering of all forty-eight members of the study cohort from most independent to least independent. No effort was made to define independence precisely—the working definition was simply a subjective judgment of the extent to which the person was living without the need for assistance from others. By following this imprecise definition, the author, and three students who had

1. For example, Cobb (1932), Storrs (1929), Little and Johnson (1932), Bronner (1933), Steckel (1934), McPherson (1935), Abel (1940), Jewell (1941), Bijou *et al.* (1943), Muench (1944), Johnson (1946), McIntosh (1949), Hartzler (1951, 1953), O'Connor (1953), Wolfson (1956), Carriker (1957), Krishef (1959), Windle (1962).

Table 6 *Mean Rank Orderings by 4 Judges of the Relative Independence of 48 Ex-patients*

Rank	ID Number and sex		IQ	Rank	ID Number and sex		IQ
Most independent							
1.	24	Male	80	25.	36a	Male	52
2.	16	Male	56	26.	14	Female	83
3	37	Male	68	27.	36b	Female	64
4.	40	Female	60	*28.	6	Female	56
5.	9	Female	77	*29.	18b	Female	70
6.	23	Female	57	*30.	26	Female	50
7	41	Female	73	*31	32	Female	74
8.	12	Female	84	32.	35	Female	65
9.	5	Male	52	33.	21a	Male	61
10.	18a	Male	70	34.	34	Male	66
11.	1	Female	48	35.	13	Male	53
12.	11	Male	51	36.	33	Female	74
13.	2a	Male	82	37.	15	Male	64
14.	19	Female	65	*38.	8	Female	70
15.	22a	Male	84	*39.	29	Male	64
16.	2b	Female	67	40.	28	Female	72
*17.	10	Female	66	41.	42	Male	47
*18.	20	Female	85	42.	43	Male	61
19.	4	Male	83	*43.	17	Male	77
20.	3	Male	85	*44.	39	Female	65
21.	31	Female	66	45.	25	Female	57
22.	22b	Female	57	46.	38	Female	56
23.	7	Male	48	47.	27	Female	64
24.	21b	Female	61	48.	30	Female	47
				Least independent			

Rank-order correlation (Spearman r) = −.21
* Indicate ties.

read all the available case material, independently rank-ordered the forty-eight ex-patients. Each ex-patient was assigned a rank from 1 ("most independent") to 48 ("least independent"). The four ranks of scores were then compared and each ex-patient was assigned the mean score of the four rankings. Table 6 gives the results of this ranking.

In terms of my own subjective judgment of the absolute degree of independence or dependence, only the first three could be considered fully independent. Numbers 4 through 10 are largely or periodically independent; 11 through 27 are heavily but not completely dependent, and 28 through 48 are, for all practical purposes, completely dependent. This conclusion may be somewhat more pessimistic than the findings of most previous studies, but since this sample does not claim to be representative, the implications of the conclusion are difficult to assess.

It should be noted that dependence upon benefactors, as here estimated, and social competence, are not exactly the same phenomenon. An individual could be relatively competent and yet be quite dependent. Ex-patient number 14 is such a person; she is more competent than her dependence rating of #26 would suggest. However, among these former patients, she is an exception. If I were to alter the rank-ordering to reflect social competence rather than dependence, I would change the relative position of no more than three or four individuals. In reality, then, what is true about the relationship of IQ to dependence is true of social competence as well.

With this in mind, we should return to the point made in chapter 1, that a number of these former patients are not "officially" retarded by the IQ criterion. In fact, fourteen of the former patients have IQs over 70. In Table 6 we find that while the most independent person among the forty-eight had an IQ of 80, many whose IQs were over 70 were quite dependent, and hence not very competent, persons. On the other hand, among the ten most independent and competent ex-patients, we find persons with IQs of 68, 56, 60, 57, and 52.

This finding leads to the point I wish to make. Throughout this study, persons in the research cohort whose IQs were over 70 have been referred to and dealt with in the same fashion as those whose IQs were 70 and below. There was nothing in the character of post-hospital lives of these ex-patients to suggest a need to distinguish between them. On the whole, the IQ of any given individual among these forty-eight former patients tells us little about what to expect from him following his return to the outside world. Even very low IQ is no sure indicator. For example, while it is true that the most dependent and incompetent person in the cohort had an IQ of 47, another person whose IQ was 48 was rated as the eleventh most independent and competent member of the cohort.

Is this because a few IQ points really do not matter where social competence is concerned? Perhaps so. Or is it because all of these persons have shared the experience of being labeled as mental retardates and have been institutionalized as such? Again, perhaps so. Or is it still more important that all of these persons have been patients in the same hospital for the mentally retarded? It is probable that all these factors, and others, contribute in some measure, but the relative contribution of these factors cannot be unraveled here. For example, only a very few of the potentially contributing factors can be measured with any objectivity. Two such are the age at which the former patient was admitted to the hospital and the length of time spent there. When either of these factors is correlated with the dependence rank-ordering shown in Table 6, the same very weak relationship results.

Possible contributing factors aside, it is clear that persons in this research cohort whose IQs were over 70 possessed no obvious adaptive advantage over those whose IQs were 70 or below. This finding matches the almost unanimous opinion of the literature that IQ is not the best criterion for predicting successful community adjustment. Other factors such as age, personality characteristics, education or training, class or ethnicity, and the like, are generally found to be much better predictors.[2]

Aid with Passing

Although the aid that benefactors provide is vitally important to the former patients' ability to cope with the practical demands of everyday life, the aid of benefactors is not limited to problems of coping. Benefactors regularly serve the ex-patients by assisting them with passing and denial. Aid with the first of these—passing—was alluded to in several of the previously presented vignettes, where words such as "protected" and "supported" necessarily implied a concern with passing as well as with coping.

In order to assist with the task of passing, the benefactor sometimes becomes an "insider," someone privy to an ex-patient's secret institutional past. In such a situation, there is an active collaboration, usually involving a benefactor who is a spouse, a relative, a professional person, or an employer. Either these persons have prior knowl-

2. Kinder and Rutherford (1927), Blackey (1930), Channing (1932), Lurie *et al.* (1932), Shimberg and Reichenberg (1933), Bronner (1933), Abel (1940), McKay (1942), Thomas (1943), Hamlett and Engle (1950), O'Connor and Tizard (1951, 1956), Hiatt (1951), O'Connor (1953), Badham (1955), Krishef and Hall (1955), Krishef *et al.* (1959).

edge of the ex-patients' diagnosis and hospitalization, or, as is the case with some spouses, the ex-patient has told them. Thirty-eight of the total of fifty regular benefactors had explicit knowledge of the ex-patient's diagnosis and past; thirty-one of these persons had prior knowledge through some official hospital source, and seven (all spouses) had been told by the ex-patient of the earlier—but, of course, wrongful—hospitalization "under the State." The remaining twelve benefactors were "outsiders" who had no explicit knowledge, but ten of these had easily made their own diagnosis of mental retardation. Only two benefactors claimed not to know "for sure," but in both of these cases it was evident that they had active suspicions.

Once a benefactor is an "insider," he is obliged to conceal the ex-patient's secret. But "outsider" benefactors are also actively engaged in the business of helping the former patient to pass. Most of these benefactors—"insiders" and "outsiders"—showed remarkable protective fervor when they were first encountered by the research workers from this study. In many instances, they were bellicose and threatening until reassured by proper identification that the researchers were from the hospital, knew the ex-patient's background, had only the best of intentions, and would permit no disclosure of the ex-patient's discrediting past. On two occasions before identification was made, suspicious benefactors called the police to request an investigation of the activities of research workers.

The "insider" benefactor is often concerned with problems of biography management, particularly with concealing the ex-patient's discrediting past. Aid with this problem can take the form of helping the former patient fill out an official form (for employment, welfare assistance, credit applications, etc.) so as to conceal past hospitalization, or simply to intervene when a stranger comes to the door, not merely to help manage the situation but also to prevent disclosure of the ex-patient's past. For example, this statement from a landlady who is an "insider":

"I keep a pretty close watch on their door, just in case some stranger comes along. You know, someone could really take them if they found out they used to be in a hospital for the retarded. Besides, I think that is their private secret and I don't think anyone should be asking questions that might make them admit something that would really shame them."

Benefactors also contribute to the concealment of deficits in everyday competence such as appearance, dress, or speech. However, the benefactors' aid most often concerns the ex-patients' inability to read, write, or manipulate numbers. Again, the emphasis can be as much upon passing as upon coping. As one "insider" employer explains:

"Well, you know John isn't too good when it comes to numbers, or any kind of writing as far as that goes. So he always comes to me with letters for me to read. Sometimes I write letters for him, too. Or if he's going to the store, I'll tell him how much something ought to cost and how much money to give them, or if I can, I even go along and handle the money so he won't be embarrassed when he has to pay the bill. It isn't so much that people take advantage of him, although that can happen too. It's more that he doesn't want to admit to people that he can't do these things."

Or, as an "outsider" benefactor put it: "She gets so embarrassed when she has to do things in public, so I go along and help her out. She always comes and asks me if I'm busy. So I go along, and that way she never feels ashamed because she doesn't know how to act in public or how to do things like read and write."

Aid with Denial

Still more important than aid in passing is the benefactors' role in aiding denial. The need to deny to oneself the humiliating admission that one is in fact mentally deficient is for these ex-patients constant and essential. As was pointed out in chapter 4, denial is accomplished, and accomplished surprisingly well, by arguing to oneself that the very fact of hospitalization is the cause of whatever current incompetence the ex-patient sees in himself. Nonetheless, the need for confirmation that one is not retarded repeatedly arises, and here the benefactor can be invaluable. A direct approach for reassurance is apparently rarely attempted, but indirection is often employed. The ex-patients' approach usually takes the form of a slip or hint—a self-deprecatory remark that is casually tossed off with the express hope that the benefactor will argue to the contrary. For example, the following exchanges between former patients and benefactors were overheard:

(Ex-patient) "When I heard my brother had died, I said, 'Why couldn't it have been me? I'm good for nothing, I'm just no good. I wish my mother had throwed me down the toilet.'" (Benefactress) "Now that's the silliest thing I've ever heard. You have no business saying such things—you've got to learn to appreciate yourself. You're just as good as anybody else." (Ex-patient) "Oh, I just don't know what to do. I can't find a boyfriend. They're all too good for me." (Benefactress) "That is just ridiculous. Now stop that! You are a very nice, sweet girl and you're going to make some lucky man a wonderful wife. You just need more self-confidence." (Ex-patient) "Oh, you're so understanding. You make me feel so much better. Sometimes I just get to feeling so, well, you know, sorry about the way I am. You make me feel so much better." (Benefactress) "Just don't worry yourself. You'll see. Everything'll be all right."

(Ex-patient, remonstrating with herself and bursting into tears about burning a shirt she was ironing) "I'm just so stupid; I can't do anything right." (Husband, a normal man) "Cut that out. Anybody can burn a shirt. Don't talk that way. You're good enough to be my wife so don't talk that way."

(Ex-patient) "My husband does all that heavy lifting, you know. I may be stupid but I'm not that stupid." (Benefactress) "You're not stupid, Beulah, why do you say that?" (Ex-patient) "Oh you're so nice. You always make me feel so good."

(Benefactor, a roommate) "Did you get the job?" (Ex-patient) "No, well, they said they'd let me know. You know that means I don't get it. Hell, nobody's gonna hire an idiot like me that don't know nothing." (Benefactor) "What d'ya mean? The whole country's full of people with no jobs. You think they're all idiots? You're as good as anybody—it's just hard times." (Ex-patient) "Yeah, I suppose that's it. I was only kiddin' anyhow. You know that. It's just that I got no luck."

(Ex-patient) "Oh, why am I so stupid?" (Husband, a normal man) "Because you're human like everybody else." (Ex-patient) "Oh, you say the nicest things."

And so it goes. The ex-patients make "slips" about their incompetence. As one benefactress—a landlady—put it: "He is always saying little things to belittle himself when I'm around, because he knows I'll tell him it isn't so. That seems to make him feel better, so I always try to build him up." When questioned specifically about their actions in this regard, every single benefactor stated that he or she typically responded to an ex-patient's deprecations by denying the validity of any implied incompetence. Indeed, several benefactors looked upon this as the most important feature of their relationship with an ex-patient.

A related contribution of the benefactors must not be overlooked. In the ex-patients' efforts to establish their worth as normal human beings, they are greatly in need of the affection and respect of normal persons. Through these affectionate responses, the ex-patient is better able to regard himself as a worthwhile person. In order to convey affection without seeming to be patronizing, the normal benefactor must be highly sensitive to the ex-patients' need for self-respect. As the preceding material should have made clear, most of the benefactors are very successful in providing affection *with* respect. The following exchange is characteristic:

(Benefactor, an employer) "Hi, Bertha, you're looking real pretty today." (Bertha, blushing happily) "Oh, you're always talking that way to the girls, I betcha." (Benefactor, smiling and walking away) "You know that's not so, Bertha. You're my girl. You look very nice today, pretty as a picture, in fact." (Bertha, to a researcher who had overheard the conversation) "He is so nice. He always makes me feel like I'm appreciated. He really is the nicest man. I'm always happy when I'm around him, because I know he likes me." Later, the benefactor made this comment to the researcher:

Sometimes, it's pathetic the way these retarded people eat up anything nice you say about them. They're like puppy dogs. They'll lap up affection as long as you can give it out. I've had half a dozen of these Pacific people work for me over the years, and they've all had such a need to be loved—I guess you could say—that it's hard to deal with them. You've got to give them attention and affection every minute or you disappoint them terribly. It's the price you've got to pay if you're going to have them around. You've got to give them love every minute and you've got to mean it. I can do it because I do like them and they know it.

Who Are the Benefactors?

It is clear that benefactors aid the ex-patients in several ways and that their aid is important. But who are these persons and why do they give their aid? At the time of the study there were fifty-one persons who were regularly and frequently giving assistance to the ex-patients. These fifty-one, then, stand in an established benefactor relationship. Thirty of them are female, twenty-one are male.

Of the female benefactors nine are employers, five are landladies, four are social workers, three are neighbors, three are sisters, three are mothers, two are stepmothers, and one is a wife. Of the males, eleven are husbands, three are employers, two are roommates, three are stepfathers, one is a lover, and one is a doctor. The mean age of the women is forty-seven; of the men, it is thirty-eight. Sixteen of the women and four of the men were known to have had prior experience with persons who were mentally ill or mentally retarded.

The question of the motivation of these benefactors is extremely difficult to answer. Between the extremes of crass exploitation and perfect altruism lie innumerable intermediate motivations, all of which are difficult to assess. The benefactors were asked about their reasons for befriending and aiding the ex-patients, but their answers were by no means either clearly or candidly phrased. When queried about their motivations for serving as benefactors, the benefactors regularly phrased their answers in terms of one or another altruistic purpose. Searching cross-examination was out of the question. However, some measure of the accuracy of their claimed motivation may be had by examining what is known of their actual conduct. Twelve of the benefactors are employers working in sanitariums or restaurants that regularly recruit employees from State hospital dischargees. Indeed, many of these places are licensed and supervised by the State. All of these employers have good practical reasons for attempting to stabilize their employees and maximize their work potential (e.g., they are very low-cost workers); but in addition, all these employers went beyond such obvious practical needs by becoming truly concerned and sympathetic benefactors. Without exception these employers showed a high degree of altruistic concern for their retarded employees.

Thirteen of the benefactors are spouses or lovers. Here, too, the motivation and necessity for benefaction can be inferred from actual conduct. Several of the eleven husbands involved admitted directly or indirectly that they were isolating or secluding their wives not simply to protect these women from public obloquy or derision but also to protect themselves from public disclosure that their wives were mentally retarded. Furthermore, most of these husbands appeared to enjoy their extremely dominant relationship with their retarded wives. Hence, it seems fair to conclude that while the motivation of the spouse-benefactor is always mixed, it is not simply altruistic.

Ten benefactors are close relatives. Here the motivations vary still more widely—from strong affectionate concern on the part of some, to a transparent desire to degrade, control, and reject in at least one case. Such variability was noted that it is impossible to characterize either the ostensible or the "real" reasons why those close relatives become benefactors.

Ten benefactors are neighbors or landladies. All the benefactors in this category are women. For the most part, these women appear to have a profound and selfless interest in the welfare of persons whom they perceive as being desperately in need of their help. In only two instances did it appear that a neighbor or landlady was exploiting an ex-patient. Five benefactors are professionals. Their "reasons" for becoming benefactors, however, always transcended professional duty. None was even remotely required to act as he or she did; each one had a sincere personal interest in the well-being of the ex-patient that somehow made the sacrifice of time, effort, and money worthwhile.

In conclusion, while it is clear enough that a few of the benefactors maintained basically exploitative motives for their benefactions (e.g., the controlling parent, the *quid pro quo* landlady, the self-protective husband, the neighbor who enjoyed psychological dominance), and perhaps all incorporated a modicum of such feeling into their reasons for acting, nonetheless, most of these persons appear to have acted out of motives that were predominantly compassionate.

If it is not obvious why the benefactors acted as they did, it is certainly clear that their aid is important. They assist with the practical problems of coping as well as with the highly delicate matters of passing and denial. In all three areas they did yeoman service. Few of the ex-patients—perhaps three, and at the very most ten—could cope with everyday life adequately without the aid of a benefactor. It is impossible to measure the importance of the benefactors' contributions to passing and denial, but it is certain that these contributions —especially toward effective denial—are important. It would not be an exaggeration to conclude that, in general, the ex-patient succeeds in his efforts to sustain a life in the community only as well as he succeeds in locating and holding a benefactor.

Since much of the activity of the benefactors is secretive, the benefactors' role might even be thought of as a conspiracy. If so, it is indeed a benevolent conspiracy.

CHAPTER SIX

Stigma and the Cloak
of Competence

The foregoing has been an attempt to provide an accumulation of detail about the lives of some former patients of a hospital for the mentally retarded. This presentation is unique in the extent to which it documents the everyday lives of mentally retarded persons who have been released from an institution to make their lives in the outside world, and, consequently, it is intended to make a substantive contribution to the sociology of mental retardation. But beyond its possible merits as a description of the lives of such folk, it is also intended to be a study of a stigma, a stigma which galvanizes the most basic feelings of these retarded persons into a single-minded effort to "pass" and to "deny." The character of this stigma and its impact upon the lives of these ex-patients is of such central importance that it requires further attention.

To find oneself regarded as a mental retardate is to be burdened by a shattering stigma. Indeed, for the former patient, to be labeled as a mental retardate is the ultimate horror. They reject it with all their will. Their own words best indicate how the stigma weighs upon them.

(A woman) When I got out of that place it was horrible. I knew everybody was looking at me and thinking that it was true what they thought I was. I couldn't stand for people to think that about me. That's a terrible thing for people to think. Nobody could stand to have people thinking about them like that. That's why I started to take dope (heroin). I used to cry all the time because of what people were thinking about me, so my friend gave me this dope and said it would make me feel better. It did, too. I didn't worry about nothing while I was on. But that's the reason I started taking it—nobody could stand what those people were thinking.

(A man) When I was in the colony I was always worried. I'll admit it. You know, I was worried did they really think I was like them others. The ones that couldn't do nothing or learn nothing. I used to think that I'd rather be dead than be like them. I found out OK that nobody thought I was really like them others. I wasn't no mental problem or nothing like them others. If I was like them others, God, I would have really killed myself. Anything's better than that. Having no mind and not being able to think or understand nothing. God, that's really the worst thing.

(A man) I don't believe that anyone from the hospital has it easy outside. There's problems from being in that place. I mean with people you meet. They take me as if I'm not a smart person. That's what makes me so provoked. And I mean they act like I don't understand things, which I do understand things. That's a terrible thing; I'd never do that to anybody. I don't know why I have to suffer like this. Sometimes I'd rather be dead than have people act like I'm not a smart person.

(A woman) I don't even want to think about that colony. Some of the people there was so odd, I don't know why. And I used to wonder, God, if I stay here any longer I'm gonna turn out the same way. That used to scare me. When the doctor sent me here I guess he thought I was mentally unbalanced, but in my part I don't think I was. Afterward I seen that I don't think I was. And that's what bothers me. Why does everything happen to me? Why did I have to go to that place? Sometimes I go to the father, but all he does is tell me to pray. The worst thing is always trying to hide it from everybody. I just don't want nobody to know I was in that mental State hospital. I'm ashamed of it. Maybe it wasn't my fault for being there but I'm ashamed that I was ever there. I pray all right. I pray that nobody will ever find out about me.

Words to the same effect were uttered by all but a few of the former patients in this study. For all of these persons, an admission of mental retardation is unacceptable—totally and without exception. As chapter 4 emphasized, the ex-patients explain neither their past institutional confinement nor their current incompetence in the community in terms of their own stupidity. They employ almost any other excuse, from epilepsy to "craziness"—excuses that are themselves highly stigmatizing. Never is mental retardation admitted.

The reasons why mental retardation should be so thoroughly unacceptable cannot be determined here, nor are these reasons explained elsewhere in the literature dealing with mental retardation or with stigma. It may be that any stigmatized person prefers to verbalize some stigma other than the one which he actually bears. However, one might speculate that no other stigma is as basic as mental retardation in the sense that a person so labeled is thought to be so completely lacking in basic competence. Other stigmatized persons typically retain some competencies, limited though they may be, but the retarded person has none left to him. He is, by definition, incompetent to manage *any* of his affairs. And, unlike the psychotic, who at times may be considered (and, in fact, may be) competent to manage his practical affairs, the mental retardate is *forever* doomed to his condition. As everyone "knows," including the ex-patients, mental retardation is irremediable. There is no cure, no hope, no future. If you are once a mental retardate, you remain one always.[1]

Whatever the reasons, self-knowledge of mental retardation is totally unacceptable to these ex-patients. These persons cannot both believe that they are mentally retarded and still maintain their self-esteem. Yet they must maintain self-esteem. Clearly, then, passing and denial are vital. This point is critical, for the stigma of mental retardation dominates every feature of the lives of these former patients. Without an understanding of this point, there can be no understanding of their lives.

In his book *Stigma* (1963), Erving Goffman has discussed several varieties of stigmata and the ways in which "blemished" people attempt to contend with their particular stigma. As Goffman's insightful discussion indicates, many stigmata are painfully discrediting, but others are somewhat less serious, and a few can even be joked about. No one whose stigma is mental retardation jokes about it. For the accused or suspected mental retardate, passing and denial are as much a life and death matter as are the deceptions of a spy behind enemy lines.

But if the need for passing and denial is great for these ex-patients, their chances of successful deception are correspondingly good. This, of course, is a result of the availability of an all-purpose excuse—the depriving experience of being in Pacific State Hospital—and the collaboration of normal benefactors.

The problem that the mentally retarded face in avoiding their stigma is unique in another way. Their efforts to evade the stigma

1. There are a few exceptions. Some conditions, such as phenylketonuria, may respond to treatment, but in the main, "cures" for mental retardation do not exist.

through the deceptions of passing and denial must proceed despite their defective brains. Students of passing usually assume that the passers, no matter how horrendous their stigma, nonetheless have adequate intelligence. The mentally retarded must provide a practical solution to their problems, even though they have already been adjudged incompetent to manage their ordinary affairs. As an inevitable consequence, their efforts to deal with their stigma are limited.

There is also a paradox about their efforts to maintain themselves that is for them not a paradox at all. The paradox lies in the contrast between their often ingenious and always strenuous efforts to pass and to deny on the one hand, and their compliant dependency upon normal benefactors on the other. For them, however, such a commingling of opposites is not paradoxical; they find it natural to seek and accept help wherever they can find it. They tend to look upon help as a right which is due them as a partial recompense for their past wrongful institutional confinement.

It should also be pointed out that it is misleading to attempt to bring the lives of these retarded persons into the perspective of "social deviance." These former patients are not social deviants who have rejected the normative expectations of the "outside," normal world. They espouse no counter-morality. Quite the contrary, their every effort is directed toward effecting a legitimate entry into the "outside" world. To do so they will lie and cheat, but they practice their deceptions in order to claim a place in the "normal" world, not to deviate from it. Their behavior, in fact, represents the very antithesis of social deviance.

Implications for Institution Programming

Institutional treatment for the mentally retarded is more than a century old in this country, but the beginnings of active social concern over the care and treatment of the mentally retarded occurred in France and Switzerland in the early decades of the nineteenth century. Much of the impetus for this concern derived from the work of Edouard Seguin and Jean Itard. The latter's work with his "wild boy," Victor of Aveyron, was particularly influential. The first actual institution to be devoted to the care and treatment of the mentally retarded was established in 1839 by a Swiss physician, Johann Guggenbühl. Guggenbühl's interest in mental retardation was piqued by his chance encounter with a cretin boy who was attempting to recite the Lord's Prayer before a wayside cross. Guggenbühl was greatly affected by this meeting, and thereafter he devoted himself to the treatment of cretins. Although his efforts to find a "cure" for the condition failed, he succeeded in establishing a residential treatment institution at Abendberg in Switzerland. This facility influenced many persons who were later to work with the mentally retarded, among them Dr. Samuel Howe who, in 1848, established the first institution for the retarded in the United States. By 1917, all but four States in America had publicly supported residential institutions for the care of the mentally retarded (Kanner, 1964).

The early advocates of institutional care for the retarded based their plea for institutional facilities upon deeply felt humanitarian beliefs which were often buttressed by religious conviction. By the end of the nineteenth century, however, both public and professional concern had shifted, from a desire to protect the retarded against society, to a determination to protect society against the retarded. The mentally retarded were portrayed as a malignant menace to society, as undesirables with a record of limitless crime, hopeless poverty, loathsome disease, moral degeneracy, and sexual promiscuity. The threat of the retarded, it was argued, could not be tolerated, and various programs were begun to limit the "breeding" of these persons. Vigorous programs of eugenic sterilization were one answer; another was an increased emphasis upon custodial confinement of the retarded, especially the mildly retarded, who were commonly thought to constitute the greatest danger to society.

Following the Second World War, the custodial period finally gave way to a renewed therapeutic interest in residential institutions. "Colonies," "schools," and "villages" became hospitals in which therapy dominated custody. Government funds were made available for research and treatment, and facilities grew and improved dramatically. Today, the many excellent State institutions for the mentally retarded are staffed by competent and sympathetic professionals.

However, almost without exception, these institutions for the retarded are crowded far beyond their present, or their projected capacities. There are only some 200,000 beds available in the 124 State-supported residential facilities for the retarded in the United States (Stevens and Heber, 1964). This means that at any given time, approximately 96 percent of the mental retardates in the United States cannot find space in public institutions.

Furthermore, mildly retarded patients such as those described in this research are becoming less and less a part of the hospital scene in this country. The trend is everywhere toward the preferred institutionalization of younger, more severely retarded patients, and as these more retarded persons begin to take up the available hospital beds, there is the inevitable need to move the mildly retarded patients from hospitals into community-based programs. This is the trend at Pacific State Hospital and at most of the large public institutions. Despite all such plans to remove the mildly retarded from institutional care, large numbers of these patients still remain within the large State institutions, and will probably continue to do so for much longer than administrators will find convenient. But whether the mildly retarded continue to occupy hospitals for some time, or their supervision rapidly becomes the burden of community officials, the problems of preparing these patients for a relatively independent life in the community must ultimately be faced.

The population of mildly retarded ex-patients from which I generalize in this research may be somewhat different from other populations of mildly retarded persons in other parts of the country. For one thing, this research cohort is somewhat higher in IQ than might be expected; for another, their careers before and after institutionalization are colored by life conditions in Los Angeles; and obviously all are affected by their experiences within Pacific State Hospital. Nonetheless, I feel that some broad general statements are both possible, and necessary.

It should be obvious to any reader of the foregoing pages that the experiences of these ex-patients at Pacific State Hospital did not equip them for life in the community as fully as they, the ex-patients, or we, the judges, might have hoped. It is abundantly clear that their training concerning money, time, work attitudes, transportation, and frustration tolerance—to mention but a few areas—was deficient. I should hastily add that such deficiencies are not limited to Pacific, where standards of care are high and the staff exceptionally competent. Furthermore, since the results of this research were reported to them in 1961, the officials at Pacific have made noteworthy changes in all these areas. But even if such programs were not already underway, they would not be difficult to develop. There would always be problems, of course, not the least of which would involve money, staff time, and criteria by which patients would be included in such a training program, but all of these problems are susceptible to administrative solution, and in many institutions around the country these problems are already being solved. The point to be made here—the critical point—involves the importance of stigma for any hospital or community program that is concerned with the training or treatment of the mildly mentally retarded.

Let me take one example. Traditional psychotherapy attempts to increase the patient's "insight" into his affliction so that he may learn to accept his "problem" and either overcome it or learn to live with it more realistically. However, when this same approach is taken with the mentally retarded, when the therapist asks *them* to accept their handicap and thus learn better to live with it, he is asking the impossible. He will surely encounter firm resistance from his retarded patient. He may meet with outright rejection, because for the mildly retarded, acceptance of their affliction is intolerable. The stigma is too great, too global, and too self-destructive. Acceptance of this affliction is incompatible with self-esteem, thus should acceptance occur, the prospect of independent community life is thereby rendered difficult, and perhaps impossible.

Institutions, therefore, not only must deal with the need of their mildly retarded patients for increased social competence, but they must also attempt to devise means for patients to deal with stigma. This will be difficult, far more difficult than the development of more customary training programs. The first step may be to forgo any efforts—therapeutic or otherwise—to convince these patients that they are in fact mentally retarded. What is needed is a stigma-free explanation that helps the retarded person to explain his relative incompetence without suggesting that his affliction is one of basic and ineradicable stupidity.

Another explanation, another word, must be found, and the word must avoid the stigma. Call the condition an "adjustment deficiency" or "educational deprivation," or provide a medical neologism. Whatever the euphemism, it must suggest that the affliction is a partial one—not an all-encompassing "mental" deficit—and that it is amenable to treatment and training. If a non-stigmatizing label can be found which can be employed consistently, then it may be possible to enlist the mildly retarded as willing participants in their own improvement. It may then be possible to deal directly with the specific behavioral incompetencies or emotional problems that each patient manifests, not merely as manifestations of a basic, global, macro-disorder called mental retardation, but as separable and partial problems that can be dealt with as such.

Perhaps no such solution is possible. Perhaps our current practices are too firmly entrenched. Perhaps our goals are not sufficiently well defined. But if our goal is for mildly mentally retarded persons to live as independently as possible, then some new steps are called for. Perhaps part of the solution may lie in abandoning the mental-medical-psychological mold into which mild mental retardation is now cast, for another more purely behavioral idiom. Then we might phrase all institutional treatment for the "behavioral" problem as "education," rather than as "treatment" for an untreatable "mental" disorder. But whatever the solution, if there is one, we must recognize that if we wish the mildly retarded to live outside of institutions in a largely independent way, then we must understand and deal with the stigma that they now face.

Even beyond this, we must recognize these ex-patients' exaggerated need for affection and for confirmation of their own self-worth. In all the material presented in this study we have seen the ex-patients' efforts—not simply to pass with other people, nor to deny to themselves that they are retarded, but more than this—to establish some personal worth in their own right. In guarding their fragile self-esteem, they seek evidence that normal persons think well of them, regard them with affection, and accept them as worthwhile human beings.

Walter Goldschmidt (1959) has argued that mankind universally has a "need for positive affect." The ex-patients in this study surely have such a need, an intense one. They cry out for the understanding, acceptance, and love of normal persons, and the receiving of such positive affect from others is essential to their self-esteem. Too often, however, the ex-patients' efforts to win approval are so clumsy and inappropriate that they drive away those who are kindly disposed toward them. We must understand that their need for positive affect is a basic one, not simply in some romantic utopia, but in our plans for equipping these patients for community living.

Their need for affection is a fundamental need. The means by which the patients might better satisfy this need are not as impossible of fulfillment as one might think. In seeking positive response from normal persons, much of the ex-patients' success depends upon appropriate grooming, dress, posture, facial expression, speech, and emotionality. Appropriate display of behavior of these kinds can to a great degree be taught directly within institutions. The more subtle modes of communication, incompetence in which deprives the ex-patients of positive affect, are more difficult to teach directly, but they can be learned, especially in the give-and-take of peer-group relations. As I have attempted to show elsewhere (Edgerton, 1963), such peer-group relations can be made available by permitting patients to interact frequently under conditions of minimal supervision. These experiences provide for the free expression and development of the subtle, social manipulations so essential for the understanding, and the internalization, of the rules for acceptable social conduct.

What I would urge, what I think the evidence points to, is a greater awareness of the impact of the stigma of mental retardation upon mildly retarded persons. This impact creates acute needs for passing, denial, and approval. If the mildly retarded are to be prepared for community living, then means for easing this burden must be found.

The Nature of Their Incompetence

What, if anything, can be concluded about the nature of the incompetence that these former patients display? In his discussion of stigma, Goffman refers to two important features: "evidentness" and "obtrusiveness."[2] The first of these—"evidentness" or "know-about-ness"—refers to how visible the stigma is, how easily it can be recognized. The incompetence of these former patients should not be particularly evident, at least not "at a glance." Their physical appearance is not distinctive and they appear to be able to move through most public places without revealing any tell-tale signs of their stigma. In this sense, then, their incompetence is not "evident." They remain "unknown about" in most of their superficial, casual, and brief appearances in the normal world. However, they do not escape detection when their public exposure becomes face-to-face, when it is prolonged, or when they must deal with problematic social

2. Goffman (1963). See especially pp. 48–49.

situations. In such instances the former patient is found out; his incompetence becomes quite evident.

Once this incompetence is recognized, it becomes obtrusive in Goffman's sense of interfering with the flow of interaction.[3] It almost inevitably results in reduction of all subsequent interaction to a less complex level than the normal person would otherwise have attempted. For example, the normal person who becomes aware of the incompetence of the former patient regularly switches his mode of speech to a condescending tone and a simplified content. The normal person "talks down" and sometimes even attempts a form of "baby talk" as might a colonial Englishman in talking to "native" servants.[4] There is also a tendency for the normal person to speak both more slowly and more loudly than he ordinarily would. Interaction is reduced to a plane upon which the normal person asks few questions, utilizes the simplest possible vocabulary, avoids complexities of humor, and assumes that the former patient has almost no knowledge of what is commonplace, much less what is intricate, in the world. Furthermore, since the normal person generally wishes not to embarrass the retardate, he exercises conspicuous tact. The result is a slowing down of interaction to the point of virtual cessation.

Another question concerns the magnitude of their disability. How great is their incompetence? It is possible to argue—as many have done—that the incompetence of the mildly retarded is of a special and partial sort; that it is limited to certain "intellectual" deficits. The evidence of this study would agree that the most conspicuous incompetence of these former patients occurs where space and time, and the numbers that relate to these matters, are concerned. As was demonstrated again and again in the course of this study, the ex-patients were most incompetent when required to deal with spatial, temporal, and numerical relationships.

Such relationships have often been considered uniquely "abstract" or "intellectual." Indeed, more than one philosopher has regarded them as *the* uniquely human attributes. That the incompetence of these retarded persons is most apparent in these "intellectual" areas leads to the conclusion that their deficit is truly a partial and limited one—a lack of intellectual competence, not a lack of social compe-

3. *Ibid.*, p. 49.
4. Edgerton (1965).

tence. In fact, however, for the ex-patient in this study, any distinction between "intellectual" and "social" competence is factitious. In the course of these ex-patients' everyday lives, the two competencies—intellectual and social—cannot be separated. Space, time, and number ineluctably intrude themselves into the everyday lives of these former patients. As Cassirer (1944) has argued, there is no escaping the demands of space, time, and number; the very language of everyday life requires that these factors be dealt with and dealt with competently. Much of the deficit in verbal skill that these former patients display is directly a result of their inability to bring a minimal control over spatial, temporal, and numerical concepts into their everyday language. So omnipresent is the sway of these three "intellectual" factors that competence in space, time, and number becomes "social" competence. It is in this sense that we must evaluate the words of the ex-patient quoted in chapter 4: "Most of us people that was at the colony just can't figure. . . . Outside you gotta learn to figure or you'll go down the old pot. Seems like most of us go down the pot."

Thus it would be more accurate to speak of the disability of these former patients as basic and inclusive rather than partial and intellectual. Their lives are suffused by displays of incompetence; that this incompetence tends to cluster around the central concern over space, time, and number, makes its magnitude no less great, and its effect no less general. These former patients do some things quite adequately, but in critical everyday demands of life, as well as at crisis points, they fail.

The Cloak of Competence

The ex-patients usually fail in their attempts to cope with the exigencies of everyday life; it would appear that, with a few exceptions, they would not be able to maintain themselves in the outside community without the assistance of normal benefactors. They usually fail to pass as well. They are often surprisingly clever in their techniques of passing and they are always dogged in their efforts. Nonetheless, they are successful in deceiving relatively few people, and they deceive these only if the ex-patients' exposure before them is brief and superficial. The normal persons with whom these former patients regularly come into contact typically "know" that the former patients are mentally deficient. Their words in this regard permit no doubt of that. But in what I have termed a benevolent conspiracy, normal persons not only avoid humiliating these retarded persons by failing to disclose that they are aware of the source of their incompetence, but they also actually help them to pass with others who may not be aware.

Thus the ex-patient is able to maintain his self-esteem by denying that his incompetence is "what it appears to be," and the masquerade continues. The masquerade is able to proceed only through the connivance of normal persons in the outside world. It would almost appear that these incompetent persons have been given a niche (earlier reserved for the "village idiot") in which they are permitted to live incompetently as long as in the course of this living they do not cause the wrong persons too much trouble. At the very least, normal persons exhibit great sympathy and tolerance for these former patients; perhaps normal persons see too clearly in them what they fear for themselves or for their children.

So the desperate search for self-esteem continues. The ex-patients strive to cover themselves with a protective cloak of competence. To their own satisfaction they manage to locate such coverings, but the cloaks that they think protect them are in reality such tattered and transparent garments that they reveal their wearers in all their naked incompetence. In a sense, these retarded persons are like the emperor in the fairy tale who thought he was wearing the most elegant garments but, in fact, was wearing nothing at all.

Conclusion

Both incompetence and stigma management are ubiquitous features of any society, for societies cannot fail to be concerned with the incompetence of their members.[5] Neither can they fail to inflict stigma upon certain, if not all, of their incompetents. Hence, some people in all societies must be both incompetent and

---

5. Goffman (1963) has given full recognition to this point. See especially p. 130.

stigmatized. The mentally retarded must very often, perhaps always, find themselves in this predicament.

In the efforts of the former patients in the present study to evade the stigma that they feel and fear, we see an eloquent testament to man's determination to maintain his self-esteem in the face of overwhelming cultural rejection and deprecation. If we accept the unanimous findings of the behavioral and psychological sciences concerning the fundamental importance of self-esteem for any human being, then we can understand the dilemma in which these former patients find themselves, and we can appreciate their achievement in finding what is for them a cloak of competence.

The most fitting epilogue for this discussion is found in the plaintive yet defiant words of one of these retarded persons: *"I've got a tendency of an ailment but it isn't what it seems."*

CHAPTER SEVEN

The Follow-up Studies

Beginning in 1972, the first systematic follow-up study of the former patients from the original "Cloak of Competence" sample was initiated. With the assistance of a senior research associate and several anthropology graduate students I began an effort to contact all forty-eight of the sample members. Over the more than a decade since the original study had been terminated, I had maintained contact with ten or eleven of the sample members but had lost touch with the others, many of whom had moved or changed jobs. By 1972, government agencies and public utilities were no longer willing to risk violating the privacy of individuals by releasing any information they might have about their whereabouts. As a result, it was not possible to locate everyone. Despite our best efforts, we were unable to collect meaningful information from eighteen persons; and therefore we have data for thirty persons, fifteen men and fifteen women. There were no statistically significant differences between the thirty people we located and the eighteen whom we did not in terms of their IQ, age, ethnicity, length of hospitalization, reliance on welfare payments, or degree of independence. Of course, there may have been other differences that we could not measure. I concluded at the time that these thirty people were probably not meaningfully different from the original forty-eight, but this is still impossible to confirm. For example, we still do not know whether those we could not find had become more independent and successful and therefore moved away to better housing or a better job, or whether they could not be located because their lives had worsened.

My associates and I collected data from these thirty people throughout 1973 (at that time, funding was exhausted and an opportunity to begin research with another, younger, and never-institutionalized sample of mildly retarded people materialized). By the end of 1973 we had managed to collect a substantial amount of information from all thirty persons. As in the 1960–1961 study, we relied on participant-observation rather than direct questioning and tried to spend time with these people in all but the most intimate and private domains of their lives. Despite the richness of the data we collected, it was quite clear that we had not gotten to the bottom of their lives. New and surprising information continued to surface even late in 1973 although with less frequency than earlier in the study. Although we recognized that there was much we did not know about these people, we concluded nevertheless that we had learned enough to make it worthwhile to report our findings, which was done in 1976 (Edgerton and Bercovici, 1976).

The first question we tried to answer was whether these individuals' lives had changed for the better or the worse. In an attempt to find the answer to this I asked two of my associates who had read all the material we recorded on each sample member to join me in rating their overall community adjustment as "better," "the same," or "worse." We agreed to make these judgments in terms of our global interpretation of the general quality of their lives as reflected in their relative independence, social competence, economic security, health, absence of antisocial behavior, enjoyment of leisure-time activities, presence of meaningful social relationships, sexual and marital adjustment, feelings of stigma, and other intuitive criteria that no doubt varied among the three raters. To my surprise, the percentage of agreement among the three raters was over 90 percent. We concluded that ten of the sample members had seen the quality of their lives worsen, twelve were very much the same, and another eight had experienced an improvement in the quality of their community adaptation.

Before the 1972–1973 research follow-up was begun, I had made systematic predictions about which members of the sample we would find to have improved, which would have remained stable, and which would have experienced a decline in the quality of their lives. After the research was completed and our ratings had been made, it was found that my predictions had been wrong somewhat more than half the time and even when my predictions proved to be in the right direction, they were often correct for the wrong reasons. In short, for the most part, my predictions were worthless. To be sure, it was not difficult to predict what was likely to happen to some of these people. For example, in 1960–1961, one man (John, no. 17, then aged thirty-nine) was often so floridly psychotic that it was difficult to imagine how the quality of his life could be expected to improve. In fact, after several short-term stays in mental hospitals, John accidentally hanged himself while masturbating, leaving behind clear evidence of his fascination with bondage. Agnes (no. 30, then aged sixty-six, IQ 47) was rated the least independent member of the sample in 1960–1961 because she was wholly dependent on a relative. Because this relative was dedicated to Agnes's care and was relatively healthy and affluent, it was not difficult to predict that Agnes's life would have changed little, and so it proved to be.

But other predictions were wildly wrong. For instance, Hal (no. 2a, then aged forty-nine, IQ 82) was a very competent member of the sample; indeed he was probably wrongly diagnosed as being mentally retarded, a phenomenon I will discuss further in the next chapter. However, he had an explosive temper and was by all accounts, including his own, not unwilling to use physical violence. This proclivity, combined with the fact that he often quarreled with his wife (another member of the sample) and worked very long, hard hours in a foundry in return for little salary, led me to predict that by 1972 he would either have lost his job or committed a seriously violent offense, or both. In reality, 1972 found him at work at exactly the same job and he had committed no offense, violent or otherwise. The only change in his life was that his wife and he had amicably separated. Another unpredictable outcome involved Bertha (no. 22b, then aged thirty-eight, IQ 57) who in 1960–1961 was heavily dependent on her older, more intelligent husband. I predicted that as long as they were married and he was healthy there would be no change in Bertha's life; were he to suffer a serious health problem or should they divorce, I predicted that her life would take a major turn for the worse. In 1967, Bertha's husband died of a heart attack. Instead of retreating into greater dependency and incompetence, Bertha immediately found a job as a maid that fully supported her financial needs, developed rewarding leisure activities, and was feeling so positive about herself that she was considering remarriage, not because she needed the man's support but because she was fond of him.

Now you may well conclude that I am simply hopelessly inept when it comes to predicting the course of human lives, and I would be inclined to agree. But there is a good reason why you should not dismiss the significance of my errant judgments completely. I would contend that prediction was difficult because the lives of many persons in this sample were marked by major fluctuations, both positive and negative in their consequences. There is some research with other populations of people with mental retardation that suggests the lives of such individuals are indeed more volatile than those of nonretarded comparison populations (Cobb, 1972). In my experience, this finding is probably correct because people with mental retardation who live largely independent lives in community settings lack access to reliable resources or support systems that are capable of stabilizing them in times of crisis. Typically, these people lack networks of concerned and capable friends or relatives, have little job security, no savings, no credit, no health insurance, and few marketable skills. As a result, when a crisis occurs—the loss of a job or benefactor, the death of a spouse or loved one—the affected person may quite literally be left without a place to live or food to eat. But conversely, good fortune in the form of a new benefactor or eligibility for welfare may rapidly restore a more positive level of adaptation. Therefore, it would appear that persons such as these often live more changeable and unpredictable lives than do people who are stabilized by job security, savings accounts, health insurance, and networks of kin or friends who can provide support.

Another reason for my failure to predict more accurately had to do with the power of dependent role relationships to mask a person's true social competence. That is to say, some people appear to be much less competent than they actually are. For example, since 1960–1961, four women lost their husbands to death or divorce. All of these women had been markedly dependent on their spouses when we studied them in 1960–1961 and although I was keenly aware of the capacity of relationships such as these to create learned helplessness in the dependent person, I nevertheless predicted that these women would have difficulty coping if their spouses were lost. Instead, with the assistance of welfare payments, all four women achieved a substantially improved quality of life in which they appeared to be more competent and confident than before. In retrospect, it is easy to say that this is what one would expect, but I did not expect it, and I doubt that few people who had seen these women in their earlier lives of dependency would have predicted it either. I am forced to conclude, and happily so, that many persons with mental retardation have personal resources that even intense and lasting participant-observation cannot readily detect.

The next issue concerned stigma and passing, matters which had so dominated their lives in 1960–1961. A decade later, it was clear that a sense of stigma and a felt need to pass as normal were no longer central concerns for most of these people. Only five of them continued to express pain and humiliation resulting from their past institutionalization; three of these individuals had nonretarded spouses from whom they were carefully guarding the secret of their past confinement. All the others, in one way or another, indicated that the issue was behind them, not completely forgotten to be sure, but not something that was very often on their minds. The tactics of passing that had been so commonplace among them ten years earlier were now seldom in evidence. However devastating the stigma of hospitalization and labeling had been earlier in their lives, these effects were not necessarily permanent.

A similar change had taken place with regard to benefactors. In 1960–1961 benefactors played a crucial role in helping most of the sample members to cope with crises as well as some routine aspects of life. Because judgments about a person's reliance on another can involve many subjective considerations, I asked another rater familiar with all the data (Sylvia Bercovici) independently to judge whether, compared to the period 1960–1961, each of the sample members was more, less, or equally dependent on one or more benefactors. With 95 percent agreement, she and I concluded that no one in the sample was more dependent in 1972–1973 than they had been a decade earlier, that eleven were dependent to the same degree, and that sixteen were less dependent. The evidence clearly indicates that the overall social competence of most sample members had risen over the years, making the need for benefactors less pressing. This same increase in the sample members' ability to master the demands of the social settings that they encountered no doubt also contributed to the reduction in their need to pass as normal. These individuals were not only many more years removed from the hospital experience, they were in fact socially far more normal.

The success of sample members in finding and holding jobs deserves special attention here. Recall that all persons in the original sample were released from the hospital only after they had demonstrated their ability to perform well in a vocational placement arranged by hospital authorities. Only after years of vocational success were they actually discharged from Pacific State Hospital. Whether as a result of this circumstance or simply because they shared the fundamental American belief that the ability to work was character defining, most sample members had a strong work ethic in 1960–1961. At that time, even the women, most of whom had married and dropped out of the work force, continued to express their conviction that their proven ability to work had stamped them with at least a veneer of virtue, and they continued to say that they could work again in the future if their spouses were to permit or encourage them to do so. During 1972–1973, only eight members of the sample were employed more or less full-time, while one woman was working part-time. Nine women and one man were married and supported by their spouses. The rest were unemployed. Five were receiving welfare payments, and an equal number relied on friends or relatives for their support. Even those individuals who had been continuously employed over the decade were making wages that were identical to or only slightly higher than they had made in 1960–1961. Because the Consumer Price Index had risen over 60 percent over this period, the loss in terms of real income was great.

Based on their employment history, it would appear that the sample members we located in 1972–1973 had undergone a major decline in the level of their community adaptation. However, as we have already noted, many were more independent, more competent socially, and were enjoying an improved quality of life. These considerations suggest that employment may not be the best criterion of success in community adaptation. One reason for this is the fact that for the women in this sample, marriage has been a more important goal than employment, and like many other American women at that time, they believed that being married exempted them from the need to work. For men, jobs were less readily available than they had been in 1960–1961, and welfare eligibility was more easily attained. What is more, several men in the sample were limited in their ability to work by chronic injury or illness. For example, three members of the sample died during the period of the 1972–1973 research, one was terminally ill, and nine others had major physical disabilities. No one in the sample was healthier than they had been a decade earlier. These persons often said that they could no longer be expected to work and that they deserved to be supported by "the welfare." Even those persons who continued to work full-time no longer commented on their ability to work as if it were a signal virtue. In 1972–1973, work was taken for granted, even grumbled about, as it was by many other Americans.

What these individuals told us in 1972–1973 and what we observed about their everyday activities made it abundantly plain that what mattered most to them was not stigma or passing, and not the ability to work, but the quality of their lives as it was reflected in leisure activities, social relationships, and meaningful interests in other people and the world around them. To confirm our impression, we asked each member of the sample to compare his or her life to a period "about ten years ago." Six people said they were less happy (all of these had major physical disabilities), seven said things were about the same, and twelve said that they were happier (one person could not decide). It is evident that being employed was not a prerequisite for happiness. When Bercovici and I commented about this issue in 1976, we wrote that at a time of high unemployment such as that which prevailed in the early 1970s, it might prove to be unwise for professionals who directed the lives of their clients living in community settings to continue to stress vocational success and the work ethic. The result, we believed, could be needlessly diminished self-esteem (Edgerton and Bercovici, 1976). We made these comments because it was apparent that the criteria of successful community adaptation then used by many professionals in the mental retardation service delivery system were not the same as those recognized by persons with mental retardation who had lived in the community for a number of years. Professionals tended to emphasize the development of social competence and independence, especially success in the workplace. Our sample members stressed personal satisfaction.

It was apparent from this research that the lives of many of the people in this sample fluctuated so markedly that unless investigators monitored these individuals frequently, it was very likely that they would reach invalid conclusions about the nature of the community adaptation they were attempting to assess. It was also clear that how persons with mild mental retardation evaluated their own lives often differed from the way we, and other outsiders, were likely to do so.

Our most fundamental conclusion was this: the lives of these people are complex and changeable; if we are to understand how they live and how they feel about themselves, we must avoid imposing our conceptions about appropriate social living on them and listen carefully to what they have to say to us about their own goals and values. The failure to do so will perpetuate a kind of imperialism in which "human service" professionals impose their values on the lives of handicapped people who, for better or worse, are determined and entitled to chart the course of their own lives.

The 1982 Follow-up

The next follow-up study took place ten years later. In 1982, my associates and I were able to locate twenty-one of the people whom we had restudied during 1972–1973 but four of them were living too far away to allow effective contact. The mean age of the remaining fifteen persons was 56, their mean IQ was 61.7. Seven of those restudied were women and eight were men. Although it is impossible to claim that these fifteen people are representative of the original forty-eight, they share some life experiences that may be typical of former patients their age who are living in the community.

After the intensive participant-observational research of 1972–1973 ended, sporadic contact was maintained with almost all of the sample members by telephone and an occasional visit. Those few who did not have telephones were difficult to stay in touch with but through cards or calls to relatives and friends it was usually possible to monitor at least the major events in their lives. By 1982, it was obvious that there had been enough changes in their lives to warrant another intensive follow-up study. Throughout that year, all fifteen persons were visited on a regular basis, and as in the earlier research, they were also taken grocery shopping, invited to restaurants for lunch or dinner, accompanied on errands, recreational activities, and many of the other routine and out-of-the-ordinary things that they did. Five of these people had led remarkably stable lives since 1973; these were not uneventful lives—far from it; but they were lives without dramatic changes. Conversely, one person's life was so much in flux that it was chaotic. For example, one person (Midge, no. 2b, then aged sixty, IQ 67) lost job after job as a cleaning woman and her relationships with men were just as unpredictable. She lived with one man for a time before he left her for another woman but invited her to join them in a menage-à-trois. She actually did so for awhile before striking up a new relationship with a man who eventually told her that he was gay and asked her to have a sex-change operation so that they could stay together. She declined. Perhaps as a result, she developed such severe bleeding ulcers that she qualified for both SSI and Medi-Cal (Medi-Care), which she soon lost because she did not understand the restrictions on additional income. She moved her residence so frequently that she referred to herself as being "just like a moving van, moving around." Fortunately, she had her elderly mother and older brother to rely on for housing and help when times became particularly trying, which they frequently did. Nevertheless, Midge was imperturbable. She was never depressed and never lost her self-confidence. As we shall soon see, these were qualities she shared with many others among these fifteen no-longer young people.

Three members of the sample had seen their lives improve quite visibly. All were single men who held full-time jobs. One man achieved virtual independence from his sometimes domineering mother, an achievement that greatly improved his self-esteem and probably contributed to his ability to be seen by his coworkers as a normal person. Two other men who had previously been quite heavy drinkers gave up alcohol on their own initiative and as a result their social relationships and their job performances improved. These success stories were balanced by the decline in life's quality for four other persons all of whom had experienced either a major loss of a benefactor or serious illness. Hal's (no. 2a) life had been surprisingly stable until a few years prior to 1982, when, at the age of sixty-one, he had lost his job, was severely incapacitated by very painful phlebitis, and was nearly destitute. Unable to qualify for SSI and too young for Social Security benefits, with no friends or relatives able to help him, he lived a hand-to-mouth existence. (As we'll see later, however, his life would soon take a turn for the better—yet another demonstration that life circumstances can change remarkably from one year, or even month, to the next.) Another man (Ricardo, no. 15, then aged sixty-eight, IQ 64) was unable to maintain his active life-style due to serious heart disease, which was soon after to lead to his death. Two other women experienced a significant drop in their standard of living as well as marked depression after their husbands died. Both were destined to recover remarkably. Soon after, this research period in 1982 ended.

Two other single women had also suffered major losses in their lives but their reactions were more complex. Lulu (no. 1, then aged fifty-two, IQ 48) had been inseparable from her nonretarded boyfriend for nine years. She had doted on him even though he was largely dependent on her. When he died in 1976, she gave up her full-time job and became dependent on her older sister. She also developed arthritis and sundry emotional complaints that led her sister to find a physician who made it possible for her to qualify for SSI. Until 1981, she adopted a sick role and became obese and depressed, but by 1982 she had lost weight, was cheerful and was looking for work and an apartment away from her sister. A final woman (Martha, no. 28, then aged sixty, IQ 72), who had always been the person in the sample most stigmatized by her hospitalization, had developed a strongly dependent relationship with a woman benefactor who died shortly before 1982. This death left Martha alone and frightened but instead of retreating into self-pitying solitude as I firmly expected, she sought out new relationships, began to work as a volunteer, and tried her best to make new friends and find a new benefactor. Sadly, her abrasive manner and her obvious desperation drove potential friends and benefactors away, but Martha continued to seek out a better life saying, " 'I want to take care of myself as long as I can and not get helpless, 'cause it's an awful thing to be helpless' " (Edgerton, Bollinger, and Herr, 1984:348).

Aside from Martha, the impact of hospitalization with its resulting stigma continued to weaken for the former patients. What is more, only two members of the sample were more dependent on a benefactor than they had been in 1972–1973. All the others were considerably less dependent. Indeed, it appeared that most of these people were no more dependent on other people or agencies for help than would be acceptable for nonretarded people of their age. As in 1972–1973, they continued to value those activities and relationships that gave them pleasure over the rewards of the workplace, and as their health worsened many were legitimately unable to work. Indeed, growing older paradoxically seemed to increase their self-esteem because their reference group now was other people of their age and declining health who were also unable to work and who were dependent on other people and agencies for assistance.

Of course, there are many ways in which all of these people differed one from the other, but they shared one dominant attribute—they were optimistic. All but one woman (Myrtle, no. 38) who was depressed (although in years to come, she too would feel more hopeful and happy), spoke and acted as if they believed that life in the future would be rewarding or more rewarding than it had been in the past, and they believed that their own actions would help to bring this to pass. However bad life might be at the moment, they indomitably believed that they would manage, and with very few exceptions they were right.

The 1985 Follow-Up

Intermittent contact with the surviving sample members continued after 1982 and by 1984 so many of these people had improved the quality of their lives that I felt it would be important once again to look carefully at this ongoing process of community adaptation. The new follow-up study began in 1985 with sufficiently generous funding to allow me to employ four research assistants with advanced degrees in anthropology, and, in most instances, previous research experience with persons with mental retardation. Two members of the 1982 sample had died before 1985 but three other former patients who were previously inaccessible were added to the sample, making a total of sixteen, including nine women and seven men. Their mean age in 1985 was fifty-nine and their mean IQ was 62. Thanks to my relatively abundant research resources, it was possible to contact the sample members as well as friends, spouses, relatives, employers, and other people who knew them with greater frequency than in any previous period of data collection. We maintained frequent contact and excellent rapport throughout the year. The resulting information was unusually detailed and complete.

The most compelling finding was that however much these people had shown themselves to be indomitable optimists in 1982, in 1985 their zest for life was even greater. It should be emphasized once again, that these sixteen people had very different talents, interests, and life circumstances. With one exception, they had no knowledge of one another's whereabouts, nor vivid memories of one another in the hospital. They were very much on their own. Where and how they lived, how they dressed and spoke, and what they found interesting in life was highly varied. Some were articulate, others spoke haltingly and stumbled over simple words. About half could neither read nor write, but many of the rest read well enough to keep up with current events. Their personalities differed tremendously as well. A few were lonely, but the majority had many personal relationships and these too were highly varied. What they had in common was their optimism and their remarkable self-reliance. Only one person had ever been dependent on SSI for her entire income, whereas two others supplemented their SSI benefits with earnings from part-time jobs. Hal (no. 2a) had turned sixty-five and was now receiving Social Security benefits, and another woman would soon do so as well; but both had worked full-time for most of their lives. Seven people were still working full-time (four men and three women), and another man had recently retired with a pension after spending thirty-one years on the same job. Four others worked part-time, and even the two women in the sample who were supported by their husbands contributed time as volunteers to church and other service organizations. Only one person now relied on a benefactor, and this would prove to be a temporary involvement following the death of this woman's husband. The remainder of the sample had no reliance on benefactors. Indeed, four men now frequently acted as benefactors toward nonretarded friends to whom they gave money, good advice, and emotional support without any expectation of reciprocity.

This raises an important point. Everyone in this sample, even the most isolated and dependent person, had some meaningful relationships with other people, most of whom were not mentally retarded. With one exception, everyone else had at least one important, long-term sexual relationship in addition to other friendships. It is impossible to convey the quality of these relationships in a few words but it was impressively obvious that these people were now, after so many years of living on their own, deeply embedded in reciprocal relationships with people who were never, as far as I know, labeled mentally retarded. These relationships were hardly idyllic, they included tension, argumentation, and quarreling, but they were also marked by affection, concern, and shared involvement in various activities of interest to both parties. No longer were these people the incompetent and dependent recipients of help from cognitively more competent people. Beyond any reasonable doubt, they were people who gave as much to others as they received in return. And this reality, perhaps beyond any other, gave their lives a legitimacy and a fulfillment that nothing else could provide and that few could have predicted in 1960.

It is also important to note that their social competence improved more dramatically in the latter stages of their lives than at any time before. No doubt this transformation was due at least in part to the fact that compared to nonretarded people of the same age and socioeconomic status, they had done relatively well, but beyond that we have the cumulative record of lives that over time have become progressively more satisfying, more secure, and more independent. Although most of these sixteen people had a shaky start in adapting to the demands of life outside the hospital, by now all demonstrated impressive mastery over the residential, vocational, and public settings in which they spent their time. A few may have run short of money at the end of the month, so the rent may have been late or the meals spartan, but there was no serious deprivation. Their living quarters were often cluttered but with one exception, they were not dirty. Their leisure time was seldom spent passively watching television. More typically they chatted with someone in person or on the telephone, played cards, pursued a hobby, or listened to music. They were all comfortable and appropriate on buses, in shopping malls, coffee shops, bowling alleys, swap meets, parks, and other public places.

Of course, their lives were not entirely trouble-free. On occasions, some novel circumstance would leave them perplexed and worried, and sometimes their needs went unmet. One of the greatest problems for them was finding affordable health care. With the exception of one woman, none of these sixteen people had a personal physician. Instead, they had to rely on clinics that treated Medi-Cal patients, county hospitals, or HMOs. Such facilities were often so difficult to reach without a car that the former patients chose to do without health care. When they felt compelled to seek health care, they often had difficulty tolerating the long periods spent in waiting rooms, had trouble explaining their symptoms, and did not fully understand the health professionals' vocabularies so that they often did not adequately comply with their instructions. Pharmacists' prescriptions, too, were problematic because they presupposed literacy. As a result, the sample members often took medication inappropriately, failed to follow dietary restrictions, and did not exercise or rest as directed. Another source of puzzlement for most of these people was the large bureaucracies with which they sometimes had to contend. Like many people who are not mentally retarded, the Social Security Administration could present them with incomprehensible demands, as could many smaller agencies or institutions that presumed their clients were literate and could grasp complicated regulations.

Despite these occasional problems, these older people managed their day-to-day lives with relative ease. Their everyday routines served them well and the problems they sometimes encountered were neither too frequent nor serious to be coped with or ignored. Day after day they met their own needs, enjoyed life, and looked forward to the next day with plans, hopes, and optimism. They complained some, of course, and they had many concerns regarding ill health, the loss of income, the well-being of loved ones, the growth of crime, and various other urban dangers, but no one dwelled on such matters morbidly. In most respects, the quality of their lives and the strength of their self-esteem were the equal of those seen among the nonretarded, older, low-income people who were their neighbors or friends. And, compared to other older persons with mild mental retardation who lived in restricted residential settings where their lives were scheduled, regimented, and supervised, these people were not only far more independent, they were more normalized in every way.

For most of these people, a variety of cognitive limitations continued to show up in their speech, numerical ability, and general capacity to process information and solve problems, but all of the sample members are nevertheless competent to deal effectively enough with the everyday demands of the various social worlds in which they live. This, then, is a story of adaptive success, slow in coming, but no less impressive for that fact. These people have done well and, as I shall discuss further in the final section of this chapter, after 1985, many of them did even better. But we must not generalize too freely from their lives. They are only sixteen of the original forty-eight. We cannot be certain that those people who dropped out of sight, or who died, were as resourceful or as successful. As I mentioned earlier, there is nothing about the IQs, independence rankings, or personal characteristics of the sixteen people I have been describing to suggest that they were more resolute, intelligent, or adaptable than the others. Even so, that possibility cannot be dismissed.

Continuing Follow-up Studies

A reduction in research funding made it necessary to end the intensive research program that had continued throughout 1985, but two research associates and I have maintained contact with sample members ever since. Some sample members have been visited an average of every two weeks, with phone calls in between, whereas others have been contacted every four to six weeks. There is still much about the lives of these people that we do not know, and could never know, but we do know a great deal, probably more than has been recorded about any other group of people once hospitalized because of their presumed mental retardation. We intend to continue our contacts with these people as long as possible and we understand, with all the resentment and resignation that the human condition imposes on us, that the day will come for them, as for us, when serious illness or death will restrict their independence or end their lives. But as this was written, late in 1992, the lives of these sample members continue to be mostly stable. With the exception of one man who died in 1988, the others continue to display impressive competence, self-confidence, and good spirits. Indeed, as these people move into their mid- or late sixties, they appear to be happier than they have ever been. It may be rewarding to look more closely at some of these people as they move through the last, or penultimate, decade of their lives.

Richard (no. 16, IQ 56) died in 1988, four years after he retired after working on the same job as a truck loader and member of the Teamsters Union for thirty-one years. He could not read or write, and some of his coworkers teased him about his often-obvious lack of intelligence, but Richard stood his ground with threats of physical retaliation and eventually was well-enough accepted. He was strong and hardworking and that was enough for the union. As a young man, he had been slim, good looking, and athletic, riding his racing bike long distances. But when he retired at the age of 65, he was ponderously overweight, wore filthy clothing, and gave off a powerful body odor that led various people who knew him to complain and urge him to bathe. His apartment was cluttered and filthy, with empty, unwashed food containers and soft drink cans covering the counters, furniture, and even the floor itself. Yet someone meeting him on the street and speaking to him when his body odor was not oppressive would have little reason to suspect that he was mentally retarded. His clothing and his ever-present Teamsters cap seemed appropriate for a normal, retired man who spent his time meandering around the neighborhood near his apartment. He spoke appropriately, too, and had the sort of knowledge of life that a man of his years should.

What is more, he had a great zest for life. His pension plus Social Security benefits gave him $1,300 a month and his apartment cost him only $400. Some of the surplus he spent on food, eating five or six formidable meals a day. Despite his weight—which was too great for hospital scales to measure and could only be estimated at nearly 300 pounds—and recurring bouts of coronary disease that led various doctors to implore him to cut back on his intake of fat and salt, he joyfully continued to eat whatever pleased him. While in the hospital for high blood pressure, he demanded five eggs for breakfast and was incredulous when his doctor told him that the cholesterol in eggs would be harmful to him. Back in his apartment and free to eat what he liked, he returned to his normal diet, which now included a large multicourse dinner delivered by the hospital's "Food-on-Wheels" program as a "healthy" replacement for his fatty diet. However, Richard saw these meals as supplements to his previous diet, not replacements for it. Rising late, Richard typically had "breakfast" sometime before noon, eating fried eggs, several pancakes, and greasy bacon. After a nap, a walk, some conversation with passersby, some time spent listening to "cowboy" music on his radio, several cold snacks also delivered by "Food-on-Wheels," coffee and donuts, and a daily ration of two large chocolate bars, he regularly ate a double cheeseburger, fries, and a diet Pepsi at 5:00 p.m. Around 8:30 in the evening, he would eat the large meal that had been delivered that morning, and just before going to bed around 11:00 he ate either a ten-ounce steak or three pork chops fried with a large amount of butter in a greasy skillet. To complete his consumption of fat, most of these meals were washed down by several glasses of milk that he mixed equally with half-and-half.

Despite five periods of hospitalization, each lasting about ten days, and endless harangues by doctors and nurses about the necessity of changing his diet, Richard did not change his food habits, saying "some things I like to eat. I can't stay away from it" (Edgerton and Ward, 1991:141). He confidently insisted that the medication he had been given for hypertension would allow him to eat what he pleased. He never admitted that his diet was unhealthy or even that he was overweight, insisting that he had seen men who were "bigger" than he was. And in the face of striking errors of judgment or failure to understand instructions, he would never admit that he was "slow," much less that he was retarded. To the end of his life, he did not know how much money he received each month, nor how much he spent or gave away; he did not even know the cost of the meals he ordered every day. He understood that his "girlfriend" who visited him every month shortly after his checks arrived to relieve him of $500 or more on one pretext or another, was taking advantage of him, but he made excuses for her and continued to hope that she would allow him a moment of sexual pleasure, something that rarely occurred. Thanks to her avarice, sometimes Richard was not left with enough money to feed himself at the end of the month.

Richard was one of the intellectually most limited people in the sample. Like many others among these people, there was much in his world that he simply could not understand, but unlike most of the people in the sample he seldom realized how little he understood, and, when he did realize it, he was unique in his willingness to ask people to explain things to him. This disingenuousnous apparently helped him to maintain his exceptionally high self-confidence. He thought well of himself, truly so, and believed that other people did so as well. He was deluding himself, but the delusion no doubt helped him through life, and we should not forget that he worked reliably and well for thirty-one years before retiring. It is almost certain that his preposterous intake of food cut short his life span, but it is nevertheless the case that he lived for sixty-eight years and at the end of his life he was happy with what he was doing and with himself. Many people cannot say as much.

Myrtle (no. 38, then aged sixty-two, IQ 56) was originally ranked as the forty-sixth least independent person among the forty-eight former patients. Myrtle has limited intelligence, as people in her life have been quick to notice and comment on. Despite her cognitive deficits and her plain, overweight appearance, she married a non-retarded, physically handicapped man who took care of her well. When he died, she professed sorrow but soon married another non-retarded man, this time a robust, physically active reformed alcoholic. In 1985, their life together, although not without its rough edges, was very much like that of a perfectly normal, working class couple.

They had friends, possessions, and enjoyed a wide range of activities and relationships. Myrtle was still largely dependent on her husband, but she was happy and coping quite well with the demands of her often hectic life.

Since then, this energetic, irascible (she calls herself "ornery") woman has managed to maintain a stable life despite her all-too-clearly limited intelligence. On one poignant occasion, Myrtle admitted that she wanted badly to be "cured" of "whatever was wrong" with her, perhaps as she said, by "better schooling," and she added that she sometimes wished to die "to get rid of my misery." If this is truly how she feels about herself she hides it well. She made this admission only once as far as we know, and despite comments by her husband such as, "She couldn't keep up with me if she was trying and I was asleep," she forges ahead seemingly untroubled and invulnerable. There are many ways to adapt to limited intelligence and for Myrtle, seeming not to feel or to care may be best. From an exterior view, Myrtle has done very well indeed; how she feels inside is another matter, one that is almost always hidden from view.

To illustrate a less complicated success story, we can turn to Roberto (no. 3, then aged sixty-five, IQ 69). "Bobby" is a gay, Mexican-American man who would rather be thought of as Italian or Spanish, as people sometimes mistake him to be. In the early years of his community adaptation, his life was an epic of drunkenness, poverty, sexual profligacy, violence, vagrancy, and short jail terms. When drunk, which was often, he was aggressive, and given his small stature he sometimes came out of these imbroglios badly injured. For years he sold his own blood as often as twice a week for $5 a pint and collected aluminum cans to survive. With the help of a woman who provided him with a place to stay, sometimes without charging him rent, he eventually became less troubled and less troubling, curbing his more promiscuous sexual encounters and drinking less. Although Bobby readily admits that he is gay and calls himself a "slow learner" who did not get enough schooling (which is certainly true), he denies that he is mentally retarded, pointing out that he can read a little as proof. And indeed there is nothing about him except his illiteracy and some difficulty with money and numbers to suggest that he is intellectually limited.

After twenty-five years of living with his often quite demanding benefactress, for whom he sometimes worked as well, in 1985, Roberto moved out and rented his own apartment. Continuing to rely on welfare benefits as he had for several years, he still does not have much money and he is not above eating a free meal now and then at a skid-row mission, but he now lives a happy, if quieter, life. He no longer drinks, or at least he drinks very seldom, and his sexual life is muted in comparison to earlier times, but he loves to ride the bus on a bus pass all over Los Angeles, looking at the sights and remembering his youth when he would impetuously jump aboard a passing freight train from time to time and travel long distances. Now he lives quietly, watching television and listening to music at night. He is in good health and if he worries about the future he will not admit it. He is very pleased with his current life and says that he has "twenty more good years to live" (Ward, 1991:99).

For two final examples of turbulent lives that have stabilized and improved late in life we could turn to a long-separated but still-married couple, Hal (no. 2a) and Midge (no. 2b). As mentioned earlier in this chapter, when Hal was laid off from the furnace-stoking job he had held so well for some twenty-six years, his self-esteem suffered. He was not only impoverished, he was disabled by painful phlebitis in his legs. His life was at its nadir. Thanks to a physician who treated his legs with some success and arranged for him to receive SSI for the physical disability left by phlebitis, Hal was soon not only physically much improved, he had a stable source of income. When he turned sixty-five in 1986, he also qualified for Social Security benefits which further increased his income. The help of a concerned physician along with his own perseverance and competence to cope with bureaucratic details allowed Hal to step back from the abyss to resume what has once again become a comfortable and rewarding life.

Hal is a small, wiry man who is always neatly dressed and clean shaven. He speaks articulately and well, reads and writes, possesses extensive knowledge of the world, and gives no indication of being mentally retarded, no doubt because he was always incorrectly diagnosed (a post-release IQ test recorded 82). Hal is fond of telling tall tales about his accomplishments and adventures, but his actual life has been far from uneventful. He has been known to settle disputes with his fists and to have a number of women friends. Some of these who have lived with him in one or another of his several small apartments or hotel rooms in a run-down, high-crime area of downtown Los Angeles have been down-on-their-luck street women, several of whom abused alcohol and drugs. When drunk, one of these women once hit Hal on the head with a hammer, causing enough bleeding that the paramedics had to be called. Like other "working men" as he calls himself, he worked hard, but he played hard, too.

Since 1986, his life has been circumscribed, in part by his still painful yet no longer disabling legs, but also by his increased age and tranquility. In 1992, at the age of seventy, Hal still rises very early, sometimes by 4:00 A.M. and has breakfast at a nearby all-night coffee shop where he also smokes, reads the newspaper, and chats with friends. During the day, he visits friends, reads, watches television, and naps. He has an early dinner and is careful to be in his apartment before dark for fear of being mugged. It is not an exciting life, but it is not as dull as these few words may make it seem. He still takes bus rides, has visitors, and becomes excited about current events (he is a Democrat who takes care to vote in all elections). With his adequate and secure income, access to a conscientious physician, and a bit of luck, Hal may enjoy life for years to come.

Hal's separated wife, Midge (no. 2b, then aged sixty-nine, IQ 67) has lived a truly volatile life that did not begin to stabilize until 1982 when she moved into a house with her mother and brother. Her mother died in 1986 after thanking her for taking care of her at the end of her life and apologizing for allowing Midge to be hospitalized as a young woman (ostensibly for surgical sterilization that her father thought was necessary to protect her). Her mother's words meant a great deal to Midge who felt vindicated. Midge's current life in a quiet lower-middle-class neighborhood seems to appeal to her. Even before her mother's final illness, Midge took care of the household chores, including cleaning and grocery shopping. She especially enjoys her walks to the market which allow her to chat with neighbors and fellow shoppers. Always something of a busybody, she knows many of her neighbors and greets them by name along with bus drivers, police officers, salespeople, and regular customers like herself. She is devoted to her infirm brother (although she bridles when he is "bossy"), and in addition to caring for his needs, paying the bills, and shopping, she spends evenings discussing current events with him, or advising (often incorrectly) about how to solve one of the jigsaw puzzles that he is constantly working on. Like her separated husband, Hal, she is interested in politics and votes Democratic, complaining that she is always surrounded by Republicans, by which she means her brother.

Midge's life has never been so predictable and comfortable. She is not worried about the future, saying that should her brother die from his steadily worsening heart condition, she would inherit the house and probably be the beneficiary of his life insurance (she was vague about this latter point, however). Whatever the future may hold for Midge, she has the optimism of a born survivor. Her feelings are well summarized by her frequent and heated declaration that whatever may happen, " 'I'm not going to stay home and feel sorry for myself 'cause I'm getting up in years like a lot of them do' " (Gaston, 1991:69). She has some obvious intellectual limitations, but her life now is more secure than anyone could have predicted for her earlier in her life. She is her own person, aggressively so, but she is also a caring, vital, happy woman who is not intimidated by what the future may hold.

These brief comments do nothing to capture the richness of the lives of these people. They are offered merely as illustrations of what has become of some of the former patients from Pacific State Hospital. More detailed accounts of these individuals have been published elsewhere (Edgerton and Gaston, 1991b), and a book-length life history of another person is in preparation. The point I have been trying to illustrate is that although most of these people have lived in ways that are far from being predictable, there has been a trend among them for their lives to improve, especially so after they have grown older, or in some cases, old. I find much to admire in their tenacity, their good spirits, and their courage. And I take heart from what they have been able to accomplish and from what they will yet accomplish in the years left to them. When we recall that officials of the state once declared all of these people to be so incompetent that they would pose a threat to themselves or others if they remained in society, what they have done in life seems truly remarkable.

CHAPTER EIGHT

Conclusion

Along with some flattering words of praise, *The Cloak of Competence* has been criticized for several failings, and some of these criticisms raise issues of general significance. When *The Cloak of Competence* was first reviewed one year after its publication by anthropologist Thomas Gladwin (1968), he took me to task for not focusing my account of these former patients in terms of culture, a concept long fundamental to anthropological inquiry. At the time, I took Gladwin's suggestion to be misguided, even formulaic, because these forty-eight people were, after all, not even in touch with one another. How could they develop a culture—a system of shared beliefs and meanings—much less convey this system to succeeding generations?

Although it is still not clear to me what Gladwin meant by this criticism, I can now see two ways in which culture was important to the lives of the former patients. First, to succeed in the world outside the institution, they had to divest themselves of the institutional culture they had come to adopt. How patients dressed, spoke, and even walked would have identified them as "different" to "outside" people, and their beliefs about many institutional practices such as work, recreation, independence, and responsibility also had to be unlearned if they hoped to conform to the expectations of people in the community. At the same time, the former patients had to learn the culture—or the various subcultures—of the communities in which they lived after release. As most of the former patients said, it took some time to understand what was expected of them, what was appropriate, in that foreign world outside the hospital. Their success, then, required unlearning one culture and learning, or in some cases relearning, another one. To do so took time.

The Cloak of Competence has also been criticized for failing to recognize that the former patients whose lives it attempts to describe were not "mentally retarded" but were instead victims of various social, economic, and political processes. This line of reasoning has been articulated best by historian David A. Gerber who has noted that many of these people were originally institutionalized during the Great Depression of the 1930s, a time when widespread economic tribulations made it likely that a low IQ was not the sole or even primary reason for their institutionalization. It is almost certainly correct that economic pressures played a role as they have done in other periods in the United States as well as in other countries. However, although social and economic factors very likely played a part in the decision to institutionalize these people, it does not follow that they therefore did not have lower IQ scores than most of their peers. Gerber also noted that the experience of institutionalization contributed to the relative incompetence of these individuals. In this regard, he is correct. Not only were these people deprived of a formal education, they were socialized into a mode of life, a culture, that did not prepare them for community living. Gerber (1990:6) concluded that as a result of these social and historical factors " . . . a plausible case may be made that these people did not possess a clinically identifiable disability."

Setting aside what exactly might be intended by "clinically identifiable," the sense of Gerber's argument is that the kinds of incompetence these people displayed when I first encountered them were the product of social processes rather than biologically based cognitive deficits. Other scholars have gone even farther by faulting me for making what they regard as the naive epistemological assumption that there is such a phenomenon as mental retardation at all (Bogdan and Taylor, 1982). Although I believe that such extreme social constructionist views are misleading, they have been made often enough in the past and are sufficiently central to many current approaches to the experience of disability that they deserve a considered answer.

When I began the research that led to *The Cloak of Competence*, it was widely understood that there were two separable categories of what I shall, for present purposes, call mental retardation. The first, which can be called "clinical" retardation, was the more severe, being usually identified early in life, involving moderately or severely impairing deficits in intelligence, and often having a specifiable etiology. The second category, then commonly called "familial" or "sociocultural," is usually not identified until the child enters school, involves only mild cognitive limitations, and seldom has a known etiology (the recent identification of Fragile X Syndrome may change this latter point in a significant number of cases). Somewhere between 75 percent and 85 percent of all persons with IQs below 70 belong in this second category. Even in 1960, it was acknowledged that within each of these two major categories of mental retardation there was enormous variability in cognitive, physical, and emotional disability. The concept of mental retardation, then, was clearly understood to be an omnibus, administrative one, not a unitary phenomenon based on a scientific nosology. In this sense, it has long been recognized that the term mental retardation refers to multiple conditions that are united only by the presence of below-normal intelligence. Although some people admittedly hypostatize the concept, I have always thought of "mental retardation" as nothing more than a conventional label for a host of phenomena that can combine to produce substandard cognitive competence.

Even in 1960, it was also recognized that where the IQ point scale was cut to designate mental retardation was arbitrary. From 1959 through 1963, the official definition of mental retardation utilized by the American Association on Mental Deficiency (the dominant scientific organization in this field in the United States) set the cutoff point at IQ 85. The decision in 1963 to lower the upper criterion to to IQ 70 was based more on financial considerations than scientific ones. The IQ 85 criterion defined 16 percent of the population as mentally retarded, creating the potential for a fiscally insupportable burden on states or the federal government to provide services for so many people. Setting the upper limit of "mental retardation" at IQ 70 reduced the numbers of individuals for whom federal or state services might have to be provided, but there was no more scientific justification for choosing an IQ of 70 than there was for an IQ of 85. It should be self-evident that how low a person's IQ must be before he or she is cognitively incompetent depends on the demands of that person's social and cultural environment.

There have been many attempts to assess what degree of "intelligence" is required to succeed in a particular environment. For example, people with IQs below 100 seldom do well in college, and to do well in a legal or scientific career, a higher IQ is almost certain to be necessary, and so may other kinds of intelligence not assessed by an IQ test. Success in some professions calls for a higher IQ than success in less-demanding occupations, and it has long been thought that even persons with very low IQs might live moderately well if they were placed in "sheltered" environments such as farm colonies. To further illustrate the relativity of "mental retardation," when close to 2 million recruits were given IQ tests during World War I, it was found that the average mental age of white American adults was only barely above age twelve, the upper limit then used to define feeble-mindedness. The absurdity of defining half the white male population of the country as feebleminded was apparent to Army authorities; they promptly inducted these men who became perfectly competent soldiers. The idea that mental retardation is relative to the demands of particular environments is an old one. This understanding is implicit in most definitions of the concept, and in 1963 it became explicit when mental retardation was defined by the American Association on Mental Deficiency (now called The American Association on Mental Retardation) as existing only if a person's IQ was below 70 *and* his or her adaptive behavior was deficient relative to the standards for that person's age and cultural group. If a person had an IQ of 55 but was considered to be perfectly normal by people in his community, he was not mentally retarded. In practice, this emphasis on adaptive behavior in defining mental retardation was often ignored, but the principle was widely accepted.

For example, consider the people of Duddie's Branch, an Appalachian "hollow" described by Rena Gazaway (1969). These 238 people were so impaired intellectually that it is quite possible to consider them all to be mentally retarded. Not only could they neither read nor write, they had no conception of either clock or calendrical time. Children could not solve even the simplest problems Gazaway posed to them, and they were largely incapable of mastering such basic manual skills as pounding a nail or sawing a board. All but a very few survived by receiving welfare payments from the State of Kentucky, but despite their reliance on the money provided by the state, most adults could not even make change and were regularly victimized by storekeepers as a result. By the standards of the surrounding communities, these people were not competent; they were also not employable, and there was nothing about their way of life that outsiders admired. Indeed, if they had been given IQ tests there is no doubt that almost all would have scored well under 70. By our standards, then, these people could be considered mentally retarded and might well have qualified for services as such.

The people of Duddie's Branch were the products of a long history of poverty, social isolation, and a lack of access to education as well as the hazards posed by a host of toxins in their environment, malnutrition, disease, nonexistent prenatal care, teenage pregnancy, and various genetic factors that may have reduced the intellectual abilities of people in this small, isolated breeding population. But whatever the extent or the causes of their intellectual limitations, their adaptive behavior was acceptable by their own standards. Indeed, they were so attached to one another and to their way of life that they refused to leave the hollow even when given the opportunity to do so. Within the hollow of Duddie's Branch, these people had adapted well enough to survive and to find satisfaction in their way of life. What is more, they thought of themselves as intellectually normal.

The former patients from Pacific State Hospital also came from deprived environments, although not as drastically so as Duddie's Branch, and all suffered more deprivation during their years in that institution; but unlike the Duddie's Branchers, each one of these people had been recognized while still a child as being slow to talk, or walk, or to behave appropriately. Or at least that is what their hospital records indicate. Of course, their parents or siblings or teachers might have fabricated these reports of delayed development for reasons of their own, or the hospital records might simply be wrong; but if these records can be believed, then these former patients were not intellectually normal members of their own families or communities. Because this is an important point, let me turn to another example in an attempt to clarify it further.

Like other investigators in the field of mental retardation research in the mid-1970s, I believed that many children from low-income racial and ethnic minority populations were wrongly labeled mentally retarded by school systems that did not understand their cultural backgrounds. I decided to explore this question by examining a sample of African-Americans from low-income neighborhoods in Los Angeles. After collecting a substantial pool of individuals all of whom had been identified by one agency or another as persons with mental retardation, forty-five were chosen for intensive study. These people were young adults (mean age = 25) without significant physical or emotional disabilities and with good language skills, all of whom had been labeled mentally retarded in school (mean IQ = 59). It was my expectation that many of these people would prove to be "six-hour retarded children"—retarded in school but adaptively normal as far as their families and friends were concerned. To my surprise, we found that almost all of these people were seen by their peers and their families as being "slow" or having a "problem" learning. In addition, our African-American field research staff consistently reported that most of these individuals were unable to perform everyday tasks involving even minimal literacy, were so limited in quantitative skills that using money at a market was problematic for them, and very often spoke in ways that left their interlocutors baffled.

Moreover, in most cases for which good evidence was available from parents or siblings, these individuals had been recognized as being slow to develop normally *before* they went to school. Their families had not thought of them as normal children. Those tasks that these young people had most difficulty mastering once they were in school—reading, writing, mathematics—continued to limit what they could accomplish in life after leaving school. Other people thought of these young adults as being relatively incompetent because they could not master these skills, and the individuals themselves suffered a loss of self-esteem because they knew that they could not perform what they perceived to be normal intellectual tasks (Koegel and Edgerton, 1982;1984). Now it is possible that these forty-five inner-city young adults are not typical of most African-Americans who were labeled mentally retarded in school, but those persons in our sample who were *not* receiving services as mentally retarded persons had the same cognitive limitations and adaptive difficulties as those who were receiving such services. This suggests that even those persons who were no longer served by agencies as mentally retarded persons did not blend into their communities as altogether normal persons.

We chose to look in greater detail at the lives and skills of twelve members of this sample because our African-American field-workers at first refused to believe that they were cognitively impaired, much less "mentally retarded." On superficial acquaintance, these men and women appeared to be perfectly normal, even rather successful, members of their inner-city communities. Upon closer inquiry, however, it became apparent that all twelve were seen by others who knew them well as "limited," "slow," or "handicapped." Moreover, although with some reluctance in most cases, these twelve people eventually acknowledged their own limitations. They questioned not only their ability to perform certain tasks, but their own overall intelligence. With great poignancy, some tearfully described how greatly they had suffered as a result and how desperately difficult it was for them to cope with the demands of their lives. These individuals had not achieved even marginal abilities in reading, writing, or arithmetic. What is more, those who knew them well agreed that they lacked normal intellectual skills, referring to their short attention spans, poor judgment, vulnerability to exploitation, and their general incapacity to understand what was taking place around them (Koegel and Edgerton, 1984).

What has this to do with the people in *The Cloak of Competence* sample? It suggests, I think, that many people whom we would expect to become victims of mislabeling may in fact be identified as retarded by their families long before any school or agency becomes involved. But the truest test of the assertion that the former patients from Pacific State Hospital were not actually retarded must be an assessment of their own cognitive abilities as these were manifested over time in their everyday lives. It is my opinion, one that I believe has been shared by the more than twenty graduate students and postdoctoral fellows who have come to know these people, that all but two or three so consistently fail to understand certain important aspects of the world in which they live, and so regularly find themselves unable to cope with some demands of this world, that we are justified in thinking of them as being cognitively inadequate to cope with significant aspects of their environments. When it comes to reading, writing, arithmetic calculations, understanding spatial and temporal relationships, and solving complex problems, especially those involving calculations of probabilities, they often need the help of others. With the exception of Hal (no. 2a) and Martha (no. 28), and the possible exception of one other person, this is true of everyone in the sample. At the same time, their *social* competence, their ability to cope with routine tasks and to interact appropriately with others, is usually adequate to meet the demands of the world in which they live.

Does this mean that we should think of them as being mentally retarded? That depends on what this concept is taken to mean, as I have noted. I suggested in 1967 that we should replace the term "mental retardation" with something less likely to humiliate. That has been done to some extent in the professions that are concerned with cognitively limited people, and less pejorative terms are a step in the right direction. But the label is only one consideration in shaping the life of a person; the socialization that goes along with it is much more formative. And this takes us to another point brought up by Gerber (1990). Even if I am correct that the people in my sample have significant cognitive limitations, and that these deficits probably existed early in childhood, the experience of institutional confinement as a person with mental retardation is almost certain to have reduced their ability to cope with life outside the hospital. Most members of the sample complained that the hospital had done too little to prepare them for life in the community and their complaints were surely justified. But neither they nor we can know just how powerfully and lastingly their social or cognitive competence was impaired by their hospitalization.

To illustrate what can sometimes happen, let us briefly consider the experiences of people who have been labeled mentally retarded and treated as such only later to be found to possess normal intelligence. As early as 1956, Lewis A. Dexter (1964) argued that labeling people as mentally retarded was a self-fulfilling prophecy. There is evidence to suggest that this is correct. For example, people with normal intelligence have been labeled mentally retarded, duly hospitalized, and socialized as persons with limited intelligence. Although this is not an everyday occurrence, it is not a rare one either. Some cases of people who were considered to be retarded one day and declared to have normal intelligence the next have been so dramatic that their stories have been told in books or television documentaries (Edgerton, 1986).

In the early 1970s, I encountered a twenty-one-year old man living in a group home for people with mental retardation. He was receiving SSI benefits as a "mentally retarded" man with "permanent brain damage," a diagnosis he had first received when he was four years old. When his intelligence was reevaluated during a routine psychological examination at the age of twenty-one, he was found to have a full-scale WAIS IQ of 102. Overnight, he became a person with "normal" intelligence, but seventeen years of living the role of a retarded person were difficult to set aside. For almost his entire life, this man had been exposed to expectations and practices that deprived him of normal experiences. He was not only secluded from most of life's dangers such as riding a bicycle, playing sports, handling tools or knives, and later, from dating, driving, or drinking, he was routinely excluded from the kind of complex conversations, jokes, and innuendo that his peers engaged in. His education was limited, and at home he was not even tutored in the use of money or the telephone, doing household chores, or planning for tomorrow.

Instead of becoming increasingly independent and competent as he grew older, he remained dependent and incapable of coping with many of life's demands. Instead of entering a world of normal experiences, he retreated into an inner world of fantasy. When he was "delabeled" and told that he had the ability to live as any other twenty-one-year old, he discovered with mounting anxiety that he was expected to seek work, cope with the demands of the workplace, make normal friends, manage his money, arise early, shave every morning, be responsible, pay bills, be sensitive to the needs of others, and be concerned with their well-being as well as his own. He was not prepared for this onslaught of normalcy and it was more than a year before he even began to assume social roles that were appropriate for a normal man of his age. The important point is this: despite a lifetime of being treated as a person with mental retardation, he retained enough cognitive competence to perform normally on an IQ test, but his social competence was seriously impaired.

Another criticism of the book was that I treated mental retardation as if it were an unalterable condition (Gerber, 1990:14). Because I did write a passage in chapter 6 of the book that conflated several points, it may be useful for me to clarify what I meant then, as well as to indicate what I think the evidence today suggests. First, it should be obvious that all organisms, no matter how impaired their central nervous systems may be, are capable of some learning. As I think the material presented in chapter 7 so clearly demonstrates, the people in *The Cloak of Competence* sample learned a great deal over the years, so much so in fact that their social competence improved considerably. However, their cognitive competence changed very little over that same period. My inference is that those neural structures and processes that control such cognitive capacities were so impaired that they were capable of only minor improvement or replacement by other complementary structures.

Let me take an example from the condition known as Down Syndrome (DS). Typically referred to as trisomy-21, this condition is caused by the inherited presence of an extra number-21 chromosome (there are other forms of DS such as mosaicism which I will not discuss here). Most individuals with this extra chromosome have IQs that range from 35 to 54, are limited in the development of language skills, and are cognitively impaired, especially in higher-order tasks involving abstraction and successive information processing. They suffer from a number of physical ailments as well. For all of these reasons, until recently physicians typically recommended that DS children be placed in institutions like Pacific State Hospital where they lived quite restricted lives and ordinarily appeared to be quite incompetent.

When I first went to Pacific State Hospital in 1959, there were many DS adults there (they were then known as "Mongoloids"). At that time, many of the more competent patients who had been utilized by the staff as helpers with the care of more severely retarded patients were being released. The people in *The Cloak of Competence* study were part of this exodus. This left the staff overburdened, so George Tarjan, the enlightened medical director of the hospital, decided to ask DS adults to help with the large task of feeding severely retarded, bedridden patients. And this they did, holding their charges upright while carefully feeding them with a spoon. These DS people typically enjoyed doing something useful and they did it tenderly and well. However, when word of this experiment in patient care reached the ears of those authorities who accredit hospitals, these concerned physicians were aghast. They *knew* that people with DS were quite incompetent, and they feared that they would feed their charges improperly, causing them to aspirate food and perhaps die.

There was an investigation and, from the perspective of the present day, it is no surprise that Dr. Tarjan was exonerated. Today, we know that many people with DS can lead semi-independent lives and enjoy a great range of community activities without supervision; indeed, some of them marry and hold down competitive jobs. Given the opportunity and appropriate support, activities like these are within the competence range of persons with trisomy-21, and it is tragic when they are denied the opportunity to live to the fullest. However, opportunity to experience life outside of institutional confinement and restraint is not sufficient to bring about significant improvement in the basic cognitive limitations that handicap DS persons. No amount of environmental enrichment or intensive teaching has yet been successful in transforming a person with trisomy-21 into a person with normal or near-normal cognitive abilities (Fischler and Koch, 1991).

Because mental retardation is a condition that includes deficiencies in both intellectual skills and adaptive behaviors, it is necessary to specify which of these one is referring to as unalterable. Adaptive behaviors can change dramatically, whereas cognitive skills change relatively little. When I wrote *The Cloak of Competence* I was not sufficiently clear about this distinction. Moreover, I frankly did not realize how much these former patients would be capable of improving their adaptive behavior over time. As the predictions I made in 1972 about the course of their lives indicated, I often underestimated how well these people would do, especially those women married to non-retarded men who lived in highly dependent relationships. I am happy that they proved me wrong.

Another criticism of the book has to do with my emphasis on stigma, passing, and denial in the lives of these former patients. It has been said that although I allowed these people to speak about their lives, I did not take seriously what they said, namely that they were not retarded and were placed in Pacific State Hospital for reasons other than intellectual deficiency (Gerber, 1990; Luckin, 1986; Bogdan and Taylor, 1982). Let me try to explain why I think these assertions are wrong. To begin, I set out to accomplish what generations of anthropologists have done, that is to hear these individual's own words and as much as possible to see their world as they themselves did. It hardly needs to be said that no anthropologist has ever fully achieved these goals. One version of this approach that was also pioneered by anthropologists (Langness and Frank, 1981) is the life history interview by means of which a member of another society is encouraged to tell the story of his or her life. Such documents can provide many important insights into another cultural system, but as anthropologists have learned—sometimes painfully—what people talk about as they reconstruct their biographies can depart considerably from the truth. Like people in Western societies who write their autobiographies, people in nonliterate societies sometimes embellish, exaggerate, or simply lie as they talk about themselves and others (Crapanzano, 1980).

After I wrote *The Cloak of Competence*, several scholars published life histories or autobiographies of people with mental retardation (Frank, 1981; Bogdan and Taylor, 1982; Atkinson and Williams, 1990; Kaufman, 1988; Meyers, 1978). These documents provide provocative insights into a world of meaning that we as outsiders can never fully enter. We should have more such biographical documents, and indeed my colleagues and I are preparing some now to follow those few we published earlier (Edgerton and Gaston, 1990). But these documents, like any other autobiography or life history, cannot be taken at face value. Everything a person with mental retardation says can reveal something about his or her life, but even so it may not be factual. People with mental retardation, like the rest of us, may put themselves in a better light than history, and other people, would support. An autobiography, like ethnographic description of the kind I attempted with the former patients, often calls for inter-pretation before it can be corroborated. In general, then, when I chose to search for patterns among the forty-eight former patients I was engaged in a perfectly conventional form of social science. When I interpreted those patterns in terms of concepts such as stigma, pass-ing, and denial, the issue is not whether it was legitimate for me to have done so, but whether these concerns accurately represented the feelings and behaviors of the former patients.

Robert Bogdan and Stephen J. Taylor have written (1982:211) that although I purported to view the former patients "through their own eyes," in fact, for me, " . . . case record entries are 'facts,' while ex-residents' accounts are fabrications or rationalizations." *Pace* Bog-dan and Taylor, as I noted in chapter 7, I was quite skeptical about hospital records, but I believed that sometimes they were accurate. Much that found its way into these files was not credible, but some records were verifiably correct. *Pace* Bogdan and Taylor yet again, I would also protest that I surely did not regard everything that the former patients said to me as "fabrications." It was only in the area of what I called "denial" that I believed I was hearing accounts that were typically not factual renderings of historical events. Finally, it must be observed that these people continue to exhibit marked cog-nitive limitations that suggest "mental retardation" and, moreover, that their own "denials" are often implausible. But this the reader can judge.

It is also possible, as another scholar has suggested, that the con-cepts of stigma, denial, and passing, which were well known at that time due to the work of sociologist Erving Goffman, were imposed on the data in a manner reminiscent of Procrustes (Gerber, 1990). Although you will have to take my word for it, as I can offer no proof, that is not what I believe happened in this case. As my associates and I spent time with the forty-eight former patients, we heard and saw repeated evidence that these people were humiliated by their involuntary stay at the hospital, that they did everything they could to have other people think of them as ordinary people, not former patients, and that they denied over and over that they were, in fact, mentally retarded. Faced by this overwhelming evidence that these were the central concerns of their lives, I searched for a way of conceptualizing the data and concluded that Goffman's formulation fitted very well.

But this is only one issue. A more fundamental question has to do with whether it was valid for me to have interpreted what these people said about not being retarded and having been institutionalized for other reasons as psychological defenses rather than statements of fact (Gerber, 1990). This is an arguable point because hospital records cannot be regarded as factual in this regard. To avoid unnecessary repetition, I will say only that because I came to believe that almost all of these people in fact had such significant cognitive limitations that they could be considered mentally retarded by prevailing standards, their denials seemed like defenses to me. If these people were in fact cognitively normal, then I was wrong in my interpretation. I have already presented my evidence for cognitive deficiencies among all but a few of these former patients, so the resolution of this issue must be left to the reader. I continue to believe that my interpretation was correct. Of course, by 1972, this emphasis on denial, passing, and stigma had lessened, and over the ensuing years it became moot.

Another question is whether by focusing attention on stigma, passing, and denial, I overlooked other more salient aspects of their lives. I did not think so at the time, but subsequent experience with these people has raised a number of doubts. As my associates and I continued to conduct research with these and other samples of people labeled mentally retarded, it became evident that even after twelve or eighteen months of intensive research, like that done in 1960–1961, further research could lead to new and surprising insights into the lives of the people being studied. That is so in part because their life circumstances change over time, but it is also true that people's lives are so complex that it is impossible to learn everything of significance about them in a year or so, and finally, because people with mental retardation, like other people, quite often withhold some kinds of information from investigators for long periods of

time. We have encountered all three phenomena many times in subsequent research, as was indicated in some of the findings discussed
in the previous chapter. People with mental retardation who live in
community settings do not lead simple lives and they surely are not
simple people. In reading the various accounts of individuals reported here, it should be kept in mind that there is always more to
be learned about them, probably much more.

For example, consider Ted Barrett, the man discussed in chapter 2
under the pseudonym of Fred Barnett (Ted cannot read but when we
told him that his real name had not been used in *The Cloak of Competence*, he was upset; we have subsequently used his real name as he
wishes). Since 1960, eleven different field-workers and I have spent
thousands of hours with Ted, or Teddy, as most of his friends call
him. Over the past five years, one field-worker (Marcia Gaston) has
visited Teddy, or been visited by him, on an average of every two
weeks, with phone conversations in between. We have also spent
many hours with his friends and relatives. It is likely that more information has been collected about Teddy and his everyday life than any
other person with mental retardation in history. We have used some
of this information to make an hour-long film about him and we are
currently writing a book-length biography of him. We have focused
this amount of time and energy on him because despite his illiteracy,
his clear cognitive deficits, and his relatively low IQ (tested as either
52 or 54), he has lived successfully on his own in a dangerous part
of central Los Angeles for over thirty years, has a wide circle of
friends and acquaintances, has worked hard and well to support himself, and continues to lead a fascinatingly complex life. Yet the circumstances of life are changeable, so we are continually learning
something new (and sometimes surprising) about his coping skills
and how he thinks about himself and life. For example, Teddy occasionally volunteers the information that he is "mentally retarded." We
know that these declarations are related to his knowledge that he has
been unable to read and write, but despite many efforts on our part,
we still do not understand at all well what else this designation
means to him. Perhaps he is not sure himself.

Today, as we try to convey a full and accurate picture of Ted and
his life, we are acutely aware that there is much about his past that
we will never know, just as there is much about how he thinks and
feels that we still do not fully understand. And we cannot claim to
know anyone else in the sample as well as we know Ted. The attempt

to understand any other human being is a truly humbling process. This is a truism, of course, but repeating it here may help to establish the essential point that the longer we do research with people who were once patients at Pacific State Hospital the more obvious it becomes that we have not gotten to the bottom of their lives and never will.

One conclusion that I reached in chapter 6 needs to be modified. In my discussion of the cognitive limitations of the erstwhile patients, I noted that these deficits most commonly involved concepts of space, time, and number and I concluded that these concepts "ineluctably" intruded into their everyday lives. Hence, I wrote that their cognitive disabilities were omnipresent and severe. Subsequent follow-up studies with these people indicated that although the former patients had only rarely and to a minimal degree improved their capacities to deal with spatial, temporal, and numerical relationships, with more experience in community living they were increasingly able to cope adequately without these skills. They sometimes needed help from others with mail, bills, addresses, and the like, but these matters seldom played a central part in their lives. Many people who have never been considered mentally retarded have managed to deal with life in urban America without being literate or being able to count very well, and the former patients have learned to do so as well. When I wrote the original book in 1965, I simply did not realize how easy it could be for the erstwhile patients to learn to live in a large city without being able to read, write, or make change.

Conclusion

As I have observed, the more we have come to know about these people who were once patients in a large hospital for people with mental retardation the more obvious it is that there is much about them still to learn. Yet, there is another, even more general point to be made. Since *The Cloak of Competence* was published some twenty-five years ago, the scholarly literature about the lives of mentally retarded people in community settings has multiplied by many orders of magnitude, and more books and articles appear every year. Based on this accumulation of knowledge—more, almost, than one can master—many scholars, myself included, have attempted to reach general conclusions about how people with cognitive limitations are able to live on their own, about what kinds of assistance they may need, and how various services should be made available to them. Although there is as yet no perfect consensus about these matters, there is widespread agreement about many of them (Edgerton, 1988*b*). It is important that all concerned continue to explore these pressing issues and to facilitate the provision of services that can contribute to a better quality of life for people with disabilities.

Unlike the mentally ill, for whom services have been drastically cut in recent years, forcing many to become homeless, services for people with mental retardation have continued to receive federal support and relatively few mentally retarded people have been identified among the ranks of America's homeless. In fact, federal funding for the mentally retarded has increased every year since 1950 (with the anomalous exception of 1975), and in 1985, federal spending for services, training, housing, research, and so forth was almost $8 billion annually. State and local authorities continue to spend funds on mental retardation as well, and the quality of life of many people with mental retardation and their families has improved as a result. All over the country programs are attempting to integrate people with mental retardation into general community activities, to teach them more adaptive behaviors including vocational skills, to provide less restrictive residential care, organize more fulfilling recreational opportunities, offer better health care, and in many other ways to enhance their quality of life (Schalock, 1990; Lakin and Bruininks, 1985; Seltzer and Krauss, 1987).

Of course, still more could and should be done, and it is important to acknowledge that there is still much to be learned about those people with mental retardation whose lives in community settings we have been examining. What is more, there may be an even greater need to learn about the lives of people with cognitive limitations who have never been studied. Those people who have been studied thus far constitute a small minority of all people with mental retardation who live in community settings. Those who have been studied have almost always been people who were diagnosed as mentally retarded in school and have continued to maintain some form of contact with the mental retardation service delivery system since leaving school. With the exception of a very few studies in the United States, the United Kingdom, and Sweden, the lives of people who were labeled mentally retarded but have not maintained contact with service providers have not been examined. When they have been, as Granat and Granat (1973) reported for Sweden, and Koegel and Edgerton (1982;1984) described in an inner city, a substantial number of these people have been found to have adaptive difficulties. They have not simply "disappeared" into normal life and become indistinguishable from their peers. Indeed, these kinds of people, people who predominantly come from very poor, ethnic minority backgrounds, are a hidden majority of all those people who probably have significant cognitive limitations. They are hidden from our view and they represent what we must presume to be a very large and culturally diverse population.

On those few occasions when people who were once labeled mentally retarded only to disappear from "official" view have been studied, the results are of exceptional interest. For example, Robert T. Ross and colleagues (Ross et al., 1985) have reported that when 160 former pupils (mean IQ = 67) of ungraded classes in San Francisco in the 1920s and 1930s were followed-up forty years later, their community adaptation appeared to have been quite positive. These individuals, most of whose parents were foreign born, had no identity as persons with mental retardation since leaving school. They were indeed "hidden." When these people were compared to their siblings and nonretarded controls (matched on age, sex, and ethnicity), they were found to have worked for lower salaries in jobs that required fewer skills, but nevertheless 80 percent of the men said that they had been regularly employed. These former special class students also reported that they had married, raised children, and stayed in stable unions. Only 20 percent needed public assistance, and few had been criminal offenders. Most of the men served in World War II although they had not risen above the rank of private or seaman. These men were not American success stories, but they had not done badly either.

Ross and his colleagues concluded (1985:149) that their lives show that " . . . it does not take as many IQ points as most people believe to be productive, to get along with others, and to be fulfilled." But they also point out that these people seemed to owe their success as "reasonably competent citizens" to factors such as their stable and supportive families, conditions of high employment (during World War II) when they first entered the labor market, and marriage to spouses of higher intellectual ability. If this is correct, then these individuals may have succeeded not only because of favorable employment opportunities but because their ethnic traditions (Italian, Chinese, and Russian, for example) provided them with supportive families and arranged marriages, forms of social support that may or may not be available in other ethnic minority communities not yet studied. A word of caution, however. Ross's findings derive entirely from interviews. How these people actually lived, and what others actually thought of them, could have been less positive than their interview responses suggested.

People with mild and severe cognitive disabilities are known in all societies, even the smallest foraging societies described by anthropologists. In some of these small-scale societies, such people were treated with contempt, were abused, and sometimes killed; in a few societies, they were treated with compassion (Edgerton, 1970). Developing societies in the contemporary world are aware of the problem that mental retardation poses, but few have the resources to provide even minimal services, although in some countries like Pakistan, the availability of services is improving. But no developing country has any clear idea about the number of its citizens who have mental retardation. Only a few countries such as the United Kingdom, the Scandinavian countries, and Finland have successfully maintained registers of all or nearly all of their people with IQs below 70. In the United States, there has been no nationwide epidemiological research to identify persons with low IQ scores.

As a result, in this country the life circumstances of poor rural whites with low IQs, like those of Latinos, Asian-Americans, and African-Americans, have seldom been documented, and never in adequate detail. New immigrant populations from Asia and the Pacific islands, Central America, the Caribbean, the Middle East, and elsewhere are rapidly growing in numbers and even less is known about them. This circumstance is unfortunate for several reasons. For one thing, many children and their families may be suffering needlessly because potentially beneficial services are not available to them. Also, new services are planned on the basis of existing knowledge, which derives almost entirely from studies of people who are already receiving services. And most fundamentally, we do not know whether, and if so how, culturally different populations in our society are able to adapt to the demands of life in their communities. A minority population that can arrange marriages between cognitively limited individuals and more competent spouses, then organize extended families in support of those couples, deserves careful study. In the absence of studies like this, conclusions about the community adaptation of persons with mental retardation must come with this disclaimer: "As far as we know, based on studies conducted with a minority of affected people and populations."

I believe that the lives of the people I have described in the previous chapters tell us a great deal about the abilities of cognitively limited people to live meaningfully. But matters should not rest here. There are many cognitively limited people in the United States and the rest of the world who live in dramatically different social and cultural worlds. Until we enter those worlds and learn from the people who live in them, we will not know what mental retardation is or what people with it can accomplish, and what they can accomplish can enlighten and enlarge us all.

Bibliography

Abel, T. M.
    1940   A Study of a Group of Subnormal Girls Successfully Adjusted in Industry and the Community. *American Journal of Mental Deficiency* 45:66–72.

Abel, T. M., and E. F. Kinder
    1942   *The Subnormal Adolescent Girl*. New York: Columbia University Press.

Atkinson, D., and F. Williams (eds.)
    1990   *"Know Me as I Am": An Anthology of Prose, Poetry and Art by People with Learning Difficulties*. London: Hodder & Stoughton.

Badham, J. N.
    1955   The Outside Employment of Hospitalized Mentally Defective Patients as a Step Towards Resocialization. *American Journal of Mental Deficiency* 59:666–680.

Baldwin, D. H.
    1990   "Two is Enough." In R. B. Edgerton and M. A. Gaston (eds.), *"I've Seen It All!" Lives of Older Persons with Mental Retardation in the Community*. Baltimore: P. H. Brookes, 101–122.

Baller, W. R.
    1936   A Study of the Present Social Status of a Group of Adults, Who, When They Were in Elementary Schools, Were Classified as Mentally Deficient. *Genetic Psychology Monographs* 18:165–244.

Bienenstock, T., and W. W. Coxe
    1956   *Census of Severely Retarded Children in New York State*. Albany: Interdepartmental Health Resources Board.

Bijou, S. W., M. H. Ainsworth, and M. R. Stockey
    1943   The Social Adjustment of Mentally Retarded Girls Paroled from the Wayne County Training School. *American Journal of Mental Deficiency* 47:422–428.

Blackey, E.
    1930   The Social Adjustment of Children of Low Intelligence. *Smith College Studies in Social Work* 1:160–179.
Bogdan, R., and S. J. Taylor
    1982   *Inside Out: Two First-Person Accounts of What it Means to be Labeled "Mentally Retarded."* Toronto: University of Toronto Press.
Braddock, I.
    1987   *Federal Policy Toward Mental Retardation and Developmental Disabilities.* Baltimore: P. H. Brookes.
Bronner, A. F.
    1933   Follow-up Studies of Mental Defectives. *Proceedings and Addresses of the American Association on Mental Deficiency* 38:258–264.
Brown, D.
    1952   The Working Convalescent Care Program for Female Patients at Rome State School. *American Journal of Mental Deficiency* 56: 643–654.
Burgess, E. W.
    1928   Factors Determining Success or Failure on Parole. In A. A. Bruce and others (eds.), *The Workings of the Indeterminate Sentence Law and the Parole System in Illinois.* Springfield: Illinois State Board of Parole.
Camp, B. M., and T. E. Waite
    1932   Report on Four Cases of Mental Deficiency on Parole. *American Association for the Study of the Feebleminded* 37:381–394.
Carriker, W. R.
    1957   *A Comparison of Post-School Adjustments of Regular and Special Class Retarded Individuals Served in Lincoln and Omaha, Nebraska, Public Schools.* Washington, D.C.: Office of Education, U.S. Dept. of Health, Education, and Welfare.
Cassirer, E.
    1944   *An Essay on Man.* New Haven: Yale University Press.
Channing, A.
    1932   *Employment of Mentally Deficient Boys and Girls.* Washington, D. C.: Children's Bureau Publication No. 210.
Charles, D. C.
    1953   Ability and Accomplishment of Persons Earlier Judged Mentally Deficient. *Genetic Psychology Monographs* 47:3–73.
Cobb, H. V.
    1972   *The Forecast of Fulfillment: A Review of Research on Predictive Assessment of the Adult Retarded for Social and Vocational Adjustment.* New York: Teachers College Press.
Cobb, O. H.
    1923   Parole of Mental Defectives. *Proceedings of the American Association for the Study of the Feebleminded* 28:145–148.
Crapanzano, V.
    1980   *Tuhami: Portrait of a Moroccan.* Chicago: University of Chicago Press.

Denny, R., and M. L. Meyersohn
    1957   A Preliminary Bibliography on Leisure. *American Journal of Sociology* 62:602–615.

Dexter, L. A.
    1964   *The Tyranny of Schooling: An Inquiry into the Problem of "Stupidity."* New York: Basic Books.

Doll, E. A.
    1930   Community Control of the Feeble-minded. *Annals of the American Academy of Political and Social Science* 149:167–174.

Edgerton, R. B.
    1963   A Patient Elite: Ethnography in a Hospital for the Mentally Retarded. *American Journal of Mental Deficiency* 68:372–385.

    1965   Some Dimensions of Disillusionment in Culture Contact. *Southwestern Journal of Anthropology* 21:231–243.

    1970   Mental Retardation in Non-Western Societies: Toward a Cross-Cultural Perspective on Incompetence. In H. C. Haywood (ed.), *Social-Cultural Aspects of Mental Retardation*. New York: Appleton-Century-Crofts, 523–559.

    1983   Failure in Community Adaptation: The Relativity of Assessment. In K. Kernan, M. Begab, and R. B. Edgerton (eds.), *Environments and Behavior: The Adaptation of Mentally Retarded Persons*. Baltimore: University Park Press, 123–143.

    1984   The Participant-Observer Approach to Research in Mental Retardation. *American Journal of Mental Deficiency* 88:498–505.

    1986   A Case of Delabeling: Some Practical and Theoretical Implications. In L. L. Langness and H. Levine (eds.), *Culture and Retardation: Life Histories of Mildly Mentally Retarded Persons in American Society*. Dordrecht: D. Reidel, 101–126.

    1988*a*   Aging in the Community—A Matter of Choice. *American Journal on Mental Retardation* 92:331–335.

    1988*b*   The Community Adaptation of Persons with Mental Retardation. In J. F. Kavanaugh (ed.), *Mental Retardation Research Accomplishments and New Frontiers*. Baltimore: P. H. Brookes, 311–318.

    1990   Quality of Life From a Longitudinal Research Perspective. In R. L. Schalock (ed.), *Quality of Life: Perspectives and Issues*. Washington, D.C.: American Association on Mental Retardation, 149–160.

Edgerton, R. B., and S. Bercovici
    1976   The Cloak of Competence: Years Later. *American Journal of Mental Deficiency* 80:485–497.

Edgerton, R. B., M. Bollinger, and B. Herr
    1984   The Cloak of Competence: After Two Decades. *American Journal of Mental Deficiency* 88:345–351.

Edgerton, R. B., and H. F. Dingman
    1964   Good Reasons for Bad Supervision: "Dating" in a Hospital for the Mentally Retarded. *The Psychiatric Quarterly Supplement* 38:221–233.

Edgerton, R. B., and M. A. Gaston (eds.)
  1991   *"I've Seen It All!" Lives of Older Persons with Mental Retardation in the Community.* Baltimore: P. H. Brookes.
Edgerton, R. B., and G. Sabagh
  1962   From Mortification to Aggrandizement: Changing Self-Concepts in the Careers of the Mentally Retarded. *Psychiatry* 25:263–272.
Edgerton, R. B., G. Tarjan, and H. F. Dingman
  1961   Free Enterprise in a Captive Society. *American Journal of Mental Deficiency* 66:35–41.
Edgerton, R. B., and T. W. Ward
  1990   "I Gotta Put My Foot Down." In R. B. Edgerton and M. A. Gaston (eds.), *"I've Seen It All!" Lives of Older Persons with Mental Retardation.* Baltimore: P. H. Brookes, 71–100.
Fairbank, R. E.
  1933   The Subnormal Child: Seventeen Years After. *Mental Hygiene* 17:177–208.
Fernald, W. E.
  1925   *The Feebleminded in the Community: The Social Aspects of Mental Hygiene.* New Haven: Yale University Press.
Fischler, K., and R. Koch
  1991   Mental Development in Down Syndrome Mosaicism. *American Journal on Mental Retardation* 96:345–351.
Fitzpatrick, F. K.
  1956   Training Outside the Walls. *American Journal of Mental Deficiency* 60:827–837.
Foley, R. W.
  1929   A Study of the Patients Discharged from the Rome State School for the Twenty-Year Period Ending December 31, 1924. *American Association for the Study of the Feebleminded* 34:180–207
Frank, G.
  1981   Venus on Wheels: The Life History of a Congenital Amputee. Ph.D. dissertation, University of California, Los Angeles.
Gaston, M. A.
  1991*a*   "That Was a Long Time Ago." In R. B. Edgerton and M. A. Gaston (eds.), *"I've Seen It All!" Lives of Older Persons with Mental Retardation in the Community.* Baltimore: P. H. Brookes, 5–43.
  1991*b*   "I'll Manage These Things as They Come Up." In R. B. Edgerton and M. A. Gaston (eds.), *"I've Seen It All!" Lives of Older Persons with Mental Retardation in the Community.* Baltimore: P. H. Brookes, 45–69.
Gaston, M. A., and D. M. Baldwin
  1991   "Keeping Hands and Mind Busy." In R. B. Edgerton and M. A. Gaston (eds.), *"I've Seen It All!" Lives of Older Persons with Mental Retardation in the Community.* Baltimore: P. H. Brookes, 151–168.
Gazaway, R.
  1969   *The Longest Mile.* Garden City, N.Y.: Doubleday.

Gerber, D. A.
　1990　Listening to Disabled People: The Problem of Voice and Authority in Robert B. Edgerton's *The Cloak of Competence*. *Disability, Handicap & Society* 5:3–23.

Gladwin, T.
　1968　Review of *The Cloak of Competence: Stigma in the Lives of the Mentally Retarded* by Robert B. Edgerton. *American Anthropologist* 70:618–620.

Goffman, E.
　1961　*Asylums: Essays on the Social Situation of Mental Patients and Other Inmates*. Garden City, N.Y.: Doubleday Anchor Books.
　1963　*Stigma: Notes on the Management of Spoiled Identity*. Englewood Cliffs, N. J.: Prentice-Hall.

Goldschmidt, W. R.
　1959　*Man's Way: A Preface to the Understanding of Human Society*. Cleveland: World Publishing Co.

Granat, K., and S. Granat
　1973　Below-average Intelligence and Mental Retardation. *American Journal of Mental Deficiency* 78:27–32.

Greene, C. L.
　1945　A Study of Personal Adjustment in Mentally Retarded Girls. *American Journal of Mental Deficiency* 49:472–476.

Gunzberg, H. C.
　1957　Therapy and Social Training for the Feebleminded Youth. *British Journal of Medical Psychology* 30:42–48.

Hamlett, I. C., and T. L. Engle
　1950　Mental Health Analyses of Furlough Patients. *American Journal of Mental Deficiency* 55:257–263.

Hartzler, E.
　1951　A Follow-up Study of Girls Discharged from the Laurelton State Village. *American Journal of Mental Deficiency* 55:612–618.
　1953　A Ten-year Survey of Girls Discharged from the Laurelton State Village. *American Journal of Mental Deficiency* 57:512–517.

Hay, L., and B. Kappenburg.
　1931　The Social Adjustment of Children of Low Intelligence. *Smith College Studies in Social Work* 2:146–174.

Heber, R. (ed.)
　1958　A Manual on Terminology and Classification in Mental Retardation. Monograph Supplement, *American Journal of Mental Deficiency* 64, No. 2.
　1961　Modifications in the Manual on Terminology and Classification in Mental Retardation. *American Journal of Mental Deficiency* 66:499–500.

Hiatt, M. S.
　1951　Casework Services in Community Placement of Defectives. *American Journal of Mental Deficiency* 56:204–211.

Hilliard, L. T.
    1954   Resettling Mental Defectives—Psychological and Social Aspects. *British Medical Journal* 1:1372–1375.

Jewell, A. A.
    1941   A Follow-up Study of 190 Mentally Deficient Children Excluded Because of Low Mentality from the Public Schools of the District of Columbia. *American Journal of Mental Deficiency* 45:413–420.

Johnson, B. S.
    1946   A Study of Cases Discharged from the Laconia State School from July 1, 1924 to July 1, 1934. *American Journal of Mental Deficiency* 50:437–445.

Jordan, M. L.
    1963   Leisure Time Activities of Sociologists, Attorneys, Physicists, and People at Large from Greater Cleveland. *Sociology and Social Research* 47:290–297.

Kanner, L.
    1964   *A History of the Care and Study of the Mentally Retarded*. Springfield, Ill.: Charles Thomas.

Kaplan, M.
    1960   *Leisure in America: A Social Inquiry*. New York: John Wiley.

Kaufman, S. Z.
    1988   *Retarded* ISN'T *Stupid, Mom!* Baltimore: P. H. Brookes.

Kinder, E. F., A. Chase, and E. W. Buck
    1941   Data Secured During a Follow-up Study of Girls Discharged from Supervised Parole from Letchworth Village. *American Journal of Mental Deficiency* 45:572–578.

Kinder, E. F., and E. J. Rutherford
    1927   Social Adjustment of Retarded Children. *Mental Hygiene* 11:811–833.

Koegel, P., and R. B. Edgerton
    1982   Labeling and the Perception of Handicap among Black Mildly Retarded Adults. *American Journal of Mental Deficiency* 87:266–276.
    1984   Black "Six-hour" "Retarded Children" as Young Adults. In R. B. Edgerton (ed.), *Lives in Process: Mildly Retarded Adults in a Large City*. Washington, D.C.: American Association on Mental Deficiency, Monograph No. 6., pp. 145–171.

Krishef, C. H.
    1959   The Influence of Rural-Urban Environment upon the Adjustment of Discharges from the Owatonna State School. *American Journal of Mental Deficiency* 63:860–865.

Krishef, C. H., and M. A. Hall
    1915   Employment of the Mentally Retarded in Hennepin County, Minnesota. *American Journal of Mental Deficiency* 60:182–189.

Krishef, C. H., M. C. Reynolds, and C. L. Stunkard
    1959   A Study of Factors Related to Rating Post-Institutional Adjustment. *Minnesota Welfare* 11:5–15.

Lakin, L. C. and R. H. Bruininks (eds.)
1985   *Strategies for Achieving Community Integration of Developmentally Disabled Citizens.* Baltimore: P. H. Brookes.

Langness, L. L., and G. Frank
1981   *Lives: An Anthropological Approach to Biography.* Novato, Calif.: Chandler and Sharp.

Little, A. N., and B. S. Johnson
1932   A Study of the Social and Economic Adjustments of One Hundred Thirteen Discharged Parolees from the Laconia State School. *American Association for the Study of the Feebleminded* 37:233–251.

Luckin, B.
1986   Time, Place and Competence: Society and History in the Writings of Robert Edgerton. *Disability, Handicap & Society* 1:89–102.

Lurie, L., L. Schlan, and M. Freiberg
1932   A Critical Analysis of the Progress of 55 Feebleminded Children over a Period of 8 years. *American Journal of Orthopsychiatry* 2:58–69.

MacAndrew, C., and R. B. Edgerton
1964   The Everyday Life of the Institutionalized "Idiots." *Human Organization* 23:312–318.

McIntosh, W. J.
1949   Follow-up Study of 1,000 Non-Academic Boys. *Journal of Exceptional Children* 15:166–170.

McKay, B. E.
1942   A Study of IQ Changes in a Group of Girls Paroled From a State School for Mental Defectives. *American Journal of Mental Deficiency* 46:496–500.

McPherson, G. E.
1935   Parole of Mental Defectives. *American Journal of Mental Deficiency* 40:162–167.

Masland, R. L., Sarason, S. B., and T. Gladwin
1958   *Mental Subnormality: Biological, Psychological, and Cultural Factors.* New York: Basic Books.

Matthews, M. A.
1922   One Hundred Institutionally Trained Male Defectives in the Community Under Supervision. *Mental Hygiene* 6:332–342.

Mercer, J. R.
1973   *Labeling the Mentally Retarded.* Berkeley, Los Angeles, London: University of California Press.

Meyers, R.
1978   *Like Normal People.* New York: McGraw-Hill.

Miles, M.
1991   *Mental Handicap Services: Development Trends in Pakistan.* Peshawar: Mental Health Centre.

Muench, G. A.
  1944   A Follow-up of Mental Defectives After 18 Years. *Journal of Abnormal and Social Psychology* 39:407–418.
Nirje, B.
  1969   The Normalization Principle and Its Human Management Implications. In R. Kugel and W. Wolfensberger (eds.), *Changing Patterns in Residential Services for the Mentally Retarded*. Washington, D.C.: President's Committee on Mental Retardation.
O'Connor, N.
  1953   The Occupational Success of Feebleminded Adolescents. *Occupational Psychology* 27:157–164.
  1957   The Successful Employment of the Mentally Handicapped. In L. T. Hilliard and B. H. Kirman (eds.), *Mental Deficiency*. London: Churchill, Ltd.
O'Connor, N., and J. Tizard
  1951   Predicting the Occupational Adequacy of Certified Mental Defectives. *Occupational Psychology* 25:205–211.
  1956   *The Social Problem of Mental Deficiency*. London: Pergamon Press.
Olin, I.
  1930   The Social Adjustment of Children of Low Intelligence. *Smith College Studies in Social Work* 1:107–159.
Ordahl, G., N. L. Keyt, and C. Wright
  1944   The Social Competence of High-grade Mental Defectives, Determined by Self-Report. *American Journal of Mental Deficiency* 48:367–373.
Parker, S. R.
  1964   Type of Work, Friendship Patterns, and Leisure. *Human Relations* 17:215–219.
Powdermaker, F.
  1930   Social Adjustment of the Feebleminded. *Annals of the American Academy of Political and Social Sciences* 149:59–69.
Rainwater, L., R. P. Coleman, and G. Handel
  1959   *Workingman's Wife: Her Personality, World and Life Style*. New York: Oceana.
Raymond, A.
  1923   Observations on the Placement and Supervision of Mental Defectives in the Community. *Proceedings of the American Association for the Study of the Feebleminded* 28:100–118.
Robinson, H. B., and N.M. Robinson
  1965   *The Mentally Retarded Child: A Psychological Approach*. New York: McGraw-Hill.
Ross, R. T., M. J. Begab, E. H. Dondis, J. S. Giampiccolo, Jr., and C. E. Meyers
  1985   *Lives of the Mentally Retarded: A Forty-Year Follow-up Study*. Stanford: Stanford University Press.
Sabagh, G., and R. B. Edgerton
  1962   Sterilized Mental Defectives Look at Eugenic Sterilization. *Eugenics Quarterly* 9:213–222.

Saenger, G.
1957   *The Adjustment of Severely Retarded Adults in the Community.* Albany: New York State Interdepartmental Health Resources Board.

Schalock, R. L. (ed.)
1990   *Quality of Life: Perspectives and Issues.* Washington, D.C.: America Association on Mental Retardation.

Seltzer, M. M., and M. W. Krauss
1987   *Aging and Mental Retardation: Extending the Continuum.* Washington, D.C.: American Association on Mental Retardation.

Shafter, A. J.
1957   Criteria for Selecting Institutionalized Mental Defectives for Vocational Placement. *American Journal of Mental Deficiency* 61:599–616.

Shimberg, M. E., and W. Reichenberg
1933   The Success and Failure of Subnormal Problem Children in the Community. *Mental Hygiene* 17:451–465.

Steckel, M. L.
1934   A Follow-up of Mentally Deficient Girls. *Journal of Social Psychology* 5:112–115.

Stevens, H. A., and R. Heber
1964   *Mental Retardation: A Review of Research.* Chicago: University of Chicago Press.

Storrs, H. C.
1929   A Report on an Investigation Made of Cases Discharged from Letchworth Village. *American Association for the Study of the Feebleminded* 34:220–232.

Tarjan, G., H. F. Dingman, R. K. Eyman, and S. J. Brown
1960   Effectiveness of Hospital Release Programs. *American Journal of Mental Deficiency* 64:609–617.

Thomas, B. E.
1943   A Study of the Factors Used to Make a Prognosis of Social Adjustment. *American Journal of Mental Deficiency* 47:334–336.

Tong, J. E., and G. W. MacKay
1959   A Statistical Follow-up of Mental Defectives of Dangerous or Violent Propensities. *British Journal of Delinquency* 9:276–284.

Town, C. H., and G. E. Hill
1929   *How the Feebleminded Live in the Community.* Buffalo: Children's Aid Society.

Ward, T. W.
1991   "I've Seen it All!. . . . Well, Just About." In R. B. Edgerton and M. A. Gaston (eds.), *"I've Seen It All!" Lives of Older Persons with Mental Retardation in the Community.* Baltimore: P. H. Brookes, 71–100.

Whitcomb, M. A.
1945   A Comparison of Social and Intellectual Levels of 100 High-grade, Adult Mental Defectives. *American Journal of Mental Deficiency* 50:257–262.

Whitney, E. A.
   1948   A Statistical Study of Children Admitted and Discharged from Elwyn. *American Journal of Mental Deficiency* 53:182–186.
Windle, C.
   1962   *Prognosis of Mental Subnormals.* Monograph Supplement to American Journal of Mental Deficiency, Vol. 66, No. 5.
Wolfson, I. N.
   1956   Follow-up Studies of 92 Male and 131 Female Patients Who Were Discharged from the Newark State School in 1946. *American Journal of Mental Deficiency* 61:224–238.
York, R. A.
   1939   The Paroled Boy: Working and Home. *American Association on Mental Deficiency* 44:254–258.

Index

Designer:	U. C. Press Staff
Compositor:	Jarrett Engineering, Inc.
Text:	10/13 Galliard
Display:	Galliard
Printer:	Haddon Craftsmen, Inc.
Binder:	Haddon Craftsmen, Inc.